Amazing Graces

MEALS AND MEMORIES FROM THE PARSONAGE

THE TEXAS CONFERENCE
UNITED METHODIST MINISTERS' SPOUSES
ASSOCIATION

Additional copies may be obtained at the cost of $14.95, plus $2.50 postage and handling, each book. Texas residents add $1.23 sales tax, each book.

Send To: **The Texas Conference United Methodist Ministers' Spouses Association**
12955 Memorial Drive
Houston, Texas 77079

ISBN: 0-9636854-0-6
LCCN: 93-60390

First Printing, 5,000
September 1993
Second Printing, 5,000
March 1995

Printed in the USA by

WIMMER
The Wimmer Companies, Inc.
Memphis • Dallas

Proceeds from the sale of this book will be used for projects that benefit children at Lakeview Conference Center. Our first project will be to build a contemporary playground and to provide monies for its upkeep.

Amazing Graces

GRACE—it's one of those words that brings to mind a wealth of images: the love of God, goodwill, beauty, elegance, kindness and even the short prayer we say before a meal. Likewise, **AMAZING GRACES: Meals and Memories from the Parsonage** is one of those books that will bring a wealth of images to your life. In it you will find the elegance of a special meal lovingly prepared, the beauty of our original artwork, the goodwill expressed in the sharing of our favorite recipes, perhaps a suitable table grace to use at family gatherings, and the love of God as seen through our stories of parsonage life.

We hope that in reading and using this book, you will encounter all these images that the word "grace" reflects. We hope, too, that you will feel as though you have been a welcome guest at the parsonage, that you have come to know us a little better. We want you to laugh with us at our stories, eat our favorite dishes, entertain with our special menus, join in a table grace with our families, pass on to your children some of our prized "p.k." (preacher's kid) recipes. In so doing, perhaps you, too, will experience those "amazing graces" that life in a parsonage can bring.

Now we graciously offer to you **AMAZING GRACES: Meals and Memories from the Parsonage**, which is not only a collection of more than 450 of our favorite "parsonage-tested" recipes, but also a look at who we, as United Methodist ministers' spouses, are. Welcome to the parsonage!

AMAZING GRACES: Meals and Memories from the Parsonage is lovingly dedicated to *Nancy Oliphint*, wife of retired Bishop Ben Oliphint, who has been an exemplary leader, an ideal example, a gracious lady, and above all, a devoted friend to all the ministers' spouses of the Texas Conference of the United Methodist Church.

Cookbook Committee

CHAIRPERSONS
Karen Bagley
Laura Neff

TREASURER
Bette Jo Smale

MEMORIES EDITOR
Janet Kennedy

SECTION EDITORS
Bonita Calhoun
Helen Diller
Cynthia H. Kethley
Carolyn Lanagan
Jaunita Lang
Anne McKay
Joyce Pace
Shirley Phillips

COMMITTEE MEMBERS
Judy Barnes
Debbie Bass
Charlse Bell
Virginia Crowe
Twana Holcomb
Merryl James
Irma Waddleton
Shirley Williamson
Cindi Woodward

HONORARY MEMBER
Elizabeth Summers

1993 MINISTERS' SPOUSES ASSOCIATION PRESIDENT
Mary Ann Thompson

The Cookbook Committee would like to express its most heartfelt appreciation to our own *Jean Cragg* (Rev. H. Eugene), who was the inspiration for our beautiful cover and section dividers; to *Patricia Tate* of Contemporary Catering in Fairfield, Texas, for selecting our menus; to *Virginia Crowe* (Rev. Tom W.) for the countless hours she spent putting our entire manuscript on computer disc; to all the ministers' spouses who contributed recipes, stories and ideas to the cookbook; to all the invaluable testers and tasters; and to our spouses for their patience, support and encouragement during the many months we have been working on this project.

 We have used a dogwood blossom to denote those recipes that are considered "light" or "heart-healthy."

4

Table of Contents

Menus 7

"We Gather Together"
Appetizers & Beverages 11

"Salt of the Earth"
Soups & Sandwiches 31

"In the Garden"
Salads & Dressings 53

"Staff of Life"
Breads 79

"Manna from Heaven"
Entrees 101

"Together We Serve"
Side Dishes 153

"Sweet Benedictions"
Desserts 185

"Let the Children Come"
P.K. Pages 255

Index 276

Order Form 287

Who Are We?

Who are the Texas Conference United Methodist Ministers' Spouses? We are mothers and fathers, husbands and wives, teachers, nurses, dance instructors, artists, accountants, homemakers, counselors, Cub Scout leaders, hospital volunteers, etc. We live all over East Texas from the Red River to the Gulf of Mexico, in cities as large as Houston or so small they don't show up on the map. We are young, old and every age in between. In spite of our great diversity, we do have one thing in common: we have all married United Methodist ministers. And that common bond is what makes our group so special. Our ministers' spouses association is the one group which shares the joys and frustrations of life in a parsonage, the hopes and dreams as well as the disappointments of being "in the ministry," the excitement of moving to a new position in a new location and the pain of leaving the old one. And that in itself is the purpose of our organization: to provide opportunities for fellowship with others who know what it means to be married to a United Methodist minister.

Due to the vast geographic area we comprise and to the busy lives we lead, we are a rather loose-knit organization and have been from the beginning. Sometime during the 1940's several ministers' spouses (usually referred to as "preachers' wives" in those days) gathered together for a luncheon at Annual Conference in May, and this soon became a yearly event. In the fall of 1954, the group held its first fall retreat at Lakeview Conference Center near Palestine, Texas, and has held one there every year since. In 1959 we published our first cookbook, entitled **East Texas Cooking**, under the leadership of the late Beryl G. Tower. The sale of the book netted $1,500, which was invested in church bonds. Interest income was used to establish the "Bess Smith Scholarship Fund" in honor of the late Bishop A. Frank Smith's wife. This fund has continued to grow and be reinvested over the years and was changed in 1968 to the "Bishops' Wives' Scholarship Fund" in order to honor all our bishops' wives. Earnings from this fund go to scholarships for female students at the Gbarnga Methodist Mission in Liberia, West Africa.

After more than 30 years, our spouses' association felt it was time to publish a second cookbook. So in 1991 a cookbook committee was established with the instructions that this book should contain not only our favorite recipes but also some of our favorite stories of parsonage life. The outcome of that decision is *AMAZING GRACES: Meals and Memories from the Parsonage*, which we now offer to you as a glimpse of who we are.

Suggested Menus for Graceful Entertaining

The following menus have been selected as a guide to Southern style and Christian hospitality. An asterisk (*) denotes recipes found in this cookbook.

New Year's Party

Texas Caviar (Black-Eyed Pea Dip)* / Chips
Jalapeño Jelly*   Buttery Crackers
Garden Vegetables/Shrimp Dip*
Swiss Crab Bites*   Cocktail Pecans*
Cream Cheese Drops*   Fudge*
Frozen Slush Punch*   Coffee

Neighborly Offerings

For a new neighbor or a sick friend

Chicken Spaghetti*
Broccoli Salad*   Cheese Garlic Biscuits*
My Cream Cheese Pound Cake*
Sliced Strawberries / Whipped Cream

Evening Elegance

Suitable for entertaining your most honored guests

Easy Chicken Cordon Bleu*
Broccoli Salad Supreme*   All-Bran Bread or Rolls*
Bean Bundles*
Pecan Praline Cheesecake*
Coffee   Tea

7

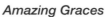
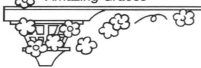

Sunrise Breakfast

Sausage Strata*
Magic Biscuits* / Strawberry Preserves*
Methodist Grits*   Apple Crisp*
Rich Sweet Bread Kolaches*
Coffee   Tea

Graduation Luncheon

Beggar's Bundles*
Salad Nicholi*   Crispy Cheese Patties*
Fresh Spring Fruit
Strawberry Squares*
Coffee   Tea

Perfect Day P.K. Party

Boiled Pebble Soup*
Peanut Butter Yummies*   Monster Cookies*
Frozen Bananas*   Homemade Clay*
Strawberry Slush*

Let's Celebrate

Perfect for a birthday meal

Garlic Chicken Parmesan*
Mandarin Salad*
Broccoli and Rice Casserole*   Fresh Yeast Bread*
Chocolate Pie with Magic Meringue*
Coffee   Tea

Dinner on the Grounds

Oven-Fried Chicken*
Marinated Vegetable Salad*   Potato Salad*
Pecan Pie*   Oatmeal Cake / Praline Icing*
Picnic Lemonade*   Tea

Mexican Fiesta

Hot Sauce* / Chips
Quick Mexican Salad*   Mexican Casserole*
Green Chili Chicken Enchiladas*   Mexican Cornbread*
Mexican Flan*
Iced Tea

Friends by the Fireside

Hot Vegetable Punch or Moctail Appetizer*
Candlelight Lasagna*
Spinach and Strawberry Salad*
Light (Crescent) Rolls*
Chocolate Crunch Supreme*
Coffee   Tea

Holiday Open House

Fresh Vegetables / All Things Good Dill Dip*
Salmon Log* / Crackers   Swedish Meatballs*
Spinach Balls*   Fresh Fruit Wedges
Aunt Selma's Spritz Cookies*   Tiny Pecan Tarts*
Parsonage Eggnog*   Christmas Wassail*

How many of you remember Bess Smith's story about how she and her husband, Frank, as newlyweds at Alto, entertained their bishop? They saved their money for weeks to purchase a special roast. Linens were freshened and silver polished. They had rehearsals on roast carving and serving. The day finally came and all were seated around the beautiful table. The bishop blessed the food. Frank stood to carve the roast, put a piece on the plate, added a vegetable and then sat down and proceeded to eat! Bess coughed to no avail, and finally said in her polite, soft voice, "Frank, if you don't mind, I believe the bishop and I are hungry, too." This story always made Bishop and Mrs. A. Frank Smith human to me.

Mary Reed (Eldon)

We Gather Together

Appetizers & Beverages

Friends! Your presence here transforms this simple meal into a banquet! As this food brings life to our bodies, so you bring inspiration to our souls. May all peoples have what we share here.

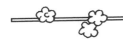

All Things Good Dill Dip

1 pint sour cream
1 pint mayonnaise
3 tablespoons dill weed

3 tablespoons chopped
   parsley
3 tablespoons diced onion
½ tablespoon seasoned salt

Mix all ingredients together. Use as a vegetable dip or dressing for salad.

Gina Sparks (Pat)

Artichoke Dip

1 cup mayonnaise
1 cup grated Parmesan
   cheese

1 (14 ounce) can artichoke
   hearts, mashed
Dash of garlic salt

Mix ingredients. Heat in 350° oven until hot. Serve with thin wheat crackers.

Cynthia Hullum Kethley (T. Paul)

Cucumber Dip

1 medium cucumber
1 (8 ounce) package cream
   cheese, softened

1 teaspoon dill weed or seed
Dash of garlic salt
2 tablespoons mayonnaise

Peel and finely dice cucumber or process in food processor. Mix with remaining ingredients. Serve with fresh vegetables.

Emma Jo Thomas (Billie)

13

Texas Caviar (Black-Eyed Pea Dip)

1 (16 ounce) package frozen
  black-eyed peas
2 cloves garlic, minced
2 tablespoons cider vinegar
3 bell peppers, diced

1 tablespoon salt
½ cup vegetable oil
3 small onions, diced
2 bay leaves

Cook, cool and drain black-eyed peas. Add remaining ingredients and mix. Refrigerate overnight. Serve with tortilla chips.

Peggy Renfroe (Rob)

Shrimp Dip

2 (8 ounce) packages cream
  cheese, softened
1 (10¾ ounce) can cream of
  shrimp soup
Garlic powder to taste

Onion powder to taste
Soy sauce to taste
Lemon juice to taste
2 (6½ ounce) cans small
  shrimp, drained

Blend first 6 ingredients in a bowl and then add shrimp. Serve with favorite crackers.

Sue Armstrong (Bill)

Party Shrimp Dip

3 pounds boiled shrimp,
  chopped
4 boiled eggs, finely chopped
3 cloves garlic, crushed
3 tablespoons dry mustard
3 cups mayonnaise or salad
  dressing

2 tablespoons paprika
3 tablespoons horseradish
2 tablespoons
  Worcestershire sauce
⅛ teaspoon salt
⅛ teaspoon pepper

Mix ingredients and chill. Serve with chips.

Note: This is good for parties and open house. For a family appetizer or snack, making half of the recipe will be adequate.

Merri Gay Biser (Roy O.)

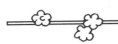
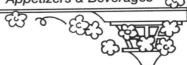

Sausage Dip

1 pound ground beef
1 pound sausage (hot or regular)
1 cup chopped onion
1 (7½ ounce) jar jalapeño relish

1 (10¾ ounce) can cream of mushroom soup
1 teaspoon garlic powder
32 ounces pasteurized process cheese spread, melted

Sauté ground beef, sausage and onion until lightly brown and crumbly. Drain fat. Add other ingredients, one at a time. Mix well after each addition. Serve hot with chips or as baked potato topping. Makes 3 quarts.

Loraine Holt (Lloyd)

Spinach Dip

1 (8 ounce) carton sour cream
1 cup mayonnaise
¼ teaspoon onion salt
½ teaspoon dill weed
¼ cup green onion, chopped

3 tablespoons red or green pepper, minced
1 (10 ounce) package frozen chopped spinach, thawed and drained

Blend together all ingredients, except spinach. Next add spinach. Chill. Serve with crackers or put inside a hollowed out loaf of bread.

Carolyn Lanagan (David)

When the REVISED STANDARD VERSION of the New Testament was first published, we could afford only one copy which our 3 boys shared. Paul, age 6, informed us one Sunday before church that it was his time to take the REVIVED STANDING VIRGIN to Sunday School.

Dorothy Schneider Dubberly (Emmett)

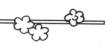

Hot Sauce

24 ripe tomatoes, peeled,
  cored and chopped
20 jalapeño peppers,
  chopped
4 onions, chopped
4 or 5 green bell peppers,
  chopped

¾ cup vinegar
4 teaspoons pickling salt
1 teaspoon garlic powder
2 tablespoons cilantro,
  chopped
4 (8 ounce) cans tomato
  sauce

To make peeling tomatoes easier, boil them for 2 minutes, then dump into cold water. Chop jalapeño peppers and leave seeds in (makes dip hotter). Use gloves, it will save your hands. Mix everything together in a large bowl or pan. Pour into quart jars. Seal jars and put them in large pan; cover with water. Bring to a boil and cook for 35 minutes. Makes about 6 quarts.

Vivian Toland (Michael)

Cheese Chili Quiches

2 eggs
⅓ cup milk
1 cup shredded Cheddar
  cheese

1 (4 ounce) can diced green
  chilies, drained
1 (10 ounce) package canned
  biscuits

Heat oven to 375°. In small bowl, beat eggs and milk; stir in cheese and chilies. Cut each biscuit into 2 pieces. Place each biscuit piece in the bottom of ungreased mini-muffin cup. Press dough to cover bottom and sides. Spoon 1 tablespoon of cheese mixture into each cup. Bake at 375° for 15-20 minutes. Freezes well. Reheat at 375° for 10-12 minutes.

Note: *This was served at a 50th Anniversary for a friend from Kosse, Texas.*

Jan Edwards (Tom)

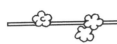

Roll-Ups

2 (8 ounce) packages cream cheese, softened
1 (2 ounce) package ranch-style dressing mix
2 green onions, finely chopped

4 (12-inch) flour tortillas
1 (4 ounce) jar diced pimiento
1 (4 ounce) can diced green chilies
1 (2¼ ounce) can sliced olives

Mix first 3 ingredients together and spread on tortillas. Drain other ingredients on paper towels. Then sprinkle evenly over cream cheese mixture. Roll tortillas up tightly. Chill at least 2 hours. Slice and put on serving dish. Makes 3 dozen.

Clara Johnson (Dee)

Easy Cheese Ball

2 (8 ounce) packages cream cheese
4½ ounces grated Cheddar cheese

1 envelope ranch-style salad dressing mix
Chopped pecans
Dried parsley

Let cream cheese and Cheddar cheese come to room temperature. Mix cheeses gradually, adding dressing mix a little at a time until entire package is used. (If too sticky, refrigerate or place in freezer 30-45 minutes.) Shape into ball and roll in chopped pecans or parsley. Can be made ahead and frozen. Makes 1 large or 2 small balls.

Wanda L. Coleman (Alvis)

Cheese Ball

1 (8 ounce) package light cream cheese, softened
1 cup small-curd low-fat cottage cheese

1 (0.7 ounce) package Italian salad dressing mix
1 cup chopped ham
Parsley flakes to taste
Chopped pecans

Mix all ingredients, except pecans, together with a wooden spoon. Chill. Form into a ball and roll in chopped pecans. Serve with crackers.

Eunice Sonneman (Bill)

17

Olive Cheese Balls

1 (5 ounce) jar sharp cheese spread
1 stick margarine, softened
1 cup all-purpose flour

1 (7 ounce) jar pimiento-stuffed olives, drained and dry (24-30 olives)

Soften cheese and mix with margarine. Work in flour until easy to handle (add more flour if needed). Pinch off and roll dough in small balls. Flatten in palm of hand and form around olive. Make sure olive is completely covered. Place on baking sheet sprayed with non-stick vegetable spray. Bake at 375° until brown, 25-30 minutes. Serve immediately while hot. Makes 24-30 cheese balls.

Eleanor Little (Don)

Spinach Balls

1 cup herb-seasoned stuffing mix
1 (10 ounce) package frozen chopped spinach
2 eggs, beaten
¼ cup Parmesan cheese, grated

¼ teaspoon pepper
½ pod garlic, chopped
1 medium onion, chopped
¼ teaspoon salt
2 teaspoons margarine

Put stuffing mix in ziploc plastic bag. Roll with rolling pin until stuffing becomes fine crumbs. Or process stuffing mix in food processor or blender. Cook spinach slightly; drain well. Add eggs and other ingredients. Mix well. Let sit at room temperature 15 minutes or until stuffing has absorbed moisture. Form into bite-size balls. (May be frozen at this point.) Place balls on greased cookie sheets. Bake at 350° about 20 minutes or until firm. Makes about 2 dozen.

Mazalene Walker (Bill)

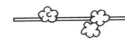

Asparagus Roll-Ups

1 (8 ounce) package cream cheese, softened
1 (2 ounce) package ranch-style salad dressing mix

1 loaf extra thin bread
Canned asparagus spears, well-drained

Combine cream cheese and dressing mix, blending well. Trim crusts from bread and roll each slice with a rolling pin to ⅛- or ¹⁄₁₆-inch thickness. Spread a thin layer of cream cheese mixture on each slice of bread. Place an asparagus spear (2, if small) at the end of each slice of bread and roll up. Cut into thirds or halves. Place on a cookie sheet seam side down. Freeze several hours on cookie sheet, then place in freezer bags and return to freezer. When ready to serve, bake at 375° for 20-25 minutes. Turn off oven and let roll-ups sit 10 minutes in hot oven to dry out. Serve warm. Serve with soups, salads or as appetizers.

Fussy Heflin (James)

Sausage Rolls

2 cups all-purpose flour
½ teaspoon salt
3 teaspoons baking powder
5 tablespoons shortening

⅔ cup milk
1 pound ground sausage, room temperature

Sift flour, salt and baking powder together; cut in shortening until mixture looks like coarse crumbs. Add milk and mix. Divide into two halves. Roll each half out until ¼-inch thick. Spread with raw sausage which will spread better at room temperature. Then roll as a jelly roll. Repeat with remaining dough. Wrap in waxed paper or aluminum foil and chill. Slice ¼-inch thick. Bake at 400° for 5-10 minutes. Do not grease pan. Freezes well. Makes 50 slices.

Sue Cantrelle (Earl P.)

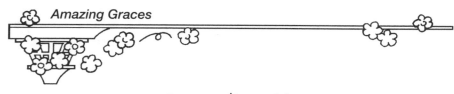

Bacon Roll-Ups

¼ cup butter or margarine
½ cup water
1½ cups packaged herb-
 seasoned stuffing mix

1 egg, slightly beaten
¼ pound sausage, uncooked
½ - ⅔ pound bacon, cut in
 thirds

Melt butter in water. Stir into stuffing. Add egg and sausage. Mix well. Refrigerate at least one hour. Shape into walnut-size balls. Wrap with bacon and insert toothpick. Bake on cookie sheet (I use a broiler pan so bacon grease will drain while cooking) at 350° for 30-35 minutes. Turn once while baking.

Clara Johnson (Dee)

Petite Porkies

1 (10 ounce) can flaky
 buttermilk biscuits
20 small cocktail smoked
 sausages

Prepared mustard seasoned
 with horseradish
Margarine, melted

Divide each biscuit in half. Spread each half with mustard. Roll biscuit halves around sausages. Place seam side down on lightly greased cookie sheet. Brush biscuits with melted margarine. Bake at 350° until brown. Serve with sweet and sour sauce for an appetizer or with honey for breakfast.

Mary Ann Stepp (Robert)

Swedish Meatballs

1 pound lean ground beef
½ cup grated breadcrumbs
¼ cup milk
1 tablespoon chopped onion

2 teaspoons butter or
 margarine
½ cup sherry
½ cup ketchup
¼ teaspoon oregano

Combine beef, breadcrumbs, milk and onion in a bowl. Form into small meatballs. Melt butter in skillet, add meatballs and cook until brown. Drain off grease and add sherry, ketchup and oregano. Simmer, covered, for 20 minutes. Serve on toothpicks as appetizers.

Bobbie Neff (Jim)

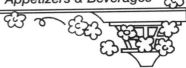

Crispy Cheese Patties

2 cups grated sharp Cheddar
   cheese
1 cup margarine
1 teaspoon salt

½ teaspoon red pepper
2 cups all-purpose flour
2 cups crispy rice cereal

Allow cheese and margarine to soften to room temperature. Combine cheese, margarine, salt and pepper. Add flour and cereal. Form into balls, using about 1 teaspoon of mixture for each, and place on ungreased cookie sheet. Flatten with a fork. Bake at 375° for 10-12 minutes or until brown. Makes about 6 dozen patties.

Kathryn Blackwell (Derwood)
Laura Winborn (Conrad)

Crescent Munchies

2 packages or cans of
   crescent rolls
1 (8 ounce) package cream
   cheese, softened
1 cup mayonnaise
1 (2 ounce) package ranch-
   style salad dressing mix

Chopped raw vegetables
   such as broccoli,
   cauliflower and green
   onions
Black olives, chopped

Open crescent rolls flat on cookie sheet and smooth out perforations. Bake according to package directions. Allow to cool. Mix together cream cheese, mayonnaise and salad dressing mix. Spread mixture on cool rolls. Sprinkle vegetables and olives on top. Cut into bite size snacks. Serve cold.

Patsy Weber (Bobbie)

Swiss Crab Bites

2 cans butterflake rolls or
 butterflake biscuits
1 cup canned crabmeat
 (check for shell)
1 cup grated Swiss cheese
½ cup mayonnaise
½ teaspoon curry powder

3 tablespoons chopped
 green onion tops
1 tablespoon lemon juice
1 (8 ounce) can water
 chestnuts (optional)
1 (2¼ ounce) jar stuffed
 green olives, sliced
 (optional)

Separate rolls or biscuits into 3 or 4 layers, placing on baking sheet. Mix next 6 ingredients thoroughly. Place a teaspoonful of mixture on each piece of roll. (If crispy texture is desired, place a thin slice of water chestnut on top.) Bake in 400° oven about 12 minutes. May be garnished with slice of stuffed olive.

Jerrie Reily (Ben)

Crab Delight

1 stick margarine, softened
1 (4 ounce) jar Old English
 cheese spread
1 (4¼ ounce) can crabmeat,
 drained

Dash of garlic powder
1 teaspoon mayonnaise
1 (6 count) package
 sourdough English muffins

Mix first 5 ingredients together and spread on English muffins. Quarter muffins and place on cookie sheet. Bake at 350° for 15-20 minutes. May be frozen in sealed freezer bags. Allow to bake a little longer if frozen.

Ginger Hood (T. Mac)
Anne McKay (Scott)

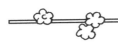
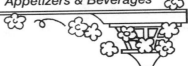

Salmon Log

1 (16 ounce) can red salmon
1 (8 ounce) package cream
   cheese, softened
1 tablespoon lemon juice
2 teaspoons grated onion
¼ teaspoon liquid smoke
¼ teaspoon salt

1 teaspoon prepared
   horseradish
¾ cup finely chopped pecans
3 tablespoons finely chopped
   parsley
1 (3 ounce) jar green olives,
   sliced (optional)

Drain and flake salmon, removing bones and skin. Combine with next 6 ingredients and mix well. Refrigerate overnight. Shape into log and roll in pecans and parsley. Serve with crackers. Can also be shaped like a Christmas tree on a cookie sheet, platter or serving tray using sliced olives as ornaments.

Audrey Barfield (John)
Laura Winborn (Conrad)

Cheese Spread For A Crowd

1 (8 ounce) package sharp
   Cheddar cheese
1 (8 ounce) package mild
   Cheddar cheese
1 (8 ounce) package colby
   cheese
1 (8 ounce) package
   mozzarella cheese
1 (4 ounce) can chopped ripe
   olives, drained

2 bunches green onions,
   chopped
1 (4 ounce) can diced
   pimiento, drained
4 ribs celery, chopped
2 jalapeño peppers, chopped
Mayonnaise to blend
Parsley

Grate all cheese and mix well. Add olives, onions, pimiento, celery and peppers. Blend with mayonnaise as desired. Make ahead for full flavor. Line large bowl with waxed paper. Spoon in the cheese spread and chill. Turn out on tray and garnish with parsley. Serve with an assortment of crackers.

Mary Thompson (James)

23

Beef and Cheese Spread

2 (8 ounce) packages cream
  cheese, softened
2 (2¼ ounce) jars dried beef

2 teaspoons Worcestershire
  sauce
3 green onion stalks,
  chopped

Mix ingredients and shape into a ball. Spread on crackers of choice. Makes enough spread for approximately 1 box of crackers.

Kathy Reiter (James)

Cucumber Vegetable Spread

4 ounces light Neufchatel
  cream cheese, softened
1 cup ricotta cheese
2 teaspoons chopped fresh
  mint leaves
2 teaspoons lemon juice

1 medium cucumber, peeled,
  seeded and chopped
½ cup finely chopped carrot
¼ cup sliced green onions
1 (2 ounce) jar diced
  pimiento, drained

In small bowl, beat cream cheese until smooth. Add ricotta cheese, mint and lemon juice; blend well. Stir in remaining ingredients. Cover; refrigerate until ready to serve. Serve with bagel chips or assortment of crisp crackers. Store in refrigerator. Makes 2⅔ cups.

Virginia Irene Crowe (Thomas W.)

Cocktail Pecans

2 tablespoons butter or
  margarine
½ teaspoon seasoned salt
2 dashes hot pepper sauce

1 pound pecan halves
3 tablespoons
  Worcestershire sauce

Put butter, seasoned salt and hot pepper sauce in a 12x8x2-inch baking dish. Place in a 300° oven until butter melts. Add pecans, stirring until all are butter coated. Bake for about 20 minutes, stirring occasionally. Sprinkle with Worcestershire sauce. Stir again and continue baking another 15 minutes or until crisp. Freezes well. Enjoy!

Gerry Millikan (Herman)

Wedding Punch

4 cups sugar
2 quarts water
1 (46 ounce) can pineapple
  juice
1 (12 ounce) can frozen
  orange juice

1 (12 ounce) can frozen
  lemonade
1 (8 ounce) bottle lemon juice
3 liters lemon-lime
  carbonated drink

Combine sugar and water. Boil for 10 minutes and let cool. Mix with all the juices. Divide into 3 (1 gallon) milk containers that have been cut around leaving the handle. Cover with foil and freeze. Remove from freezer about 1½ hours before time to serve. Place one frozen slush mixture and 1 bottle of lemon-lime drink in punch bowl. Mix into slush consistency and serve. Serves 60.

Mary Margaret Smith (Lawrence)

Frozen Slush Punch

1 (6 ounce) package gelatin,
  any flavor and color
2 cups sugar
2 cups boiling water
3 cups cold water
1 (46 ounce) can pineapple
  juice

5 ounces lemon juice
1 (½ ounce) bottle almond
  extract
3 (2 liter) bottles ginger ale,
  chilled

Mix gelatin, sugar and boiling water and stir until sugar and gelatin are completely dissolved. Add all other ingredients except ginger ale and mix thoroughly. Put in quart-size freezer containers and freeze. Set out to defrost 1 or 2 hours before serving. When punch can be broken up into mush with a heavy spoon, add 1 (2-liter) bottle of ginger ale to each quart of concentrate. Ginger ale should be chilled, so that you do not need ice for the punch. Serve in a punch bowl. Makes about 72 ½-cup servings.

Note: *This is great for a wedding or anniversary punch because you can make it any color desired.*

Bette Jo Smale (Bill)

Red Satin Punch

2 (32 ounce) bottles lemon-lime carbonated drink

1 quart apple juice
1 quart cranberry juice

Pour one bottle of lemon-lime carbonated drink into ice cube trays and freeze. Chill rest of ingredients. When ready to serve, mix together in a large punch bowl. Add prepared ice cubes. Serves 36.

Kathleen Megill (Greg)

Gelatin Punch

4 (3 ounce) packages gelatin (any flavor)
2 quarts water
2 (46 ounce) cans pineapple juice
2 (12 ounce) cans frozen orange juice (mixed as directed)

4 (12 ounce) cans frozen lemonade (mixed as directed)
60 ounces lemon-lime carbonated drink or ginger ale

Dissolve gelatin in hot water according to package directions and cool. Add and mix all remaining ingredients except bottled drinks. Add lemon-lime or ginger ale at serving time. Makes about 4½ gallons.

Sharon Fisher (Robert)

Orange Slush

1 cup sugar
2 cups boiling water
1 (6 ounce) can frozen orange juice, undiluted
1 cup crushed pineapple, undrained

3 bananas, sliced
1 (10 ounce) jar maraschino cherries, drained
½ cup lemon juice

Mix together and put into a 13x9x2-inch pan. Refrigerate 24 hours, stirring occasionally. Freeze. Before serving, allow to thaw to a slush. Goes great with a breakfast casserole.

Jean Waldman (Bob)

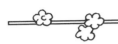
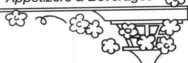

All Occasion Punch

1 (3 ounce) box lime or
   strawberry gelatin
2 cups hot water
2 cups sugar
1 (14 ounce) can pineapple
   juice

1 (1 ounce) bottle almond
   extract
Green or red food coloring
1 quart ginger ale

Dissolve gelatin in hot water. Add sugar and stir until dissolved. Add pineapple juice and almond extract. Stir in 3 drops of food coloring. Pour half pineapple mixture into freezer container. Freeze until firm. Refrigerate other half until ready to serve. Place frozen pineapple mixture into punch bowl. Pour remaining mix over top and add ginger ale. Serve immediately.

Irma Waddleton (Don)

Picnic Lemonade

½ cup light corn syrup
½ cup sugar
7⅔ cups water, divided
2 tablespoons lemon rind

3 trays of ice cubes
1¼ cups fresh lemon juice
Cherries and lemon slices

Combine syrup, sugar, ⅔ cup water and lemon rind. Bring to boil and boil 5 minutes. Strain and cool. Place ice cubes in large glass pitcher. Pour syrup mixture in pitcher and add lemon juice and remaining water. Garnish with cherries and lemon slices. Serves 10.

Cynthia Hullum Kethley (T. Paul)

Parsonage Eggnog

Vanilla bean ice cream,
   softened

Eggnog mix, chilled
Nutmeg

Mix equal parts of soft vanilla bean ice cream and commercial eggnog mix. Serve in punch bowl. Sprinkle with nutmeg. Delicious for open house at Christmas!

Beverly Duree (Sam)

Coffee Pot Tea

3 cups cranberry juice
1 quart apple cider
¼ cup brown sugar

¼ teaspoon salt
2 whole cinnamon sticks
¾ teaspoon whole cloves

Place juices in bottom of percolator. In basket put sugar and spices. Plug in percolator. Enjoy.

Shirley Phillips (Richard)

Christmas Wassail

2 quarts sweet apple cider
2 cups pineapple juice
1½ cups orange juice
¾ cup fresh lemon juice

1 cup sugar
2 sticks whole cinnamon
1 teaspoon whole cloves

Combine all ingredients and bring to a boil. Serve hot. Makes 25 to 30 ½-cup servings.

Jeannine Lamb (Lee)

Hot Cranberry Punch

2 quarts water
½ cup sugar
2 teaspoons whole cloves
3 teaspoons cinnamon red hot candy
2 or 3 (1-inch) cinnamon sticks
3 cans jellied or whole cranberry sauce

2 (46 ounce) cans pineapple juice
2 (6 ounce) cans frozen lemonade, thawed
2 (6 ounce) cans frozen orange juice, thawed
Red food coloring

Bring to a boil water and sugar. Add a tea caddy filled with cloves, red hots and cinnamon sticks. Let simmer for 15 minutes. Remove spice bag. Dissolve cranberry sauce. Add to first mixture. Add pineapple juice, lemonade and orange juice. Food coloring may be added for extra color. Heat or serve cold. Will keep well in refrigerator.

Dorothy Dubberly (Emmett)

Hot Mulled Cider

1 gallon apple cider
4 sticks cinnamon

Apple wedges

Combine cider and cinnamon sticks in pan. Bring to a boil and simmer 30 minutes. Serve in mugs and garnish with apple wedges.

Note: The first time I made this, I mistakenly put in 14 sticks of cinnamon. We were all "sippin' cider" that open house!

Helen Diller (David)

Hot Chocolate Mix

25 ounces powdered milk
3 ounces powdered creamer

½ pound Nestles' Quik
¼ box powdered sugar

Combine all ingredients and mix well. To make hot chocolate, add ⅓ to ½ cup mix to 1 cup of hot water.

Lydia Anderson (Charles)

Hot Vegetable Punch or Moctail Appetizer

8 cubes beef bouillon
3 cups boiling water
¼ teaspoon pepper
1½ teaspoons celery salt
¾ teaspoon garlic juice

Dash of hot pepper sauce, if desired
1 (46 ounce) can cocktail vegetable juice

Dissolve bouillon cubes in boiling water. Add other seasonings and cocktail vegetable juice. Heat and mix well. Serves 12-15.

Note: I first tasted this hot vegetable punch at a district dinner when Dr. Richard Robinson was our District Superintendent on the Houston Southwest District. Jessie Mae, his wife, made it. She shared the recipe with me. She used 3 cups of broth made from boiling beef soup bones. I shortened it to use the beef bouillon cubes.

Vivian White (Donald)

29

Her words are forever in my memory, although they were spoken to me in November, 1939. Mrs. Stanford was a widow who lived in a shelter made of discarded tin signs at the Galveston City Dump. She walked a long distance to attend services at Crockett Place Methodist Church. We were about to leave our house to attend the evening service, when there was a knock at the door. As I greeted her, Mrs. Stanford thrust a much used paper sack into my hands with these words: "I brung you something. It's a 'invitation' cut glass dish and Lenore paid 75 cents for it at Kresses in Fort Worth. It's the best thing I have and I'll never again have a dining table to set it on, so I wanted you and Brother Summers to have it." The pressed glass bowl was caked with dirt in every crevice. When it was cleaned, it sparkled like diamonds and was in perfect condition. For 53 years, that gift has been a daily reminder of my most humbling experience.

Elizabeth Summers (Edwin T.)

When our second son went to his first parsonage, there was an old cook stove with a door that would not close. He asked his brother, who had preceded him in the ministry by 3 years, how to get it over to his congregation that they needed a new stove. His brother agreed this was a difficult problem, but a professor of his at Perkins had said, "You should not spur the horse until you are in the saddle!" Shortly after moving in, my 9-year-old granddaughter wanted to make some cookies. Her father told her she could not use the stove, but she could go over to the church to do her baking. Afterwards she and her mother went to visit a lady in the church, and of course, she wanted to take along some cookies. As my granddaughter presented her goodie gift, she explained that she had to bake them in the church kitchen and added, "Because Daddy says you can't spur the horse until you're in the saddle!" Her mother got her out of the house. When they got home, she told her husband that he had better explain things to his daughter. It was not 15 minutes later before the phone rang, and the lady told them that a new stove was on the way.

Amy Webb (William C.)

Salt
of the Earth

Soups & Sandwiches

For food and all thy gifts of love,
We give Thee thanks and praise.
Look down, O Father, from above,
And bless us all our days. Amen.

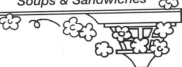

Cabbage Patch Stew

1 pound ground beef
2 onions, chopped
½ cup chopped celery
2-3 cups water
½ head cabbage, chopped

1 (12 ounce) can tomatoes
  with chilies
1 (15 ounce) can ranch-style
  beans
Salt and pepper to taste
¼ cup vegetable oil (optional)

Sauté beef, onion and celery together in a 6-quart covered pot. Cook over medium heat until meat turns gray. Add water, cabbage, tomatoes, beans, salt, pepper and oil (if desired). Continue to cook over medium heat for about 45 minutes. Serve. Serves 8.

Mamie Shelton (B. R.)

Portuguese Soup

2 onions, chopped
6 cloves garlic, chopped
6 teaspoons vegetable oil
1 pound smoked sausage
4 (16 ounce) cans beef broth
1 (14 ounce) bottle ketchup
½ teaspoon pepper
Salt to taste

1 (16 ounce) can kidney
  beans, undrained
1 head green cabbage, cored
  and shredded
12 very small new potatoes,
  unpeeled and quartered
¼ cup vinegar

Sauté onion and garlic in oil. Slice sausage ¼-inch thick and add to onion and garlic; brown slightly. Add all remaining ingredients; bring to a boil and stir well. Reduce heat and simmer one hour. This keeps well in the refrigerator and is really better the second day.

Cookbook Committee

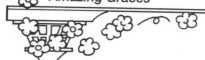
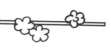

Hamburger Soup

1 pound ground beef
4 large potatoes
2 carrots
1 (14½ ounce) can stewed
tomatoes, undrained

2 cups water
1 (17 ounce) can whole
kernel corn

Brown ground beef in a skillet. Peel and chop potatoes and carrots. In a large stew pot, combine potatoes, carrots, stewed tomatoes and water. Cook until potatoes soften, then add corn and browned ground beef. Heat and serve.

Melissa Sarver (David)

Taco Soup

2 pounds ground beef
1 onion, chopped
1 (15 ounce) can ranch-style
beans
1 (15 ounce) can pinto beans
1 (16 ounce) can whole
kernel corn
1 (16 ounce) can stewed
tomatoes

1 (1¼ ounce) package taco
seasoning
2 ounces mild green chilies,
diced
1 teaspoon salt
1 teaspoon black pepper
1 (1 ounce) package
buttermilk salad dressing
mix
1-2 cups water

Brown ground beef and onions. Drain excess fat. In a large pot, combine meat, beans, corn, tomatoes, taco seasoning, chilies, salt, pepper and buttermilk dressing mix. Stir in 1-2 cups water. Simmer about 30 minutes, uncovered. This soup is extra good with jalapeño cornbread. Serves 15-20.

Variation: Use ground turkey for lower fat. Try a can of hominy or kidney beans for a different taste.

Doris Cheney (John)
Sharon Fisher (Robert)
Margie Holt (Bill)
Frances Love (Elza)
Pat Petty (Steve)

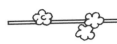
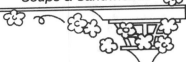

Full Meal Deal Soup

1½ pounds ground chuck
1 onion, chopped
1 (15 ounce) can ranch-style
beans
3 (10½ ounce) cans
minestrone or vegetable
soup

1 (16 ounce) can stewed
tomatoes
1 (16 ounce) can tomatoes
with chilies
2-3 cans water

Sauté meat and onion. Add the remaining ingredients and simmer 20-30 minutes. Serves 12-15.

Mary Reed (Eldon)

Preacher Soup

1 pound ground turkey or
lean ground beef
1 onion, chopped
2 garlic cloves, chopped
4 cups water
2 tablespoons
Worcestershire sauce
1 (16 ounce) can tomatoes
1 (8 ounce) can tomato sauce

1 (10 ounce) can tomatoes
with green chilies
3 carrots, sliced
2 celery stalks, chopped
2 potatoes, peeled and diced
1 (16 ounce) can corn,
drained
1 (16 ounce) can green
beans, drained
½ cup uncooked macaroni

Brown ground meat, onion and garlic in a large pot. Drain off grease. Add all other ingredients except corn, green beans and macaroni. Simmer, covered for about 30 minutes or until vegetables are tender. Add remaining ingredients and simmer about 10 minutes or until macaroni is cooked.

Note: This is easily doubled or tripled to feed a crowd. May be frozen.

Laura Neff (Jerry)

Tasty Turkey Soup

1 turkey carcass
4 quarts water
1 cup margarine
1 cup all-purpose flour
3 medium onions, chopped
2 large carrots, diced
2 celery stalks, diced

1 cup uncooked long-grain
  rice
2 teaspoons salt
¾ teaspoon pepper
2 cups half-and-half or
  2% milk

Place turkey carcass and water in a large pot; bring to a boil. Cover, reduce heat and simmer 1 hour. Remove from broth and pick meat from bones. Set broth and meat aside. Measure broth and add water if necessary to measure 3 quarts. Heat margarine in a large Dutch oven; add flour and cook over medium heat. Stir constantly for about 5 minutes. (Roux will be a very light color.) Stir onion, carrot and celery into the roux and cook over medium heat for 10 minutes. Stir often, then add broth, turkey, rice, salt and pepper. Bring to a boil. Cover and reduce heat. Simmer for 20 minutes or until rice is tender. Add half-and-half or 2% milk, and cook until thoroughly heated. Makes 4½ quarts. Serves 8-10.

Note: *It's a great and tasty way to use left-over holiday turkey. Serve it with hot cornbread or French bread and it will surely satisfy all who eat it.*

Millie Feller (Verlon)

Split Pea Soup

1 cup dried split peas
Water
2 cloves garlic, chopped
1 medium onion, chopped

1 teaspoon salt
2 carrots, grated
2 ribs celery, chopped

Wash the split peas. Place in a 1½-quart saucepan. Cover with water about 2 inches above peas. Bring to a boil, reduce heat. Add garlic, onion and 1 teaspoon of salt. Cook for about 2½ hours or until tender, adding water as needed. When peas are done, add carrots and celery. Cook until these are tender, about 15 minutes more.

Variation: *Substitute lentils for split peas.*

Helen Diller (David)

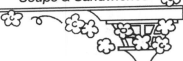

Tortilla Soup

2 tablespoons vegetable oil
1 onion, chopped
1 (4 ounce) can chopped mild
  green chilies, drained
2 garlic cloves, chopped
1 (10½ ounce) can beef broth
2 (14½ ounce) cans stewed
  tomatoes
1 (10½ ounce) can chicken
  broth
1 (10¾ ounce) can tomato
  soup

1½ cups water
1 teaspoon salt
1 teaspoon sugar
1 teaspoon cumin
1 teaspoon chili powder
½ teaspoon lemon pepper
1 teaspoon hot pepper sauce
2 teaspoons Worcestershire
  sauce
12 corn tortillas

Sauté onions, chilies and garlic in oil. Add remaining ingredients, except tortillas. Simmer 1 hour. Cut corn tortillas into strips and add. Good served over avocado chunks and topped with cheese.

Jane Fenn (Charles)

Vegetable Rice Soup

1 medium onion, chopped
1 cup chopped celery
1 cup sliced carrots
2 garlic cloves, minced
2 (14 ounce) cans chicken
  broth

1 (16 ounce) can tomatoes
½ cup mild picante sauce
½ cup uncooked rice
2 teaspoons basil
¼ cup fresh parsley
1-2 cups water

In a large pot, combine all ingredients except water and simmer for 20 minutes. Add water to desired consistency and simmer 10 more minutes. Serves 6-8.

Variation: Add 2 cooked chicken breasts, chopped into small pieces. Substitute dried parsley for fresh.

Jackie Browning (Gus)

Zucchini Soup

3 medium zucchini
2 medium (baking or red)
  potatoes
1 medium onion
½ cup margarine, melted

1 (14 ounce) can chicken
  broth
1 (12 ounce) can evaporated
  milk
1 rounded teaspoon Creole
  seasoning

Medium slice the zucchini, potatoes and onion. Then place in large pot and add margarine. Cook vegetables until tender, stirring to prevent sticking. Do not add water. Vegetables will make their own liquid. Remove from heat and add chicken broth, evaporated milk and Creole seasoning. Puree together in blender. May be frozen.

Note: *Given to me by Estelle Dameron, a retired minister's widow in Pineville, Louisiana.*

Jean Haskell (William A.)

Mr. D's Potato Soup

1 (10¾ ounce) can cream of
  mushroom soup
1 (10¾ ounce) can cream of
  chicken soup
1 (10¾ ounce) can creamy
  onion soup

3 soup cans of milk
1 soup can of water
8-10 halved and boiled
  potatoes
1 chicken bouillon cube
Salt and pepper to taste

Mix soups, milk and water in a 5-quart pot. Peel and dice potatoes and add to soup mixture. Season with one chicken bouillon cube and salt and pepper to taste. Cook uncovered over medium heat until soup is thoroughly heated. Do not boil.

Variation: *May add cooked bacon pieces, sautéed celery or grated cheese.*

Kathy Danheim (Dan)

Bean Soup

2 (16 ounce) cans pinto beans
2 (16 ounce) cans navy beans
1 (16 ounce) can pinto beans with jalapeños

2 (10¾ ounce) cans bean and bacon soup
2 cloves garlic
1 small onion, chopped
Salt and pepper to taste
1-2 pounds link sausage, sliced

Mix beans, soup, garlic, onion, salt and pepper to taste. Cook on low setting 30 minutes. Mash some beans when stirring. Add sausage and cook another 30 minutes. Good served with green salad and jalapeño cornbread.

Wanda Coleman (Alvis)

Eight-Bean Soup

1 pound black-eyed peas
1 pound barley
1 pound green split peas
1 pound lentils

1 pound great northern beans
1 pound black beans
1 pound navy beans
1 pound kidney beans

Combine dry beans. Place only 3 cups of combined beans in large pot. Cover with water and bring to boil for 1 minute. Remove from heat and let stand overnight. Drain. Remaining beans may be stored for future use.

2 quarts water
1 green or red pepper, chopped
1 large onion, chopped
1 cup chopped celery
1 (24 ounce) can tomatoes

1 garlic clove, minced
1 pound chopped smoked sausage
¾ cup hickory smoke sauce
Salt and pepper to taste
1 tablespoon lemon juice

Add the above ingredients to beans and simmer up to 5 hours.

Jane Cambre (Allison)

Mary's Louisiana Cajun Gumbo

¾ cup vegetable oil
6 tablespoons all-purpose
   flour
1 green bell pepper, chopped
4 celery stalks, chopped
3-4 onions, chopped
1 bunch green onions,
   chopped
1 pod garlic, chopped
1 (16 ounce) can chopped
   tomatoes
3 quarts water, divided

1 tablespoon salt
1 teaspoon pepper
1 teaspoon thyme
4 bay leaves
2 pounds meat (sausage,
   cooked chicken, shrimp,
   crabmeat or combination)
1 cup chopped parsley
6 dashes hot pepper sauce
1 teaspoon seasoned salt
   flavor enhancer
2 tablespoons gumbo filé

Make a roux by mixing the oil and flour in a cast iron skillet or dutch oven. Cook over low heat. Stir constantly until mixture thickens and is very brown, about 20 minutes. Be careful not to burn the roux as this will give the gumbo a bitter flavor. Add bell pepper, celery, onion, green onions, garlic and tomatoes to roux. Then add 1-2 cups of hot water and cook until vegetables are limp. Meanwhile, in a separate 8-quart pot, bring the remaining water to a boil and add the salt, pepper, thyme and bay leaves. When vegetables are limp, add vegetables and roux to water and spices. Add choice of meats and simmer about 20 minutes. Before serving, add parsley, pepper sauce, seasoned salt and filé. Serve over cooked rice.

Mary Parker (Lynn)

During the first year of our marriage one of our church members brought us a nice big fish. I decided to surprise Ben and bake it for supper. I got out my favorite cookbook and thought I'd really found the perfect recipe — complete with lemon butter sauce. When Ben came home, I proudly asked him to please see if the fish was done. It didn't take him long to discover the fish still had scales and had not been cleaned! So, I cried while he cooked us an omelet for supper. To this day if we have fish I let Ben take complete charge: He catches them, cleans them _and_ cooks them!

Nancy Oliphint (Ben)

Corn Chowder

1 cup chopped celery
1 small onion, chopped
½ cup margarine, melted
4 cups milk
4 cups water

4 cups diced, cooked
   potatoes
Salt and pepper to taste
2½ cups whole kernel corn
1 tablespoon parsley

Sauté celery and onion in melted margarine. Add remaining ingredients. Simmer.

Variation: Add chopped ham, other vegetables or pasteurized processed cheese.

Gina Sparks (Pat)

Quick and Easy Clam Chowder

3 (10¾ ounce) cans cream of
   potato soup
3 (10¾ ounce) cans New
   England-style clam
   chowder
1 (10¾ ounce) can cream of
   celery soup

1 (6½ ounce) can minced
   clams, undrained
1 quart half-and-half or
   2% milk
10 slices cooked bacon,
   crumbled

Combine the soups, clams and milk; cook slowly over medium heat. Stir often and do not boil. Serve hot and sprinkle 1 teaspoon crumbled bacon on each serving. This is good with crusty French bread. Serves 10.

Elizabeth R. Summers (Edwin T.)

My five-year-old just returned from Grandma's. "Mom, how old are you?" I replied, "21." "You are older than Grandma," he said, "because she won't be 21 until her next birthday."

Helen Walker (Derwin)

Creamy Fish Chowder

1-2 stalks celery, chopped
1 medium onion, chopped
3 medium potatoes, chopped
Salt and pepper to taste
2-3 pounds fish fillets
1 (12 ounce) can evaporated milk
1 cup milk
1 (8 ounce) package cream cheese, diced

Cook celery, onion and potatoes seasoned with salt and pepper in a small amount of water until tender. Drain. Add fish, evaporated milk, milk and cream cheese. Simmer for 20 minutes, stirring occasionally, or until fish is done. Do not boil, as evaporated milk will curdle.

Jaunita Lang (Fred)

Shrimp Chowder

1 medium onion, chopped
3 slices bacon
1 (16 ounce) can tomatoes
1 (16 ounce) can cream-style corn
1 (16 ounce) can French-style green beans
Garlic powder
Salt and pepper to taste
1 pound cleaned and deveined shrimp
1 quart milk

Brown and drain onion and bacon. In a large pot, mix together browned onion, bacon, tomatoes, corn and green beans. Season to taste with garlic powder, salt and pepper. Add shrimp and milk. Simmer one hour. DO NOT BOIL, because milk will curdle.

Jeannine Lamb (Lee)

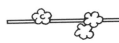
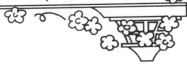

Quick White Chili

2 tablespoons olive oil
1 pound boneless, skinless chicken breasts, diced
3 shallots, peeled and chopped
3 cloves garlic, peeled and chopped
1 (18 ounce) can tomatillos, drained and cup up (fresh tomatillos are excellent)
1 (14½ ounce) can tomatoes, undrained
1 (10½ ounce) can low-sodium chicken broth
1 (7 ounce) can diced green chilies
½ teaspoon crumbled dried oregano
¼ teaspoon ground cumin
2 (15 ounce) cans white kidney beans (cannellini), drained
Juice of 1 lime
Salt and pepper
Chopped red onion, cilantro, jalapeños, tomatoes and/or avocado, sour cream, shredded Monterey Jack cheese and/or lime wedges (optional)

In large saucepan, heat olive oil. Add chicken and cook, stirring often, just until it starts to brown. Remove chicken from pan and set aside. Add shallots and garlic to pan and sauté until soft. Stir in tomatillos, tomatoes with liquid, chicken broth, green chilies, oregano, and cumin. Bring to boil, then reduce heat and simmer about 30 minutes. Return chicken to pan with drained beans and cook about 5 minutes. Chicken should be cooked and beans hot. Add lime juice and season to taste with salt and pepper. Red onion, cilantro, tomato and/or avocado, sour cream, etc. can be served at the table to add to chili as desired. Serves 4-6.

Kathleen Modd (Thomas R.)

While Kenneth was serving in Haskell, Texas, in the early 1940's, I received a phone call one morning from 84-year-old "Mother Sanders," loving matriarch of the church. She asked if there were a black leather sofa in the hall. "No," I replied. She then inquired if one were upstairs. Again I responded, "No." With a touch of consternation in her voice, she said, "I gave one to the parsonage 27 years ago. I wonder what preacher's wife sold it."

Catherine Copeland (Kenneth)

Heart-Smart Chili

1 pound 97% fat-free ground beef
2 (14½ ounce) cans tomatoes, chopped
1 tablespoon cumin
Salt and pepper to taste
¼ cup salsa or to taste

Brown the ground beef in a dutch oven. Add remaining ingredients being sure to include the tomato juice with the tomatoes. Bring to a boil, reduce heat, and simmer for 15 minutes to blend flavors, stirring occasionally. If chili is too thin, continue to simmer until it reaches desired consistency. Chili may be frozen for later use.

Katie Anderson (Jerry)

Beef Stew

3 pounds stew meat or rump roast, 1-inch cubes
3 large carrots, sliced
1 (6 ounce) can mushrooms, undrained
1 (15 ounce) can tomato sauce or canned tomatoes
1 (16 ounce) can whole onions or a box of fresh boiling onions
1 (10 ounce) package frozen peas
1 teaspoon salt
1 teaspoon pepper
1 teaspoon sugar
½ cup instant tapioca
2 bay leaves
½ cup consommé

Combine all ingredients in a large covered casserole or dutch oven. Cook in 300° oven for about six hours. Stir once or twice. Can be served over noodles or rice. Serves 8.

Frances Love (Elza)

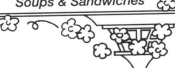

Quick Parsonage Potluck Stew

1 pound ground beef per 5-6
  guests expected
1-2 large onions, chopped
Salt and pepper to taste

Canned vegetables (each
  guest should bring 1 can of
  his/her choice)

In a large pot, brown meat and chopped onion. Drain grease. Season moderately with salt and pepper. As guests arrive, open each can and add to stew, juice and all. Water may be added to make this stretch for a bigger-than-expected crowd.

Note: *This is great for a quick "get-together" or committee meeting supper. All you need to make this a complete meal is a bottle of hot pepper sauce and your favorite crackers. This recipe always turns out right.*

Richard Hendrick (Carolyn)

Berry Turkey Sandwich

2 (3 ounce) packages cream
  cheese, softened
½ cup chopped pecans
8 slices whole wheat bread

1 cup sliced fresh
  strawberries
8 ounces deli-sliced turkey
Leaf lettuce

In a small bowl, combine cream cheese and pecans. Spread each slice of bread with cream cheese and nut mixture. For each sandwich, cover one slice of bread with sliced strawberries. Place 2 ounces of turkey on top of strawberries and put leaf of lettuce on top of turkey. Top with other slice of bread. Makes 4 sandwiches.

Cookbook Committee

Berry Bananawich

1 croissant	1 tablespoon peanut butter
1 tablespoon marshmallow creme	½ banana ⅓ cup strawberries

Slice croissant lengthwise and microwave on HIGH for 15 seconds. Spread marshmallow creme on top half of croissant. Spread peanut butter on bottom half of croissant. Slice banana and layer on top of peanut butter. Slice strawberries and layer on top of banana. Put croissant halves together. Cut sandwich in half. Eat with a glass of milk. Serves 1.

Pat Petty (Steve)

Frozen Chicken Salad Sandwiches

2 cups cooked diced chicken	1 cup chopped water
1 tablespoon finely chopped onion	chestnuts, drained
½ teaspoon salt	20 slices sandwich bread, crust removed
1 cup chicken gravy or packaged gravy mix	2 tablespoons milk
1 cup diced celery	3 eggs, beaten
2 tablespoons chopped pimiento	½ pound margarine, melted
1 (10¾ ounce) can cream of mushroom soup	1 (10 ounce) package potato chips, crushed

In a medium mixing bowl, combine first 8 ingredients and mix well. Spread mixture on 10 slices of bread. Add top slice and wrap sandwiches individually in plastic wrap. Freeze for at least 12 hours. When ready to serve, combine milk and eggs in a flat dish large enough to hold a piece of bread. Remove the sandwiches from the freezer, unwrap and dip each one in the melted margarine, then in the mixture of eggs and milk. Then coat with crushed potato chips and place on a greased cookie sheet. Bake in a 300° oven for 1 hour. Turn the sandwiches after the first 30 minutes. Serve hot.

Sue Gibbs (Walter)
Elnor Lamb (Joseph)

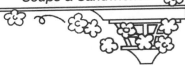

Italian Chicken Sandwiches

1 chicken breast fillet
1 teaspoon olive oil
¼ cup water
Salt and pepper to taste
1 whole wheat or sour dough
  roll

Italian creamy garlic salad
  dressing
Lettuce
Tomato slices
Black olives, sliced

Sauté the chicken breast fillet in olive oil and water. Season to taste with pepper and salt. Allow to cool. Slice chicken breast; coat roll with salad dressing. Add chicken, lettuce, sliced tomato and olives. Enjoy!

Note: *Leftover chicken works great! Makes 1 sandwich, but can be multiplied easily for a crowd.*

Kay Lynn Fenn (Marlin)

Ham or Chicken Salad Sandwiches

1 cup chopped, cooked ham
  or chicken
½ cup chopped celery
2 tablespoons mayonnaise
2 tablespoons sweet pickle
  relish

1 teaspoon prepared mustard
1 tablespoon minced green
  pepper
¼ teaspoon salt
Lettuce
Bread

Combine meat, celery and mayonnaise in a medium bowl. For ham sandwiches, add the pickle relish and mustard. For chicken sandwiches, add only green pepper and salt. Mix ingredients well. Spread on bread of choice. Add lettuce to each sandwich. Makes 6 sandwiches.

Helen Diller (David)

Spinach French Loaf

1 (10 ounce) package frozen
  chopped spinach, thawed
1 (16 ounce) loaf French
  bread
1 envelope dry vegetable
  soup mix

1 (8 ounce) can water
  chestnuts, drained and
  chopped
1 (8 ounce) jar good quality
  mayonnaise
1 (16 ounce) carton sour
  cream
1 onion, chopped

Drain spinach well and blot with paper towels. Cut French bread in half lengthwise. Hollow out the center of the bread and discard. Mix all remaining ingredients in a bowl. Use to fill the hollowed-out bread halves. Replace top half of bread on bottom half. Wrap in foil and refrigerate for several hours. When ready to serve, slice loaf as you would a plain loaf of French bread.

Kathy Danheim (Dan)

Pizza Bagels

4 bagels
8 ounces pizza sauce
8 slices mozzarella cheese

1 (3½ ounce) package sliced
  pepperoni

Slice bagels in half lengthwise and spread each half with pizza sauce. Place on a paper towel on a microwave safe plate. Top with cheese and pepperoni. Microwave on HIGH about 1 minute. Turn dish and microwave for another minute or until cheese is bubbly. The bagels may be cooked in oven on a metal baking sheet instead. Broil for about 2 minutes or until cheese is bubbly. Makes 8.

Variation: Use Cheddar or Monterrey Jack cheese. May use mixture of cheeses. Pepperoni may be replaced with ham, sliced mushrooms, chopped green peppers or chopped onions.

Cookbook Committee

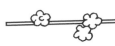
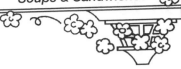

Quesadillas

2 (6-8 inch) flour tortillas
¼ cup shredded Cheddar
   cheese

¼ cup shredded Monterey
   Jack cheese
Picante sauce

Cut tortillas in half and place on microwavable plate. Sprinkle cheese over half of each tortilla. Dot with picante sauce. Fold tortillas in half. Microwave on HIGH for 1 minute or until cheese melts. Cut each tortilla into 3 pie shaped wedges. Serves 1-2.

Mary Hicks (David)

Baked Ham Sandwich

2 (8 count) packages French
   rolls
½ - ¾ cup margarine,
   softened

2-3 tablespoons mustard
1 pound sliced boiled ham
1 pound sliced Swiss cheese

Split rolls. Mix margarine and mustard; spread mixture on both halves of rolls. Put slice of ham and slice of cheese on bottom half of each roll. Put rolls together and place on baking sheet and bake for 15-20 minutes at 350°.

Variation: *Try other types of rolls or small dinner rolls. May use hot mustard.*

Joyce Pace (Rudy)

Seminary Sandwiches

1 (5½ ounce) can mixing
   chicken with broth
1 (8 ounce) package cream
   cheese, softened

2 tablespoons mayonnaise-
   type salad dressing
¼ cup chopped olives

Drain chicken broth into cream cheese. Add salad dressing. Mix well with electric mixer. (You may add a little milk if not soft enough.) Add chicken and olives stirring well. Use as a sandwich spread on bread of your choice.

Violet Waters (Bob E.)

49

French Toast Sandwiches

1 loaf French bread
½ pound thinly sliced ham
½ pound sliced mozzarella
  cheese

4 eggs
1 cup milk

Slice loaf of French bread into half-inch thick slices. On half of slices, place a slice of ham and a slice of cheese. Top with remaining bread slices. In a medium bowl, beat eggs with a fork, add milk and mix well. Spray a skillet with non-stick vegetable spray and place over medium heat. Dip sandwiches one at a time in egg-milk mixture, making sure both slices of bread are saturated. Cook sandwiches on hot skillet; turn with a spatula when bottom of sandwich is golden brown. Remove when both sides are brown. May be served with maple syrup. Serve warm. Makes 7-8 sandwiches.

Laura Neff (Jerry)

Reuben Sandwiches

8 slices rye bread
Margarine
Mustard
4 slices corned beef

4 slices Swiss cheese
1 cup Bavarian-style
  sauerkraut

Spread both sides of bread slices with small amount of margarine. Toast each slice on both sides in a skillet over medium heat. For each sandwich spread 1 side of a slice of toasted bread with mustard, add 1 slice of corned beef, 1 slice of cheese and ¼ cup of sauerkraut. Top with second piece of toasted bread and heat until cheese is melted. You can complete this last step in the microwave if you wish. Serve with chilled kosher dill pickles. Makes 4 sandwiches.

Note: *Years ago a treat at Annual Conference was to eat at a great delicatessen on South Main Street in Houston. You couldn't get a Reuben just anywhere, so we experimented with various combinations to get the taste we liked. After that we didn't have to wait until the next conference!*

Joyce Pace (Rudy)

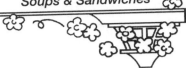

Cream Cheese Raisin Sandwich

1 (8 ounce) package cream
  cheese, softened
½ cup chopped nuts
¼ cup seedless raisins

¼ cup drained, crushed
  pineapple
Scant ⅛ teaspoon hot pepper
  sauce
8 slices whole wheat bread

Mix first 5 ingredients together. Spread on 4 slices of bread and place other slices on top. Makes 4 sandwiches.

Loraine Holt (Lloyd)

Green Chili Open-Faced Sandwiches

1 loaf French bread
½ cup margarine, softened
1 (4 ounce) can chopped
  green chilies, drained

¼ pound grated Monterey
  Jack cheese
½ cup mayonnaise
⅛ teaspoon garlic powder

Split bread lengthwise. Combine margarine and green chilies. Spread on both halves of bread. Mix cheese and mayonnaise; spread over other ingredients. Sprinkle with garlic powder. Place each half on ungreased baking sheet. Bake uncovered in a 350° oven for 20 minutes. Do not brown — it is done when bubbly. Slice and serve. May be stored in refrigerator for several hours before baking.

Karen Chance (Dale)

Bacon and Egg Sandwiches

4 slices bacon
3 hard boiled eggs, chopped

¼ teaspoon salt
2 tablespoons mayonnaise

Fry bacon until crispy, drain and crumble. Combine with chopped eggs and remaining ingredients. Use as a spread for sandwiches on bread of your choice. Makes 6 sandwiches.

Cookbook Committee

Corned Beef Sandwich Spread

1 can chilled corned beef
5 hard boiled eggs, chopped
1 cup chopped celery
½ teaspoon salt (optional)

1 cup finely chopped nuts
½ cup mayonnaise-type
 salad dressing
½ cup chili sauce or ketchup

Place the corned beef in a food processor and chop up. Pour into a mixing bowl and add remaining ingredients. Mix to desired consistency. Spread on sandwich bread. A good choice is nut bread. Makes lots.

Violet Waters (Bob)

My parson husband and I, along with our 3-month-old son, arrived in Navasota, Texas, on a bleak November night in the 1930's. We had left our former pastorate at dawn and traveled over rugged roads. I was sure there would be in this cultural little city a special delegation to welcome us. Alas! All was totally dark. My parson was thin and agile; consequently he found a parsonage window ajar, crawled in and unlocked the front door. All of our earthly possessions were placed on the living room floor. Once our baby was settled in the center of the room on his mattress, we swiftly set to work to have order. With pride, the impractical parson's wife demanded that our new chime doorbell be placed up first, certain that very soon the delegation would arrive to say, "Welcome!" She had not learned what her husband had told her, "We go where we are sent and often on short notice." Nevertheless, my ear was attuned to listening for the chime to sound. Hours passed and passed. We worked and waited. The town clock chimed 12 o'clock! A moment later the bell rang. With my churchy smile, I ran to the front door. There standing alone was a short little man with a charming grin on his face. He slowly drawled, "H-e-l-l-o. I am Bob Bill Dean. I just came to see who we got!" The parson's wife had learned a valuable truth. She dare not think she is very significant for she is just the companion of her parson husband in his Methodist career, and she is just passing through.

Mary Grace Dent (Frank)

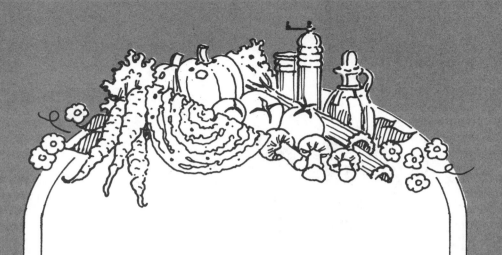

In the Garden

Salads & Dressings

Give us, Lord, a bit o' sun,
A bit o' work, and a bit o' fun;
Give us all in the struggle and sputter
Our daily bread, and bit o' butter;
Give us health, our keep to make
An' a bit to spare for others' sake.

Amen.

Strawberry Fruit Delight

1 (8 ounce) package cream cheese, softened
1 (16 ounce) can crushed pineapple, undrained
1 (16 ounce) package frozen strawberries, drained and sliced
1 (6 ounce) package miniature marshmallows
1 cup chopped pecans
1 (8 ounce) carton frozen whipped topping, thawed

Mix all ingredients together in a medium bowl and refrigerate. This may be used as a salad or is great served as a dessert with old fashioned pound cake.

Shirley Phillips (Richard)

Creamy Fruit Salad

1 (6 ounce) package vanilla instant pudding mix
1 pint buttermilk
1 (12 ounce) carton frozen whipped topping, thawed
1 (11 ounce) can mandarin oranges, drained
3 bananas, sliced
1 pint fresh strawberries, sliced
1 cup chopped nuts

Combine pudding mix with buttermilk in a large bowl. Stir in whipped topping. Add fruit and nuts. Mix well and refrigerate. Serves 8.

Kathy Danheim (Dan)

Fruit Salad

3 apples, chopped
3 bananas, sliced
1 (20 ounce) can chunk pineapple, drained
2 (16 ounce) packages frozen strawberries, thawed and drained
1 (20 ounce) can peach pie filling

In a medium salad bowl, layer ingredients in the order listed. Chill and serve.

Christine M. Garoutte (Victor)

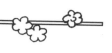

Arkansas Cherry Salad

1 (21 ounce) can cherry pie
  filling
1 (14 ounce) can sweetened
  condensed milk
1 (15¼ ounce) can crushed
  pineapple, drained

1 cup coconut
1 cup chopped pecans
1 (16 ounce) carton frozen
  whipped topping, thawed

Combine the pie filling, sweetened condensed milk, pineapple, coconut and pecans. Mix well in a large salad bowl. Fold in the whipped topping. Chill. Serves 30.

Lois Burnett (Ralph)
Ollie Phifer (Ernest)
Harriet Willis (Edwin)

Variation: Substitute 2 cups of miniature marshmallows for the 1 cup of coconut.

Nan Stein (Bernie)

Variation: Omit coconut. Increase chopped pecans to 1½ - 2 cups. Put in a 13x9x2-inch pan. Refrigerate or freeze.

Pam Besser (Robert)

Cherry Fruit Salad

1 (15¼ ounce) can chunk
  pineapple, partially drained
1 (21 ounce) can cherry pie
  filling

2 cups miniature
  marshmallows
½ cup chopped pecans
⅛ teaspoon almond extract
Frozen whipped topping

Mix first 5 ingredients together in a bowl. When serving, put a dollop of whipped topping on each serving.

Sue Bratz (Charles)

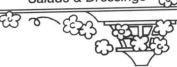

Fruit Medley

1 (29 ounce) can sliced pears
1 (16 ounce) can sliced peaches
1 (16 ounce) can sliced apricots
1 (20 ounce) can pineapple chunks
2 oranges, thinly sliced and unpeeled

1 (3 ounce) package any flavor gelatin (cherry is pretty)
1 cup sugar
½ cup vinegar
5 cloves
3 cinnamon sticks

Drain liquid from all the canned fruits, reserving about ½ the peach juice, ½ the apricot juice and all of the pineapple juice. (You will need 2½ cups reserved juice.) Set aside. Put oranges in saucepan and cover with water; boil until peel is tender. Drain well and set aside. To make marinade mix together in a large saucepan the 2½ cups reserved juice, gelatin, sugar, vinegar, cloves and cinnamon sticks. Simmer for 30 minutes (watch carefully as this will boil over quickly). Combine well-drained fruits in a large bowl. Pour hot marinade over all and chill for 24 hours or longer. Stir occasionally to tint all fruit.

Jean Cragg (Gene)

Pink Fluff

2 (8 ounce) containers pre-stirred strawberry yogurt
1 (8 ounce) container frozen whipped topping, thawed

1 (16 ounce) package whole frozen strawberries (fresh, when in season)

Stir yogurt and whipped topping together in 10-cup bowl until mixed together and smooth. Fold in frozen strawberries. Cover and refrigerate until needed. Serves 6-8.

Variation: *To make a heart-healthy version use nonfat yogurt and low-fat whipped topping.*

Eleanor Little (Don)

Hot Pineapple Salad

1 (20 ounce) can pineapple
  chunks, drained (reserve 3
  tablespoons juice)
½ cup sugar
3 tablespoons all-purpose
  flour

1 cup shredded sharp
  Cheddar cheese
½ cup melted margarine
1 cup round buttery crackers,
  crushed

Drain pineapple; add sugar and flour and stir in reserved juice; add cheese to pineapple mixture. Mix well. Spoon into a greased 1-quart dish. Combine melted margarine and crushed crackers and sprinkle over top. Bake in a 350° oven until lightly browned for approximately 20-30 minutes. Serves 6.

Kathleen Modd (Thomas R.)

Dreamy Frozen Fruit Salad

2 (3 ounce) packages cream
  cheese, softened
¼ cup lemon juice
1 (14 ounce) can sweetened
  condensed milk
1 cup chopped pecans

1 (15 ounce) can pineapple
  tidbits, drained
1 (21 ounce) can cherry pie
  filling
1 (12 ounce) container frozen
  whipped topping, thawed
Paper muffin cup liners

Combine cream cheese and juice; beat until smooth. Stir in milk, pecans and pineapple. Fold in pie filling and whipped topping. Place 24-30 paper liners in muffin tins. Spoon filling into liners and freeze. When frozen, remove from tins and place in plastic freezer bags until needed. Remove from freezer 30 minutes before serving. Serves 24-30.

Katie Anderson (Jerry)

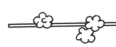
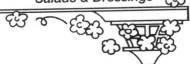

Frozen Fruit Salad (Papercup Salad)

2 cups sour cream
2 teaspoons lemon juice
½ cup sugar
⅛ teaspoon salt
1 (8 ounce) can crushed
    pineapple, drained

1 banana, diced
4 drops red food color
1 can Bing cherries, drained
Paper muffin cup liners

In a large mixing bowl, combine all ingredients. Spoon into paper muffin cups. Freeze.

Susan Helm (Cy)

Pretzel Salad

2 cups crushed pretzels
¾ cup margarine, melted
3 tablespoons sugar
1 (12 ounce) carton frozen
    whipped topping, thawed
1 (8 ounce) package cream
    cheese, softened

1 cup sugar
2 (3 ounce) packages
    strawberry gelatin
2 cups boiling water
2 (10 ounce) cartons frozen
    strawberries

Mix together crushed pretzels, margarine and 3 tablespoons sugar. Press into a 13x9x2-inch pan. Bake at 400° for 8 minutes. Meanwhile, mix frozen whipped topping, cream cheese and 1 cup sugar and spread over cooled bottom layer. Next, mix gelatin with 2 cups boiling water and stir until dissolved. Add frozen strawberries to gelatin mixture and stir until thawed. Let sit for 10 minutes, then pour over first two layers. Cover and refrigerate for several hours.

Note: *This may be used for a salad or dessert.*

Charlse Bell (J. Stewart)
Susan Johnson (Bob)

Mama's Fruit Salad

1 (8 ounce) can crushed
   pineapple, drained
1 (8 ounce) carton frozen
   whipped topping, thawed
1 (3 ounce) package lime or
   strawberry gelatin

2 tablespoons sugar
½ cup chopped pecans
1 (16 ounce) can fruit cocktail
   (optional)

Combine crushed pineapple, frozen whipped topping and gelatin together in a large bowl. Stir together until gelatin is dissolved. Add sugar, pecans and fruit cocktail. Stir well. Refrigerate for at least 15 minutes before serving.

Alynda Jones (Matthew)

Orange Gelatin Salad

1 (16 ounce) carton cottage
   cheese
1 (3 ounce) package orange
   gelatin
1 (12 ounce) carton frozen
   whipped topping, thawed

1 (16 ounce) can crushed
   pineapple, drained
1 (11 ounce) can mandarin
   oranges, drained

Place cottage cheese in mixing bowl. Sprinkle gelatin over cottage cheese and mix. Add frozen whipped topping and mix thoroughly. Then add crushed pineapple and mandarin oranges. Pour into a 13x9x2-inch glass casserole dish and chill overnight. Cut into squares and serve on a lettuce leaf.

Julia Miller (William A. "Buddy," Sr.)
Renna Williamson (W. J.)

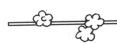

Holiday Salad

1 (6 ounce) package sugar-free cherry gelatin
1 (8 ounce) can crushed pineapple
1½ cups pineapple juice and water
1 (10 ounce) package frozen strawberries
1 cup nonfat vanilla yogurt
1 cup mashed bananas

Drain juice from pineapple and add water to equal 1½ cups. Bring to boil and add to gelatin. Mix well. Add frozen strawberries. Stir occasionally while strawberries thaw and gelatin thickens. Pour about ½ cup gelatin into yogurt and stir until blended. Pour remaining yogurt mixture into the gelatin. Add bananas and pineapple and chill until firm in a 9x9x2-inch square dish. Serves 8-10.

Doris Parrott (Bob)

Cranberry Salad

1 (16 ounce) can crushed pineapple
1 (3 ounce) box cherry gelatin
1 (3 ounce) box orange gelatin
1 (16 ounce) can jellied cranberry sauce
1 (8 ounce) carton frozen whipped topping, thawed
¼ cup confectioners' sugar
¼ cup mayonnaise
1 (3 ounce) package cream cheese, softened
1 cup chopped pecans (optional)

Drain pineapple and save juice. Add enough water to juice to make 2 cups liquid. Heat to boil and add gelatin. Stir until dissolved. Add cranberry sauce and crushed pineapple. Pour into 13x9x2-inch casserole dish. Let set in refrigerator. Add confectioners' sugar to whipped topping, then mayonnaise and cream cheese. Mix well. Spread on top of gelled mixture. Sprinkle with chopped pecans. Cut into squares. Serve on lettuce leaves.

Joye Chamness (Ben)

Orange - Cranberry Salad

1 package fresh cranberries
1½ oranges, quartered and
   seeded

1½ cups sugar
1 (6 ounce) package
   raspberry gelatin

Finely grind cranberries and oranges in a food grinder. Add sugar and stir well. This makes a relish. Set aside. Prepare raspberry gelatin according to package directions. If the relish mixture has extra juice, it may be used as part of liquid for gelatin. Place gelatin in refrigerator to cool. As it begins to gel, add 1½ cups of the relish mixture to the gelatin; stir to mix. Place gelatin in individual molds or in a larger salad mold. The remaining relish may be served as a complement to any meal. Store in refrigerator.

Nancy Oliphint (Ben)

Dark Bing Cherry Salad

1 (15¼ ounce) can crushed
   pineapple
1 (16½ ounce) can pitted dark
   Bing cherries
1 (6 ounce) package black
   cherry gelatin

2 cups cola-flavored
   carbonated drink
1 (8 ounce) package cream
   cheese
1 cup small pecan pieces

Drain juices from pineapple and cherries through a strainer and save. Heat juices and pour over gelatin in metal bowl and stir until dissolved. Add cola-flavored carbonated drink and refrigerate. In a 12x8x2-inch glass casserole dish, layer crushed pineapple, cherry halves, marble-sized pieces of cream cheese and pecans. When gelatin begins to gel, pour over layers and refrigerate overnight.

Note: *Edna Bennett, wife of the late Rev. Eugene D. Bennett III of the Texas Conference, gave me this recipe when I married. Not only is she a lovely person and concert-caliber pianist, but she also taught me piano from an early age and won my heart at the same time.*

Susan Hageman (Randy)

Apricot Gelatin Salad

1 (16 ounce) can fruit
  cocktail, undrained
1 (20 ounce) can crushed
  pineapple, undrained

2 (3 ounce) packages apricot
  gelatin
1 (12 ounce) carton frozen
  whipped topping, thawed

Put all fruit in a saucepan. Heat to boiling and sprinkle in gelatin. Stir until dissolved. Cool. Fold whipped topping into fruit mixture. Pour into a 13x9x2-inch pan. Chill until firm.

Fay Cannon (Neal)

Apricot Cheese Delight

1 (16 ounce) can apricots,
  drained and chopped
  (reserve juice)
1 (16 ounce) can crushed
  pineapple, drained (reserve
  juice)
2 (3 ounce) packages orange
  gelatin

2 cups boiling water
1 cup reserved fruit juices
¾ cup miniature
  marshmallows
Topping (recipe below)
¼ cup grated cheese

Drain fruits and chill fruit juices. Dissolve gelatin in boiling water and add 1 cup reserved juice. Chill until slightly congealed, then fold in fruits and marshmallows. Pour into 13x9x2-inch dish. Chill until firm. Spread topping (recipe below) on congealed salad; sprinkle with cheese.

Topping:
½ cup sugar
3 tablespoons all-purpose
  flour
1 egg, beaten well
1 cup reserved fruit juices

2 tablespoons margarine
1 package whipped topping
  mix, prepared according to
  package directions

Cook together sugar, flour, egg, fruit juices and margarine until thick over medium heat. Fold in 1 package prepared whipped topping mix. Serves 12-15.

Wanda Andrews (Andy)

63

Buttermilk Salad

**1 (6 ounce) package peach
gelatin
1 (20 ounce) can crushed
pineapple, undrained**

**2 cups buttermilk
1 (16 ounce) carton frozen
whipped topping, thawed**

Heat and dissolve gelatin in pineapple; cool completely. Whip buttermilk and frozen whipped topping together, then add to pineapple and gelatin mixture. Pour into a 13x9x2-inch pan or large crystal bowl. Refrigerate until set. Serves 12-15.

**Sylvia R. Blankenship (V. O.)
Kay Frazier (James)**

Cranberry - Raspberry Salad

**1 (6 ounce) package
raspberry gelatin
2 cups boiling water
½ cup cold water**

**1 (16 ounce) can whole berry
cranberry sauce
1 (12 ounce) package frozen
raspberries**

Dissolve gelatin in 2 cups of boiling water, then add ½ cup cold water. Stir in cranberry sauce and partially thawed raspberries. Refrigerate until congealed in a 9x9x2-inch pan. Serves 16.

Marty Sholars (Nick)

Variation: *Substitute 1 cup of applesauce for cranberry sauce; add ½ cup pecans and top with frozen whipped topping.*

Betsy Stutes (Robert)

Festive Cream Cheese Salad

1½ cups hot water
2 (3 ounce) packages any
 flavor gelatin
2 cups cold water
2 (3 ounce) packages cream
 cheese
1 (8 ounce) can crushed
 pineapple

2 cups miniature
 marshmallows
½ cup coarsely chopped
 pecans
5 or 6 chopped maraschino
 cherries

Dissolve gelatin in 1½ cups hot water. Add 2 cups of cold water. Soften cream cheese with small amount of dissolved gelatin. Combine all ingredients and refrigerate. After mixture begins to thicken, stir to evenly distribute the solid ingredients. Pour into 12x7x2-inch glass casserole dish and chill until firm. Cut into squares and serve on lettuce leaves.

Margaret Hall (A. Sherrill)

Grape - Blueberry Salad

2 (3 ounce) packages grape
 gelatin
2 cups boiling water
1 (20 ounce) can crushed
 pineapple
1 (16 ounce) can blueberry
 pie filling

1 (8 ounce) package cream
 cheese, softened
1 cup sour cream
½ cup sugar
1 teaspoon vanilla
½ cup chopped pecans

Add 2 cups boiling water to gelatin to dissolve. Add pineapple with juice and blueberry filling to gelatin. Pour into 13x9x2-inch pan and let set in refrigerator. Mix the next four ingredients with mixer. Spread over congealed salad. Top with pecans. Cut into squares and serve on bed of lettuce.

Barbara Carter (Fred F., Jr.)

65

Cranberry - Raspberry Congealed Salad

2 (3 ounce) packages
  raspberry gelatin
2 cups boiling water
1 (14 ounce) can whole
  cranberries

1 (8 ounce) can crushed
  pineapple, undrained
1 apple, peeled and chopped
  in small pieces
½ cup chopped celery
½ cup chopped nuts

Dissolve gelatin in boiling water; add remaining ingredients, chill and serve. Prepare in 12x8x2-inch or 2-quart casserole dish.

Elnor Lamb (Joe Ed)

"Christmas Salad" - Pineapple Cream Cheese Mold

½ cup water
½ cup sugar
1½ envelopes unflavored
  gelatin
½ cup cold water

1 (16 ounce) can crushed
  pineapple, drained
1 (8 ounce) package cream
  cheese, softened
½ cup chopped pecans
Red and green food color

Boil ½ cup water and ½ cup sugar in 2-quart saucepan. Dissolve 1½ envelopes of gelatin in ½ cup cold water. Add gelatin mixture into warm sugar water. Add crushed pineapple. Pour ½ of this mixture into clear glass 9x9x2-inch baking pan. Color green for festive look and refrigerate until gelled. Combine cream cheese and nuts and spread on gelled layer. Top with remaining pineapple mixture colored red. Refrigerate until top layer is gelled. Double recipe for 13x9x2-inch pan.

Note: *This is the traditional "Christmas Salad" in the Meadows' family. However, I use this recipe for other holidays, such as Easter and Thanksgiving, using different colors.*

Patti Meadows (David)

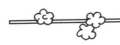
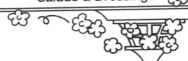

Apricot Dream - Cream

1 (6 ounce) package apricot
  gelatin
1 cup water
1 (20 ounce) can crushed
  pineapple, undrained
2 junior size jars apricot baby
  fruit

1 (14 ounce) can sweetened
  condensed milk
1 (8 ounce) package cream
  cheese, softened
½ cup chopped nuts

Combine in saucepan and bring to boil the apricot gelatin and water. When dissolved, remove from heat and stir in crushed pineapple and apricot baby fruit. While this is cooling, combine sweetened condensed milk with cream cheese (do not use ready-soft cream cheese). Beat smooth and stir in gelatin mixture. Add chopped nuts and pour into a 2-quart baking dish or individual molds and chill.

Note: *Stands up well without becoming "weepy" and is complimentary to any entree.*

Dorothea Fort (Joe W., Sr.)

Seafood Pasta Salad

1 (12 - 16 ounce) package
  rainbow rotini
1 - 2 cucumbers, peeled and
  chopped
2 bunches green onions,
  finely sliced
1 cup sliced black olives

1 (6 - 10 ounce) package
  flaked crab meat
Seasoned salt and pepper to
  taste
1 cup ranch-style salad
  dressing

Cook rotini according to directions. Drain and toss with all other ingredients except seasoned salt, pepper and dressing. Add seasonings to taste and mix well. Then toss with dressing. Chill well.

Mary Jane Petty (Ron)

Egg Cracker Salad

6 boiled eggs, chopped
½ cup chopped onion
½ cup chopped bell pepper
1 (2 ounce) jar pimiento,
   drained

1 cup sweet pickle relish
1 pint mayonnaise
1½ stacks long buttery
   crackers

Mix all ingredients together except the crackers and chill for several hours or overnight. Just before serving crumble crackers and sprinkle over the top.

Clairette Ratcliff (John)

Quick Mexican Salad

1 (16 ounce) can ranch-style
   beans, drained and washed
1 (8 ounce) package grated
   mild Cheddar cheese
6 fresh tomatoes, chopped
1 head lettuce, torn into bite-
   size pieces

1 (8 ounce) bottle Catalina
   French salad dressing
1 onion, chopped (optional)
1 (10 ounce) bag nacho
   chips, crushed

Mix everything together except the nacho chips and refrigerate until ready to serve. Just before serving stir in the nacho chips.

Note: *This is good for covered dish dinners because you don't have to worry about serving your hot food cold. It is also good for moving day since there are no left over ingredients. You use the entire bottle of dressing, the whole head of lettuce, etc.*

Belinda Carter (Thad)

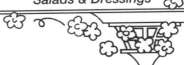

Fruity Chicken Salad

1 (15¼ ounce) can pineapple tidbits
4 cups cubed cooked chicken
1 (11 ounce) can mandarin oranges, drained
1 (8 ounce) can water chestnuts, sliced and drained
1 (2½ ounce) package sliced almonds, toasted

1 cup sliced celery
1 cup seedless grapes, halved
1 or 2 bananas, sliced
1½ cups mayonnaise
1 teaspoon lemon juice
1 teaspoon soy sauce
1 teaspoon curry powder
1 (3 ounce) can chow mein noodles

Drain pineapple, reserving 2 tablespoons juice. Combine chicken, oranges, water chestnuts, almonds, celery, grapes, bananas and pineapple in a 13x9x2-inch baking dish. Combine the 2 tablespoons pineapple juice, mayonnaise, lemon juice, soy sauce and curry powder. Stir into chicken mixture and chill. Stir in chow mein noodles just before serving. Serves 10.

Doris Parrott (Bob)

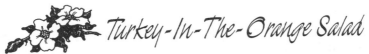

Turkey-In-The-Orange Salad

½ cup low-fat lemon yogurt
3 tablespoons fat-free mayonnaise or salad dressing
2 tablespoons frozen orange juice concentrate, thawed
Dash of salt
4 oranges, peeled and sliced

½ pound thinly sliced smoked turkey, cut into ¼-inch strips
1 purple onion, sliced and separated into rings
Fresh spinach
Cracked black pepper

Combine first 4 ingredients; cover and chill. Arrange orange slices, turkey and onion on spinach-lined salad plates. Drizzle with dressing and sprinkle with pepper. Serves 6.

Note: *Great for afternoon meetings with UMW!*

Lisa Reeves (R. Dean)

Potato Salad for 50

20 pounds potatoes, boiled
  or baked
2 dozen hard-boiled eggs
1 large onion, finely chopped
1 cup sweet relish
4-5 large dill pickles,
  chopped

2 tablespoons seasoned salt
1 tablespoon salt
1 tablespoon black pepper
½ - ¾ cup prepared mustard
1 quart mayonnaise

Peel and cut potatoes into bite-size chunks; set aside. Chop eggs and mix with remaining ingredients. Gently stir dressing mixture into potatoes. Season to taste. Chill before serving. Serves 50.

Note: *One of Longview celebrity Barbara Richardson's many contributions to Hallsville United Methodist Church! This recipe is a gem, because the ingredients can easily be halved, doubled or tripled to accommodate hungry crowds of any size.*

Kay Lynn Fenn (Marlin D.)

Cloggers' Delight Salad

1 (3 ounce) package beef
  ramen oriental noodles,
  uncooked and broken up
1 (12 ounce) package cole
  slaw mix

1 (2¼ ounce) package
  slivered almonds, toasted
¼ cup salted sunflower
  seeds
2-3 green onions, chopped
Dressing (recipe below)

Mix all ingredients except dressing together and set aside.

Dressing:
⅓ **cup apple cider vinegar**
½ **cup oil**
¼ **cup sugar**

**Beef seasoning from
  package of noodles**

Mix dressing ingredients and add to first mixture. Chill. Keeps well for days.

Martha Matthis (Leon)

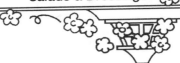

Calico Cheese Salad

1 (16 ounce) can red beans,
   rinsed and drained
1 (16 ounce) can whole
   kernel corn, drained
1 cup sliced celery

¼ pound Cheddar cheese,
   cut into ½-inch cubes
½ cup low-calorie Italian
   salad dressing

Mix all ingredients at least 3 hours before serving. Refrigerate and serve on lettuce leaves. Serves 4.

Betty Greening (John)

Fiesta Corn Salad

1 (15¼ ounce) can whole
   kernel corn, drained
1 cup chopped fresh tomato
1 cup chopped peeled
   cucumber
½ cup chopped celery

½ cup diced green bell
   pepper
2 green onions, sliced
½ cup low-fat Italian salad
   dressing

Combine all ingredients in a medium sized bowl and chill several hours before serving. Serves 4-6.

Mary Hicks (David)

Copper Pennies

6 carrots, pared and sliced
1 small onion, peeled and
   sliced
1 small bell pepper, seeded
   and sliced
½ cup tomato sauce
¼ cup orange juice

2 tablespoons cider vinegar
½ teaspoon Worcestershire
   sauce
½ teaspoon dry mustard
Salt and pepper to taste
2 tablespoons brown sugar

Simmer all ingredients for 10 to 15 minutes until the carrots are tender and crunchy. Serve warm or in glass bowl chilled. Serves 6-8.

Mary Lee Steger (Eugene)

Valley Salad

1 (10 ounce) package frozen peas
1 (10 ounce) package frozen broccoli
1 medium avocado, peeled and chopped
1 bunch green onions, chopped
1 medium cucumber, peeled and chopped
1 package ranch-style buttermilk dressing mix

Thaw frozen vegetables and drain well. Cut broccoli into smaller pieces. Combine all vegetables in a 2-quart glass casserole dish and mix well. Prepare 1 package buttermilk dressing mix according to package directions. Mix with vegetables and serve.

Laurie Hubert (Godfrey)

Layered Salad

1 medium head lettuce, chopped
1 cup chopped celery
1 red onion, sliced
1 (10 ounce) package frozen English peas, thawed and drained
1 (8 ounce) can sliced water chestnuts, drained
1 cup chopped cauliflower
2 cups mayonnaise
1 teaspoon lemon juice
1 teaspoon salt
1 teaspoon pepper
1 teaspoon Worcestershire sauce
2 cups shredded mozzarella cheese
½ cup shredded Parmesan cheese

Layer the following ingredients into a 13x9x2-inch casserole dish in the following order: lettuce, celery, onion, peas, water chestnuts and cauliflower. In a small mixing bowl, mix together mayonnaise, lemon juice, salt, pepper and Worcestershire sauce until well blended. Pour over layered vegetables, covering entirely and sealing edges. Sprinkle cheeses over the top. Cover with plastic wrap and refrigerate for 24 hours.

Virginia Jones (William F.)

Broccoli Salad Supreme

4 cups chopped raw broccoli
1 cup chopped celery
¼ cup chopped green onion
1 cup seedless green grapes
1 cup seedless red grapes
⅓ cup sugar
1 cup good quality
  mayonnaise

1 tablespoon red wine
  vinegar
½ pound bacon, fried crisp
  and crumbled
⅔ cup slivered or sliced
  almonds, toasted

Toss together the vegetables and grapes in a large salad bowl. Mix the sugar, mayonnaise and vinegar in a separate small bowl to make dressing. Pour dressing over vegetables and grapes and stir gently to allow dressing to coat evenly. Refrigerate overnight before serving, if time allows, for flavors to mix. Just before serving, add crumbled bacon and toasted almonds. Serves 10-12.

Note: *This recipe, along with the Beggar's Bundles, was given to me by a special friend while we lived in Fairfield. They have become favorites, and I love to prepare them for family and friends.*

Karen Bagley (Bert)

Broccoli - Raisin Salad

1 head fresh broccoli
1 cup mayonnaise
3 tablespoons minced onion
1½ tablespoons vinegar

3 tablespoons sugar (or to
  taste)
½ cup raisins
½ cup roasted peanuts

Separate broccoli into individual flowerets, cutting ½ to 1 inch below the flower. Mix in a separate bowl mayonnaise, onion, vinegar and sugar. Add raisins and pour all over the broccoli, mixing thoroughly. This should marinate overnight, if possible. Add peanuts shortly before serving.

Claudia Dvorak (Otto)

Broccoli Salad

2 bunches broccoli broken
  into small flowerets
¼ cup chopped red onion
1 pound bacon, cooked crisp
  and chopped

½ cup raisins
1 (2 ounce) package raw
  sunflower kernels (not dry
  roasted)
Dressing (recipe below)

Mix broccoli flowerets and onion together in a bowl. Cover and store in refrigerator overnight. Two hours before serving, add remaining ingredients to broccoli and onions and toss with dressing (recipe below). Serve well chilled.

Dressing:
1 cup mayonnaise
½ cup brown sugar

2 tablespoons red wine
  vinegar

Mix all dressing ingredients in a small bowl and store overnight in refrigerator.

Lydia Anderson (Charles)

Cole Slaw

6 cups finely chopped
  cabbage
2 cups ice water and cubes
1 teaspoon salt

1 cup sugar
½ cup vinegar (white or
  cider)
½ cup water

Soak cabbage in salted ice water overnight. Next day bring sugar, vinegar and water to boil to make dressing. Remove from stove and let cool. Drain cabbage well and add dressing. Chill.

Variation: Add any or all of the following: ½ cup chopped green peppers, 1 cup celery slices, ½ cup grated carrots.

Patricia K. Eifert (Richard)

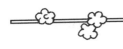

Sweet-and-Sour Kraut Salad

¼ cup vinegar
1 cup granulated sugar
1 (32 ounce) jar sauerkraut
¼ cup diced celery

½ cup chopped green bell pepper
1 small onion, chopped
2 tablespoons chopped pimiento

Combine vinegar and sugar in small saucepan. Boil, then set aside to cool. Drain sauerkraut thoroughly. Add remaining ingredients and pour vinegar-sugar mixture over all. Cover and place in refrigerator until serving time. Salad may be stored in refrigerator for 1 week.

Cynthia Hullum Kethley (T. Paul)

Orange Avocado Salad

¼ cup vegetable oil
2 tablespoons red wine vinegar
½ cup fresh orange juice
½ teaspoon grated orange peel
¼ teaspoon salt
2 tablespoons sugar
1 tablespoon fresh lemon juice

1 head red leaf or Romaine lettuce, torn into small pieces
1 (11 ounce) can mandarin oranges, drained
2 avocados, peeled and sliced
1 cucumber, sliced
1 red onion, sliced and separated into rings

To make salad dressing, combine the oil, red wine vinegar, orange juice, peel, salt, sugar and lemon juice. Mix well. Store in the refrigerator. Just prior to mealtime, toss together the remaining ingredients. Pour salad dressing over all and stir gently. Serve.

Hint: This salad travels well if just before you leave the house, you mix all ingredients except lettuce in a Tupperware container with tight lid. Carry lettuce in ziplock bag. Mix when you arrive.

Kay Lynn Fenn (Marlin D.)

Mandarin Salad

½ cup sliced almonds
3 tablespoons sugar
½ head iceberg lettuce
½ head romaine lettuce
1 cup chopped celery
2 whole green onions,
  chopped

1 (11 ounce) can mandarin
  oranges, drained and
  chilled (may use more, if
  desired)
Mandarin Salad Dressing
  (recipe below)

In a small pan over medium heat, cook almonds and sugar, stirring constantly until almonds are coated and sugar dissolved. Watch carefully as they will burn easily. Cool and store in airtight container. Tear lettuce into bite-size pieces and mix with celery and onions. Just before serving, add almonds and chilled oranges. Toss with Mandarin Salad Dressing. Serves 8-10.

Mandarin Salad Dressing:
½ teaspoon salt
Dash of pepper
¼ cup vegetable oil
1 tablespoon chopped
  parsley

2 tablespoons sugar
2 tablespoons vinegar
Dash of hot pepper sauce

Mix all dressing ingredients in a small bowl. Cover and chill until ready to use.

Cookbook Committee

At one of our early pastorates in the Oklahoma Panhandle, the wonderful people there would give us an old-fashioned "pounding" about twice a year. Invariably, someone would bring a live chicken. Now I was a "city gal" who had never killed or dressed a chicken (after all these years, I still have not). I had to do something about that chicken. I finally had nerve enough to ask an elderly widow friend across the street to do it for me, my excuse being that I had an appointment and didn't have time to do it myself. She agreed, but I'm sure I was the talk of the day at the next Farm Women's Club meeting. Anyway, after that she just automatically came and took care of the live chickens that were given to us. What a friend!

Bennie Crutchfield (Finis)

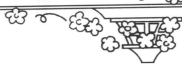

Spinach and Strawberry Salad

12 ounces fresh spinach
2 tablespoons sesame seeds
¼ cup safflower oil
2 tablespoons salad vinegar
  or white wine vinegar
2 tablespoons sugar

2 tablespoons minced green
  onions
1 teaspoon salt
Dash of pepper or paprika
Dash of hot pepper sauce or
  Worcestershire sauce
1 pint strawberries, sliced

Wash, trim, and dry spinach; refrigerate. Toast sesame seeds on a pan in a preheated 350° oven, until golden, about 10 minutes. Let cool. Combine remaining ingredients, except strawberries, in a tightly covered container and shake until sugar and salt are dissolved. Refrigerate. When ready to serve, toss spinach, sesame seeds, dressing and strawberries together. Serves 4-6.

Audrey Anne Barfield (Audrey and John)
Pam Besser (Robert)

Variation: For a larger salad, add other types of salad greens, such as romaine, endive, green leaf lettuce, to the spinach. Increase dressing ingredients as follows: 1 cup oil, ½ cup vinegar, ½ cup sugar, 3 teaspoons salt (may use part garlic salt and part celery salt). One cup of cashew nuts can be used in place of the sesame seeds. Follow directions above. Serves 10-12.

Ann Miller (Dan L.)

Marinated Vegetable Salad

1 (15 ounce) can French-style
  green beans, drained
1 (15 ounce) can English
  peas, drained
1 (15 ounce) can white
  shoepeg corn, drained
½ cup diced bell pepper
½ cup chopped celery

1 bunch green onions,
  chopped
1 (2 ounce) jar chopped
  pimiento, drained
½ cup vegetable oil
½ cup vinegar
½ cup sugar
Salt and pepper to taste

Combine first 7 ingredients in a 2-quart airtight container. Set aside. In a small bowl, mix last 4 ingredients together. Stir vinegar mixture into combined vegetables. Prepare at least 24 hours ahead. Cover and refrigerate. Keeps for a couple of weeks.

June Moore (Jim)

Salad Nicholi

1 head romaine lettuce
1 head red-tip lettuce
1 (10 ounce) bag spinach
10 slices bacon, cooked and
  crumbled

3 green onions, slivered
1 (16 ounce) carton cottage
  cheese
Dressing (recipe below)

In a salad bowl combine washed greens, bacon, onions and cottage cheese. Set aside.

Dressing:
½ cup cider vinegar
¼ cup sugar
1 teaspoon dry mustard
1 teaspoon salt

3 tablespoons chopped
  green onions (include tops)
⅔ cup vegetable oil

Combine vinegar, sugar, mustard, salt and onion in blender and mix on high speed. With blender on low speed, slowly add oil. Pour dressing over salad and toss.

Carol Crawford (James)

Zesty Salad Dressing

2 cups vegetable oil
⅔ cup red wine vinegar
2 cloves garlic, chopped
2 tablespoons Italian herb
  blend

¼ cup grated Parmesan
  cheese
1 tablespoon sugar
1 tablespoon salt
1 teaspoon cracked pepper

Combine ingredients. Beat. Serve over green salad.

Merle Williams (Charles)

Staff of Life

Breads

God is great; God is good;
Let us thank Him for our food.
By His hands we are fed;
Thank you, Lord, for daily bread.
Amen.

Sour Cream Cornbread

1 cup yellow cornmeal
1 teaspoon salt
½ teaspoon baking soda
⅓ cup melted shortening or
  vegetable oil
3 eggs, beaten

1 cup cream-style corn
1 cup sour cream
1 cup (4 ounces) shredded
  Cheddar cheese
4 - 5 jalapeño peppers,
  minced (fresh, if available)

Preheat oven to 300°. Combine cornmeal, salt and soda. Mix well. Stir in melted shortening, beaten eggs, corn and sour cream. Spoon ½ of mixture into a hot, greased 12-inch heavy skillet. Spread cheese and peppers in a layer, then cover with other half of mixture. Bake at 300° for 40 minutes uncovered.

Mildred Wallace (Paul)

Delicious Cornbread

2 cups yellow cornmeal,
  divided
2 tablespoons shortening
1 cup boiling water
½ teaspoon baking soda

½ teaspoon salt
1 teaspoon baking powder
1 cup milk
2 eggs, beaten

Blend together 1 cup of cornmeal and shortening. Pour boiling water into mixture; stir briskly. Sift the remaining cup of cornmeal together with soda, salt and baking powder. Add milk and eggs. Add to the first mixture; mix well. Pour into a greased 9x9x2-inch pan. Bake at 450° for 30 minutes.

Sue Hutchins (David)

W*hen asked by her granddaughter if the furniture in the parsonage at the new appointment was French Provincial, Rita Watson (Mrs. B. A.) replied, "No, it is Methodist Providential!"*

Beverly Duree (Sam)

Hot Water Cornbread

½ cup all-purpose flour
1 cup cornmeal
½ teaspoon salt

Boiling water (approximately
   ½ cup)
Hot vegetable oil

Mix together the flour, cornmeal and salt. Pour boiling hot water over mixture until thick consistency, stirring constantly. (BE CAREFUL — don't use too much water!) Mixture should stick together to form 1-inch balls. Flatten slightly. Drop into hot oil and fry until golden brown. Drain and serve immediately.

Alynda Jones (Matthew)

Mexican Cornbread

1½ cups cornmeal
½ cup all-purpose flour
½ teaspoon salt
2 tablespoons sugar
1 teaspoon baking powder
½ teaspoon baking soda
⅔ cup buttermilk
½ cup water
2 eggs

3 tablespoons corn oil,
   divided
1 bell pepper, chopped
1 jalapeño pepper, chopped
1 cup grated Cheddar cheese
1 (2 ounce) jar chopped
   pimiento
1 onion, chopped
1 (12 ounce) can corn

Mix dry ingredients. Add buttermilk, water, eggs and 1½ tablespoons of corn oil; mix well. Add peppers, cheese, pimiento, onion and corn; stir well. Pour cornbread mixture into a hot pan, containing the remaining corn oil. Bake in a 13x9x2-inch oblong pan at 400° for 30 minutes. Cut into squares and serve hot. Makes 15-20 servings.

Note: *In the fall of 1979, I baked this cornbread and entered it in the Pioneer Days event at Pittsburg, Texas. First Place earned me a trophy and a check for $25.*

Helen President Thomas (Darnell)

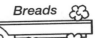

Mary Ann's Mexican Cornbread

1 (14½ ounce) can cream-
  style corn
1 egg, well beaten
1 cup milk
½ teaspoon baking soda
¾ teaspoon salt
½ cup bacon drippings
1 cup cornmeal

½ pound ground meat
1 large onion, chopped
4 (4 ounce) cans green chili
  peppers
½ cup grated Cheddar
  cheese
Pimientos

Mix corn, egg, milk, baking soda, salt, bacon drippings and cornmeal in a large bowl. Brown meat with onion and peppers. Add cheese to melt. Stir meat mixture into corn mixture, then add pimientos. Bake in a greased 9-inch square baking pan at 350° for 45-50 minutes.

Rebecca Faulk (Robert)

Heart-Healthy Cornbread

1 cup yellow cornmeal
1 cup all-purpose flour
2 tablespoons sugar
4 teaspoons baking powder

¾ teaspoon salt
1 cup skim milk
2 units egg substitute
⅓ cup applesauce

Combine dry ingredients in a large mixing bowl. Add milk, egg substitute and applesauce; blend. Pour into 12x9x2-inch baking dish sprayed with non-stick vegetable spray. Bake at 425° for 20 minutes or until lightly browned. NO FAT & NO CHOLESTEROL! Makes 12 servings, 100 calories each.

Alice A. Dawson (Ferd, III)

Broccoli Cornbread

2 (8½ ounce) boxes
   cornbread mix
4 eggs, beaten
1 cup cottage cheese

1 (10 ounce) package frozen
   chopped broccoli, cooked
   and drained
2 sticks margarine, melted
1 small onion, chopped

Mix all ingredients together and pour into a greased 13x9x2-inch pan. Bake at 350° for about 1 hour. Excellent with soup!

Peggy Laing (Charles)

Black-Eyed Pea Cornbread

1 pound sausage, browned
   and drained
2 cups grated Cheddar
   cheese
1 (4 ounce) can chopped
   green chilies
1 (15 ounce) can black-eyed
   peas, undrained
1 (15 ounce) can cream-style
   corn

1 cup cornmeal
1 cup all-purpose flour
1 cup finely chopped onion
1 teaspoon salt
½ teaspoon baking soda
2 eggs
1 cup buttermilk
1 - 2 tablespoons vegetable
   oil

Mix together and pour into 2 greased 9-inch square baking pans. Bake at 350° for 55 minutes. Cornbread will not be thick.

Hazel Hampton (Jed)

When we married in 1942, I had many luncheon cloths which I felt should be used. I decided that in order to be able to enjoy all these cloths, I must change to a clean one each day. That went well until one windy day the clothes line broke with many cloths in the wash. I decided then, after picking all the grassburrs out of the wash, I did not need to change the table so often.

Kay Kellow (Keith)

Bishop's Favorite Muffins

1 cup all-purpose flour
½ cup brown sugar, tightly
  packed
4 teaspoons baking powder
½ teaspoon salt (optional)

¼ cup vegetable oil
⅓ cup egg substitute
½ cup skim milk
½ cup chopped dates
2 cups raisin bran

Mix all ingredients except raisin bran and dates until well blended. Add chopped dates and fold in raisin bran. Spray muffin pan with non-stick vegetable spray. Fill muffin cups about ⅔ full. Bake at 400° until golden brown for about 25 minutes. Serve warm. Makes 1 dozen muffins.

Anne Hearn (J. Woodrow)

California Muffins

1 apple, peeled and cored
9 pitted prunes
9 pitted dates
2 small ripe bananas
3 eggs
¼ cup margarine, softened
1 teaspoon vanilla
1 teaspoon salt
¼ cup orange juice

1½ cups whole wheat flour
½ cup sunflower kernels
1 cup rolled oats
½ cup chopped walnuts
⅓ cup nonfat dry milk
2 teaspoons baking powder
1 teaspoon baking soda
⅓ cup unsweetened
  shredded coconut

In a blender, chop apple, prunes and dates. Add bananas, eggs, margarine, vanilla, salt and orange juice; blend. In a large mixing bowl, mix together the remaining ingredients. (It's easy to make ahead and store the dry ingredients in an airtight container until needed.) Pour blender mixture over dry ingredients and mix well. Pour into greased muffin cups. Bake at 350° for 20-25 minutes. (Or use mini-muffin tins and bake for 10 minutes.) Makes 1½ - 2 dozen muffins.

Note: Excellent for snacks & no sugar!!

Lea Bynum (Jonathan)

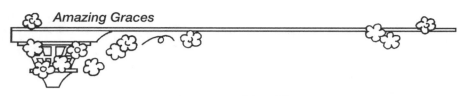
Orange Muffins

½ cup vegetable shortening
1 cup sugar
2 eggs, beaten
2 cups all-purpose flour
1 teaspoon baking soda

1 cup buttermilk
½ cup white raisins
½ cup grated orange rind
1 cup brown sugar
Juice of 1 orange

Cream shortening and sugar; add beaten eggs. Add flour, sifted with soda. Alternating with buttermilk, add raisins and orange rind. Bake at about 375° in small muffin cup tins until lightly browned. When done, dissolve brown sugar in orange juice; heat until hot but not boiling. Dip each muffin in hot sauce.

Mary Grace Dent (Frank)

Strawberry Muffins

1 cup strawberries
½ cup water
⅔ cup nonfat dry milk
3 eggs
½ teaspoon cinnamon

¼ teaspoon nutmeg
¼ teaspoon artificial
  sweetener
2 cups unprocessed bran
2 teaspoons baking powder

Preheat oven to 350°. Put the first 6 ingredients in a blender at medium speed. Place sweetener, bran and baking powder in a large bowl. Add batter; mix thoroughly. Spray 16 muffin cups with non-stick vegetable spray; spoon in batter. Bake for 15-20 minutes. Makes 16 muffins, 52 calories each.

Audrey Jones (Harold)

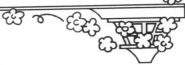

Banana Nut Muffins

½ cup butter flavor vegetable
  shortening
1¼ cups sugar
2 eggs
3 ripe bananas, mashed

1 teaspoon vanilla
2 cups biscuit baking mix,
  sifted
1 cup chopped pecans

In a large mixing bowl, cream shortening and sugar. Add eggs, bananas and vanilla. Add biscuit mix 1 cup at a time. Add pecans. Pour into greased muffin cups. Bake for 20 minutes at 350°.

Variation: Pour batter into a greased 9x5x3-inch loaf pan and bake for 30 minutes at 350°.

Maurine McDaniel (Edwin)

Strawberry Bread With Spread

2 (10 ounce) packages frozen
  sliced strawberries, thawed
3 cups all-purpose flour
1 teaspoon baking soda
1 teaspoon cinnamon
2 cups sugar

1 teaspoon salt
1¼ cup vegetable oil
4 eggs, well beaten
1 teaspoon red food coloring
Spread (recipe below)

Measure out ½ cup strawberry juice and reserve for spread. Mix all dry ingredients together. Make a hole in center of mixture. Pour strawberries, oil and eggs into the hole. Mix by hand until all ingredients are combined. Add food coloring. Mix well. Pour into 2 greased and floured 9x5x3-inch loaf pans. Bake at 350° for 1 hour. Cool thoroughly.

Spread:
½ cup reserved strawberry
  juice

1 (8 ounce) package cream
  cheese, softened

Mix until spreading consistency is obtained. Spread on cooled slices of strawberry bread.

Lydia Anderson (Charles)

Zucchini Bread

3 large eggs
2 cups sugar
1 cup vegetable oil
2 cups grated zucchini
3 teaspoons vanilla extract

3 cups all-purpose flour
1 teaspoon salt
¼ teaspoon baking powder
1 teaspoon baking soda
3 teaspoons cinnamon

Mix eggs, sugar, oil, zucchini and vanilla. Sift dry ingredients. Stir into zucchini mixture. Blend well; add nuts. Divide into 2 greased and floured 9x5x3-inch loaf pans. Bake at 350° for 45-60 minutes. Makes 2 loaves.

Betty Hawkins (James)

Cherry Pecan Bread

1 egg
1 (4 ounce) bottle
maraschino cherries
1 cup sugar
2 tablespoons melted butter
or margarine
¼ cup reserved maraschino
cherry juice

¼ cup orange juice
¼ cup water
2 cups all-purpose flour,
sifted
3 teaspoons baking powder
¼ teaspoon baking soda
¾ teaspoon salt
1 cup chopped pecans

Beat egg. Drain cherries and keep the juice. Chop cherries; add to egg. Stir in sugar and melted butter. Add cherry juice, orange juice and water. Sift together flour, baking powder, baking soda and salt. Add these to wet mixture and beat well. Add chopped nuts. Bake in a greased 9x5x3-inch loaf pan at 350° for about 45 minutes-1 hour.

Note: *This makes a very nice gift at Christmas time.*

Linda Jordan (Clinton)

Cranberry Nut Orange Bread

2 cups all-purpose flour,
  sifted
1 cup sugar
1½ teaspoons baking powder
½ teaspoon baking soda
½ teaspoon salt
¼ cup shortening

¾ cup orange juice
1 teaspoon grated orange
  peel
1 egg, well beaten
½ cup chopped nuts
1 - 2 cups halved fresh
  cranberries

Sift dry ingredients, then cut in shortening. Combine orange juice, orange peel and beaten egg. Pour into dry ingredients; stir just to moisten. Add nuts and cranberries. Pour into a greased 9x5x3-inch loaf pan. Bake at 350° for about 1 hour.

Gussie Vance (Nolan)

Poppy Seed Bread

3 cups all-purpose flour
2 cups sugar
3 eggs
1½ teaspoons baking powder
1½ tablespoons poppy seeds
1½ teaspoons salt

1½ cups milk
¾ cup vegetable oil
1½ teaspoons vanilla extract
1½ teaspoons almond extract
Glaze (recipe below)

Preheat oven to 350°. Combine flour, sugar, eggs, baking powder, poppy seeds, salt, milk, oil, vanilla and almond extracts. Beat for 2 minutes. Pour the batter into 2 greased 8x4x2½-inch loaf pans. Bake at 350° for 1 hour. Cool the bread in the pans for 5 minutes before removing. Prepare glaze from recipe below and drizzle glaze mixture onto loaves while hot. This bread freezes well. Makes 24 slices.

Glaze:
1 cup sifted confectioners'
  sugar
1 tablespoon soft margarine

4 teaspoons vanilla extract
¼ teaspoon almond extract
Hot water

Cream sugar with margarine. Add vanilla and almond extracts. Add hot water to desired consistency.

Daisy Green (Reubin)

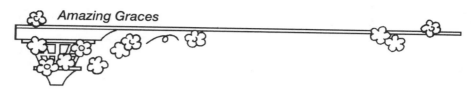

Pumpkin Bread

1⅔ cups all-purpose flour
1½ cups sugar
¼ teaspoon baking powder
1 teaspoon baking soda
¾ teaspoon salt
½ teaspoon cloves
½ teaspoon nutmeg
½ teaspoon cinnamon

½ cup vegetable oil
½ cup water
1 cup pumpkin
2 eggs, beaten
1 cup chopped nuts
1 cup chopped dates or
  raisins

Sift dry ingredients and set aside. Combine oil, water, pumpkin and eggs and add to flour mixture. Do not over blend. Fold in nuts and fruit (raisins or dates). Bake in a greased and floured 9x5x3-inch loaf pan at 325° for 1 - 1½ hours.

Note: *This bread is nice and moist. Be careful not to overbake it!*

Juanita Jonté (Eugene)

Sugarless Banana Bread

1 cup all-purpose flour
1 cup whole wheat flour
2 teaspoons baking powder
1 teaspoon baking soda
¼ teaspoon cinnamon
¼ teaspoon nutmeg

¼ teaspoon salt
2 eggs
⅓ cup oil
¾ cup mashed banana
½ cup water

Sift dry ingredients together. Mix eggs, oil, banana and water together. Add to dry ingredients. Bake in a greased 9x5x3-inch loaf pan at 325° until well done, about 45 minutes, being careful not to overbake it. Makes 1 loaf.

Marie Beckendorf (Calvin)

Banana Bread

½ cup margarine
1 cup sugar
2 eggs, beaten
3 very ripe bananas, mashed

1 teaspoon baking soda
2 cups all-purpose flour
Pinch of salt
½ cup chopped nuts

Cream margarine and sugar. Add remaining ingredients in order listed. Mix well, but not too hard. Pour batter into greased 9x5x3-inch loaf pan and bake for 50-60 minutes in a 375° oven. Cool in pan for 5 minutes before turning out onto a cake rack. Freezes well.

Barbara Carter (Fred F., Jr.)

One Pan Banana Bread

⅓ cup vegetable oil
1½ cups mashed ripe
   bananas (about 3 bananas)
½ teaspoon vanilla extract
3 eggs

2⅓ cups buttermilk biscuit
   baking mix
1 cup sugar
½ cup chopped nuts

Generously grease the bottom of a 9x5x3-inch loaf pan. In the loaf pan, combine all ingredients and stir with a fork until moistened. Beat vigorously for 1 minute. Bake at 350° for 55-65 minutes until wooden pick inserted in the center comes out clean. Cool 5 minutes. Run knife or metal spatula around side of pan to loosen and remove.

Frances Jammer (C. C., Sr.)

Light Rolls

2 packages dry yeast
1 cup slightly warm water
1 cup shortening or
vegetable oil
1 cup milk, skim if desired

½ cup sugar
2 teaspoons salt
2 eggs, well beaten
6 cups all-purpose flour,
sifted

Pour warm water over yeast to soften; set aside. In a saucepan, heat shortening, milk, sugar and salt until steamy hot, not boiling. Pour into large mixing bowl. Add yeast. Add eggs that have been beaten well. Add flour, half at a time. Mix well until dough forms. Place in airtight covered container and refrigerate. This dough may be stored in refrigerator for up to 1 week. About 2 hours before baking time, remove from refrigerator, make into one of the following types of rolls, let rise until doubled in size in a warm place and bake as directed.

Pull-Apart Round:
Roll out ⅓ of dough on floured surface. Cut into round pieces with biscuit cutter. Dip each piece in melted margarine and stand up in a tube pan arranged in a circular pattern. Let rise. Bake at 400° for 20 minutes.

Crescent Rolls:
Divide dough into thirds. Roll out on floured surface into pie shape, rather thin. Cut into 12 wedges. Dip in melted margarine and roll into crescents. Place on cookie sheets. Let rise. Bake at 400° for 15 minutes.

Sweet Rolls:
Roll dough into small balls and dip into melted margarine. Then dip in a mixture of 2 cups sugar to 2 tablespoons of cinnamon. Place on cookie sheets. Let rise. Bake at 400° for 15 minutes. Dribble with glaze made of confectioners' sugar and milk if desired.

Jane Cunningham (William R.)

Sour Cream Crescent Rolls

½ cup butter or margarine
1 (8 ounce) carton sour
  cream
½ cup sugar
2 packages dry yeast

½ cup warm water (105-115°)
2 eggs, beaten
4 cups all-purpose flour
1 teaspoon salt

Place ½ cup butter in small sauce pan and bring to boil. Remove from heat; stir in sour cream and sugar. Cool. Dissolve yeast in warm water in a large bowl; let stand 5 minutes. Stir in sour cream mixture and eggs. Combine flour and salt; gradually add flour mixture to yeast mixture, mixing well. Cover and refrigerate at least 8 hours (or overnight). Punch dough down and divide into 4 parts. Roll each portion into a 10-inch circle on a floured surface; brush with melted butter. Cut each circle into 12 wedges; roll up each wedge beginning at wide end. Place on greased baking sheet, point side down. Cover and let rise in warm place, free from drafts, until doubled in bulk (about 1 hour). Bake at 375° for 10-12 minutes or until golden brown. Makes 4 dozen rolls.

 *Note: Dough may be shaped and baked in any shape you like. For the health conscious, 8 ounces of low-fat plain yogurt may be substituted for the sour cream and egg substitute for the eggs.*

Eunice Sonneman (Bill)

When we were first married and Finis was serving as an Assistant Pastor, our income and food often seemed to run out before the month did. On one such occasion, I kept watering down the soup trying to make it stretch. Finally, I decided I had to do something to flavor it. Not having any tomatoes in the pantry, I added ketchup. We never forgot the day I put ketchup in the soup. Fortunately, the next morning the church received a call from the State Funeral Directors and Embalmers asking for someone to come open their meeting with a prayer. Finis was sent. As he walked off the stage after his prayer, someone handed him an envelope. He immediately opened it, quickly ran to call me and said, "We eat!" The envelope contained 2 one dollar bills. We had tangible proof that the Lord provides!

Bennie Crutchfield (Finis)

Magic Biscuits

5 cups all-purpose flour
1 teaspoon baking soda
1 - 3 teaspoons baking
powder
1 teaspoon salt

5 tablespoons sugar
¾ - 1 cup shortening
2 cups buttermilk
1 - 1½ packages dry yeast
3 - 4 tablespoons hot water

Mix dry ingredients; cut in shortening. Add buttermilk and yeast which has been dissolved in hot water. Put in oiled bowl, cover and refrigerate. You don't have to wait for rising. Bake in desired manner at 400° for 10 minutes.

Judy Barnes (Jay)

Batter Bread

3 cups all-purpose flour
1 teaspoon salt
1 package yeast

1⅓ cups water
4 tablespoons vegetable oil
2 tablespoons honey

Measure flour, salt and yeast into a mixing bowl and stir. Into a 4-cup glass measuring cup, pour water, oil and honey. Heat liquid to almost-boiling in the microwave. Stir and add to dry ingredients. Stir 3-4 minutes. If mixture is too stiff, add a few tablespoons water. If it is too runny, add a little flour. Let it sit about 30 minutes or more until it has just about doubled in size. Punch it down and knead for about 5 minutes. Turn into a well-greased loaf pan; smooth the top with a little water. Let rise in a warm place for about 30 minutes or until it reaches to top of the pan. Bake at 350° for 20-25 minutes until well browned on the top. Turn out to cool on a rack. Makes 1 loaf.

Variation: For a little different flavor, substitute 1 cup of whole wheat flour for 1 cup of the all-purpose flour. Sugar can be used instead of honey. Again, it will change the flavor a little. Just for fun toss in a few raisins, chopped pecans and a little cinnamon on the last stirring. This may increase the quantity, in which case an additional baking pan may be needed.

Marjorie Willis (Don)

Fresh Yeast Bread

1 cup scalded milk
½ cup shortening
⅔ cup sugar
1½ teaspoons salt

⅔ cup cold milk
1 yeast cake
⅓ cup warm water
6 - 7 cups all-purpose flour

Combine scalded milk, shortening, sugar and salt. Heat and stir until shortening is melted. Add cold milk. When mixture is lukewarm, stir in yeast that has been dissolved in the warm water. Gradually work in flour. Knead for 8-10 minutes. Cover with cloth and let rise until double in bulk. Press down, divide in half, place in 2 greased 9x5x3-inch loaf pans and let rise until double in bulk. Bake at 350° about 45 minutes or until done. Makes 2 loaves.

Mary House (Morris)

Oatmeal Bread

1½ cups boiling water
1 cup rolled oats
1 teaspoon salt
1 package dry yeast
¼ cup warm water

⅓ cup light molasses
1½ tablespoons vegetable oil
4 - 4½ cups sifted all-purpose
 flour

Pour boiling water over oatmeal. Add salt; stir and cool to lukewarm. Dissolve yeast in warm water. Add molasses, oil and dissolved yeast to oatmeal mixture. Gradually add flour until dough is stiff enough to handle. Knead dough for about 5 minutes until smooth and elastic. Place dough in lightly oiled bowl, turning to coat all sides. Cover and let rise in a warm place until double in size. Punch down and knead for a few minutes. Shape in loaf and place in well oiled 9x5x3-inch loaf pan. Cover and let rise again 1 hour or until double in size. Bake at 375° for 50 minutes.

Laura Winborn (Conrad)

Rich Sweet Bread Dough

¾ cup milk
½ cup sugar
1 teaspoon salt
½ cup margarine
½ cup warm water (105-115°)

2 packages or cakes of yeast
1 egg
4 cups all-purpose flour,
   sifted

Scald milk; stir in sugar, salt and margarine and cook over low heat until sugar and margarine are dissolved. Cool to lukewarm. Measure warm water into a large, warm bowl. Sprinkle or crumble in yeast and stir until dissolved. Stir in the lukewarm milk mixture, the egg and half the flour; beat until smooth. Stir in remaining flour to make a stiff batter. Cover tightly with plastic wrap or foil. Refrigerate dough at least 2 hours or up to 3 days. To use, cut off amount needed and shape as desired. This recipe can be used for sweet rolls of any kind, including the recipes for Kolaches and Pecan Sticky Buns below.

Kolaches:
½ recipe Rich Sweet Dough
   (see above)

Choice of cream cheese, fruit
   or sausage

Cut the dough into 16 pieces. Form into small balls and place on a greased baking sheet about 2 inches apart. Flatten with palm of hand. Cover and let rise until double in bulk. Press center of each ball down with small glass, leaving a rim around the edge. Fill with choice of cream cheese, fruit or sausage. Bake at 350° for 30 minutes. You may dust with confectioners' sugar after removing from oven. Makes 16 Kolaches.

Pecan Sticky Buns:
1 cup margarine
2½ cups brown sugar,
   divided

2½ cups chopped pecans,
   divided
1 recipe Rich Sweet Dough
   (above)

Melt margarine. Stir in 1½ cups brown sugar and 1 cup chopped pecans. Spoon equally into 24 greased muffin cups. Combine remaining 1 cup brown sugar and 1½ cups chopped pecans. Divide dough in half. Roll out each half into a 12-inch square. Sprinkle each half with the brown sugar-pecan mixture. Roll up lengthwise as for a jelly roll. Cut

(Rich Sweet Bread Dough, continued on next page)

(Rich Sweet Bread Dough, continued)

into 1 inch slices and place in prepared muffin cups. Cover; let rise in warm place until doubled in bulk (about an hour). Bake at 350° for 25 minutes. Turn buns immediately out onto waxed paper so that sugar and butter mixture won't harden in pans. Makes 24 buns.

Jaunita Lang (Fred)

All-Bran Bread or Rolls

1 cup all-bran cereal
½ cup sugar
¾ cup vegetable shortening
1½ teaspoons salt
1 cup boiling water

2 packages dry yeast
  (or yeast cakes)
1 cup lukewarm water
5½ cups all-purpose flour,
  sifted
2 eggs, beaten

Place bran cereal, sugar, shortening and salt in large mixing bowl. Pour in the boiling water and stir. Cool. Dissolve yeast in the lukewarm water. Add to first mixture. Add half of the flour and mix; add eggs and remaining flour, mixing well. Let rise until double in size (about 1 hour). Punch down and divide into 3 parts and place in greased loaf pans. Let rise until double again (about 1 hour). Bake at 350° for 25-30 minutes. Remove from pans to cooling rack in about 10 minutes. Makes 3 loaves of bread.

Variation: *To make rolls, increase the shortening to 1 cup. Use same mixing procedure. After dough has risen the first time, take about ⅓ of it at a time and roll out on lightly floured surface and cut with large cutter (about 3"). Rub a little melted margarine on each side of roll and fold in half. At this point freeze them for later use, or let rise 1 hour and bake at 350° for 12-15 minutes. If frozen, allow 4 hours to rise. Makes approximately 44 rolls.*

Hint: *The amount of flour for bread loaves or rolls can vary a little. If dough is sticky and hard to handle, add a little flour. Be careful, too much flour affects taste and texture. The bread loaves can be sliced, buttered, wrapped in foil and frozen. Then when you are ready to use it, just thaw and warm.*

Beth Haygood (Hooper)

Cheese Garlic Biscuits

2 cups all-purpose flour
⅓ cup grated Parmesan
   cheese
2 tablespoons parsley flakes
2 tablespoons baking powder
¼ teaspoon salt

⅓ cup margarine
1 cup (4 ounces) shredded
   mozzarella cheese
¾ cup evaporated milk
½ cup water
4 cloves garlic, minced

Preheat oven to 450°. Mix flour, Parmesan cheese, parsley, baking powder and salt. Cut in margarine until mixture resembles fine crumbs. Stir in remaining ingredients. Drop by tablespoonsful onto well greased baking sheets. Bake for 10-12 minutes. Makes 2 dozen biscuits.

Pat Petty (Steve)

Quick Onion Bread

2 cups biscuit baking mix
½ cup cold water
1 tablespoon instant minced
   onions

2 tablespoons melted
   margarine
Poppy seeds

Stir baking mix, water and onion to soft dough. Roll (or pat) dough on greased baking sheet into a 10x8-inch oblong shape. Spread dough with margarine and sprinkle with poppy seeds. Bake at 450° for 10 minutes. Serve hot.

Jane Cambre (Allison)

French Pancake

¼ cup margarine
1 cup all-purpose flour

1 cup milk
4 eggs, separated

Melt margarine in 8-inch iron skillet. Mix flour, milk and egg yolks. Fold in beaten egg whites. Pour into skillet. Bake 20 minutes in 400° oven. Serve with honey, syrup or preserves.

Note: *Great breakfast! I use whole wheat stone ground flour.*

Lola Fosburg (Robert)

Overnight French Toast

1 loaf French bread
5 eggs
¾ cup milk
¼ teaspoon baking powder
1 tablespoon vanilla extract

1 (20 ounce) bag frozen
   whole strawberries
3 or 4 sliced, ripe bananas
1 cup sugar
Cinnamon

Cut bread into 8 thick slices. Combine eggs, milk, baking powder and vanilla. Pour over bread. Cover and refrigerate overnight. The next morning, combine the frozen strawberries, bananas and sugar. Put in greased 13x9x2-inch baking dish and top with prepared bread. Sprinkle with cinnamon. Bake at 450° for 20-25 minutes.

Mary Hicks (David)

Cinnamon Buns

Chopped nuts (amount
   determined by taste)
Raisins (amount determined
   by taste)
1 (25 ounce) package frozen
   dinner rolls

Cinnamon
1 (3 ounce) package vanilla
   pudding mix (do not use
   instant)
½ cup brown sugar, packed
¼ cup melted margarine

Grease 1 Bundt or tube pan well. Place nuts and raisins as desired in bottom of pan. Roll each dinner roll (no need to thaw) in cinnamon. Place frozen rolls over nuts and raisins. Sprinkle vanilla pudding mix over rolls. Sprinkle brown sugar over pudding mix. Drizzle melted margarine over brown sugar. Cover with towel and let sit overnight. In the morning, bake at 350° for 25-30 minutes. Let set in pan for 5 minutes before turning out.

Susan Johnson (Bob)

Crackers or Matza

2 cups whole wheat flour
1 teaspoon salt
½ teaspoon baking soda
¼ cup butter (or vegetable oil)

½ cup buttermilk or ½ cup milk mixed with 2 teaspoons lemon juice
1 large egg

Combine flour, salt and soda; cut in butter or stir in oil. Add milk and egg; blend to make stiff dough. Whole wheat flour varies so you may need to add more flour at this point. Knead thoroughly. Roll ⅛-inch thick on floured board. Be sure to roll them thin enough. Cut into squares (I usually roll into large sheets and break apart when cooked) and place on lightly greased cookie sheet. Prick with fork. Sprinkle coarse salt, caraway seeds or sesame seeds on top, if desired. Bake in 400° oven until lightly browned, about 10 minutes.

Note: *Once my husband David wanted me to make real matza for communion. I had never attempted it before, and so I mixed some water, flour and salt. It was a real disaster — hard as brick; he could hardly break it apart. The people were afraid to eat it. Needless to say, communion was comical that Sunday! Now, I use this recipe; it's much better!*

Helen Diller (David)

In the early days of our ministry, we were appointed to a 4-point circuit and to a typical rural parsonage of the day. The time arrived for our Charge Conference, and the Presiding Elder (District Superintendent) was to spend the night at the parsonage. There were 2 beds in the guest room; both had very thin matresses and old uncovered springs. I hoped to make our guest more comfortable, so we moved 1 bed out and put both mattresses and springs on 1 bed. The next morning our guest who was "a jolly good fellow" said, "Sue, I've not rocked in a cradle in many years, but I did last night. I know what you did. Where is the other bed hidden?" I was embarrassed, but I learned a lesson and we had a good laugh. Girls, appreciate your lovely, modern homes.

Sue Gibbs (Walter C.)

Manna
from Heaven

Entrees

The Wesleyan Grace

Be present at our table, Lord;
Be here and everywhere ador'd.
These creatures bless and grant that we
May feast in paradise with Thee.

We thank Thee, Lord, for this our food,
But more because of Jesus's love.
Let manna to our souls be given,
The bread of life sent down from heaven.

Company Casserole

1 (6 ounce) package long
 grain and wild rice mix
1 pound bulk pork sausage
1 pound ground beef
1 large onion, chopped
1½ teaspoons salt
½ teaspoon pepper
1 teaspoon garlic powder

2 tablespoons
 Worcestershire sauce
1 (1 pound) can tomatoes
1 (8 ounce) can tomato sauce
1 (8 ounce) can sliced
 mushrooms, drained
1 (8 ounce) can sliced water
 chestnuts, drained
1 cup grated Cheddar cheese

Cook rice according to package directions, then set aside. Cook pork sausage, ground beef and onion over medium heat in a large skillet until meat is brown, stirring to crumble. If necessary, drain off drippings. Add seasonings, Worcestershire sauce, tomatoes and tomato sauce. Heat until mixture returns to boiling. Add rice, mushrooms and water chestnuts. Spoon into ungreased 13x9x2-inch baking dish. Sprinkle with grated cheese. Bake at 350° for 45 minutes or until heated through.

Bennye Smith (Aldous)

Best Spaghetti Sauce

1¼ pounds ground beef
1 large onion, chopped
3 cloves garlic, minced
3 tablespoons basil leaves
1 tablespoon oregano
1 tablespoon anise seeds (or
 fennel)

2 (6 ounce) cans tomato
 paste
1 (16 ounce) can tomatoes
1 (46 ounce) can tomato juice
Salt to taste
Pinch of baking soda

Brown ground beef with onion and garlic. Add remaining ingredients and simmer 1 hour or more.

Vera Sparling (Jack)

Candlelight Lasagna

1 pound ground beef
1 small onion, chopped
1 (28 ounce) can tomatoes, undrained
1 (12 ounce) can tomato paste
1 tablespoon sugar
1½ teaspoons salt
½ teaspoon oregano
½ teaspoon thyme leaves
½ teaspoon crushed red pepper
¼ teaspoon garlic salt
1 bay leaf
⅔ (16 ounce) package lasagna noodles
2 eggs
1 (15 ounce) carton ricotta cheese
1 (16 ounce) package mozzarella cheese, diced

In 5-quart Dutch oven over high heat, cook ground beef and onion until all pan juices evaporate and beef is well browned, stirring often. Add tomatoes and their liquid, tomato paste, sugar, salt, oregano, thyme, pepper, garlic salt and bay leaf. Heat to boiling, stirring to break up tomatoes. Reduce heat to low, cover and simmer for 30 minutes, stirring occasionally. Discard bay leaf. Spoon off any fat. Prepare noodles as label directs. Drain. In a 13x9x2-inch baking dish, arrange half of noodles, overlapping to fit. Combine eggs and ricotta cheese and spoon half of mixture over noodles, sprinkle with half of mozzarella, top with sauce. Repeat. Bake at 375° for 45 minutes. Remove and let stand 10 minutes. Serves 8.

Susan Bruster (Tim)

Meat Loaf For Two

½ pound ground beef
1 large onion, chopped
1 egg, beaten
Salt and pepper to taste
All-purpose flour
1 (8 ounce) can tomato sauce
1 can water

Combine ground beef, onion, egg, salt and pepper. Add enough flour to mixture to shape it into a loaf. Place in baking dish. In a small bowl, mix together the tomato sauce and water. Pour over the loaf. Bake at 350° until brown on top.

Annie N. Robinson (H. R.)

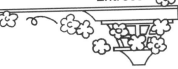

Microwave Italian Zucchini Meatloaf

1½ pounds ground beef
2 cups shredded zucchini
 (about 2 small)
1 small onion, chopped
1 egg
½ cup quick-cooking rolled
 oats
½ cup milk

⅓ cup Parmesan cheese
1 teaspoon Italian seasoning
1 teaspoon instant beef
 bouillon
¼ teaspoon salt
⅛ teaspoon pepper
2 tablespoons ketchup, if
 desired

Combine all ingredients except ketchup in mixing bowl. Mix well. Press into ungreased microwave safe 9x5x3-inch loaf pan. Cover with waxed paper. Microwave (medium-high-70%) 24-26 minutes or until center is done (about 170°), rotating dish twice. Let stand about 5 minutes. Transfer to serving plate. Brush with ketchup. Slice just before serving. TIP: With Full Power, microwave 18-20 minutes, rotating dish every 5 minutes. Makes about 8 servings, 300 calories each.

Elodie Breaux (Clarence)

Porcupines

½ pound ground beef
¼ cup rice
¼ cup milk
2 tablespoons chopped
 onion
½ teaspoon salt
¼ teaspoon celery salt

⅛ teaspoon garlic salt
Dash of black pepper
1 tablespoon shortening
1 (8 ounce) can tomato sauce
½ cup water
1½ teaspoons
 Worcestershire sauce

Mix beef, rice, milk, onion and seasonings. Form into 4 medium balls. Fry in melted shortening, turning frequently, until light brown (but not crusty) on all sides. Add tomato sauce, water and Worcestershire sauce. Cover and simmer 45 minutes over low heat. Add a small amount of additional water if liquid cooks down too much. Serves 2, but may be doubled or tripled for larger groups.

Loretta Jenkins (William)

Plantation Stuffed Peppers

1 pound ground beef
1 cup chopped onion
1 clove garlic, chopped
1 teaspoon salt
½ teaspoon pepper
2 teaspoons chili powder

2 (10¾ ounce) cans
condensed tomato soup
½ pound sharp Cheddar
cheese, shredded or sliced
1½ cups cooked converted
rice
8 medium green bell peppers

Cook ground beef, onion and garlic in skillet until meat is browned. Add seasonings and tomato soup; simmer, covered, 10 minutes. Add cheese. Cook slowly, stirring occasionally until cheese melts. Stir in cooked rice. Cool. Cut peppers in halves lengthwise. Remove membranes and seeds. Cook in boiling salted water to cover until barely tender, about 3 minutes. Drain and cool. Place peppers on baking sheet or in shallow pan. Stuff with rice mixture. Cover with foil and bake in hot oven (400°) for 20-25 minutes. To freeze, place in freezer until peppers are frozen. Remove, wrap frozen peppers in foil or plastic wrap. Seal, label, date and return to freezer. Recommended storage time: 2-3 months. To serve, remove wrapping, place partially thawed peppers in shallow pan. Cover with foil. Bake in hot oven (400°) 30-45 minutes.

Ann Nihart (John)

Sombrero Taco Cups

1 pound ground beef
1 (1¼ ounce) package taco
spices and seasonings
¾ cup water
¼ cup salsa

2 (8 ounce) packages
refrigerator biscuits
½ cup grated Cheddar
cheese

In medium skillet, brown ground meat until crumbly; drain fat. Add taco spices and water; blend well. Bring to a boil. Reduce heat and simmer, uncovered, 10 minutes. Stir in salsa. Separate biscuits and press each biscuit into an ungreased muffin cup. Spoon equal amounts of meat mixture into each muffin cup. Sprinkle each with cheese. Bake uncovered for 12 minutes at 350° or until biscuits are browned and cheese melts. Makes 12.

Laura Millikan (Charles)

Cornbread Casserole

1 pound ground beef
½ cup chopped green bell pepper
½ cup chopped yellow bell pepper
2 small onions, diced
1 jalapeño pepper, diced
1 (15 ounce) can pinto beans

2 tablespoons chili powder
1 (16 ounce) can stewed tomatoes
Pinch of salt
1 (6 ounce) package cornbread mix
¼ cup sugar

Cook beef, green and yellow bell peppers, onion and jalapeño pepper in skillet. Drain. In another pan, heat beans, chili powder, stewed tomatoes and salt. Pour beans into 12x8x2-inch baking pan. Sprinkle meat mixture over beans. Prepare cornbread mix according to package directions, adding ¼ cup sugar, and pour over meat. Bake at 425° for 25-30 minutes or until golden brown. Serves 6-8.

Irma Waddleton (Don)

Mexican Casserole

1 pound ground beef
1 bell pepper, chopped
1 medium onion, chopped
1 (15 ounce) can pinto beans
1 (15 ounce) can Spanish rice

1 (10 ounce) can tomatoes with chilies
6 - 8 ounces grated Cheddar cheese

Sauté meat, pepper and onion. Add beans, rice and tomatoes. Simmer until liquid is slightly reduced. Pour into 13x9x2-inch baking pan. Cover with grated cheese. Bake at 350° until cheese is bubbly. Serve over corn chips with shredded lettuce on top. Serves 8-10.

Note: *Wonderful for a bunch of hungry teens! Some will ask for hot sauce on top.*

Sue Gilpin (Clayton)

Chili Casserole

1½ pounds ground beef
1 large onion, chopped
1 (16 ounce) can chili
1 (12 ounce) can tomatoes
   with chilies
1 (10 ounce) jar taco sauce
1 (10¾ ounce) can cream of
   mushroom soup

½ cup milk, mixed with the
   soup
Salt and pepper to taste
1 (20 ounce) package corn or
   flour tortillas
4 ounces shredded Cheddar
   cheese

Cook ground meat and onion in large skillet or wok, and drain. Add the rest of the ingredients except tortillas and cheese, and let simmer 10 minutes. Cut tortillas in strips and line ungreased 13x9x2-inch baking dish. Pour half of the chili mixture into the baking dish. Add more tortilla strips, then add the rest of the chili mixture. Before baking, sprinkle with the cheese. Bake uncovered at 350° for 45 minutes. This can be made ahead of time and set in the refrigerator until ready to bake. Also freezes well. Serves 12.

Virginia Harris (Jesse)

Ranch-Style Hash

1 pound ground beef
3½ cups canned tomatoes
1 cup chopped green bell
   pepper
½ cup chopped onion
½ cup uncooked rice

¼ teaspoon basil
½ teaspoon salt
Dash of pepper
Pasteurized process cheese
   slices

Brown meat and drain. Add tomatoes, green pepper, onions, rice, basil, salt and pepper. Cover and simmer for 25 minutes. Top with cheese slices and heat until melted.

Patricia Bingham (John)

Cattleman's Hash

¾ cup instant rice
2 pounds ground beef
¼ cup chopped onion
1 tablespoon chili powder
1 (8 ounce) can tomato sauce

1 (10¾ ounce) can cream of
  mushroom soup
½ pound grated Cheddar
  cheese

Cook rice according to directions. Brown meat; add onion, chili powder and tomato sauce. Steam for 20 minutes. Add cooked rice and mix. Pour into greased 2-quart baking dish. Top with soup, then cheese. Bake at 350° for 30-40 minutes or until cheese bubbles.

Elaine Proctor (Michael)

Okra Gumbo

1 pound lean ground beef,
  browned and drained
Salt and pepper to taste
Dash of sugar
1 can whole kernel corn,
  drained

1 (8 ounce) can tomato sauce
2 cups diced raw potatoes
1 (10 ounce) package frozen
  okra (cut or whole)
½ cup water

Brown and drain meat and season to taste. Add corn, tomato sauce, potatoes, okra and water and simmer over low heat for about 45 minutes in a covered saucepan. Serves 4-5.

Hint: You might like to try chicken instead of ground meat or use canned whole tomatoes instead of tomato sauce.

Twana Holcomb (Michael)

Potato - Meat Casserole

1½ **pounds ground beef**
1 **onion, sliced**
4 **small potatoes, peeled and sliced**

1 **(10¾ ounce) can cream of mushroom soup**

Cook meat in skillet until done. Drain off fat. Spray a casserole dish with non-stick vegetable spray, then put in a layer of meat, then a layer of onions and potatoes. Pour the soup over top, then bake in 350° oven for 45 minutes or until potatoes are done.

Lola Fosburg (Robert)

Dinner In A Dish

1 **small onion, chopped**
1 **clove garlic, chopped (optional)**
1 **bell pepper, chopped**
1½ **teaspoons vegetable oil**
1 **(2½ ounce) jar stuffed green olives, chopped**
1 **(2 ounce) can mushrooms, drained**
1 **(10¾ ounce) can tomato soup**

¾ **cup water**
½ **teaspoon Worcestershire sauce**
½ **teaspoon salt**
Cayenne and paprika to taste
1 **pound ground meat**
1 **(17 ounce) can whole kernel corn, drained**
8 **ounces spaghetti, cooked**
½ **cup grated cheese**
½ **cup buttered breadcrumbs**

Sauté chopped onion, garlic and bell pepper in oil until golden brown. Add chopped olives, mushrooms, tomato soup, water, Worcestershire sauce and seasonings. Simmer about 5 minutes. Add meat thinned with 2 tablespoons cold water to prevent lumping. Continue to simmer until meat is done. Add corn and cooked spaghetti. Place in ungreased 2-quart casserole dish. Cover with cheese and buttered breadcrumbs. Bake at 350° about 20 minutes until browned. Serves 12.

Joe Watt (Sharon)

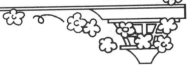

Three Cheese Tetrazzini

1 tablespoon margarine
½ cup chopped onion
(optional)
1½ pounds lean ground beef
1 teaspoon salt
¼ teaspoon pepper
1 (15 ounce) can tomato
sauce
1 (8 ounce) package cream
cheese

1 cup cottage cheese
¼ cup sour cream
¼ cup chopped green pepper
¼ cup sliced green onions
8 ounces spaghetti, cooked
and drained
¼ cup fresh grated Parmesan
cheese

Sauté onion in melted butter until tender. Add beef and brown until crumbly. Drain off. Add salt, pepper and tomato sauce. Simmer 10 minutes. Remove from heat. Beat together cream cheese, cottage cheese and sour cream. Add green pepper, green onions and spaghetti. Spread sour cream-spaghetti mixture in bottom of greased 3-quart 13x9x2-inch casserole dish. Pour meat sauce over top. Sprinkle with Parmesan cheese. Bake for 30 minutes at 325°. Can be refrigerated overnight and baked uncovered for 45 minutes.

Note: *Gets rave reviews at church fellowship dinners!!*

Virginia Irene Crowe (Thomas W.)

Hearty Meal

1 pound lean ground beef
1 medium onion, chopped
1 (10½ ounce) can vegetable
soup

1 (15 ounce) can ranch-style
beans
1 soup can of water

Brown meat and onion and drain. Season to taste. Add soup, beans and water. Simmer 30 minutes.

Dorothy Faulk (C. W.)

Chuck O' Luck

1 pound ground beef
1 (8 ounce) package shell
   macaroni
½ cup chopped onion
½ cup chopped celery
½ cup chopped bell pepper
1 (10¾ ounce) can cream of
   mushroom soup
1 (12 ounce) can light
   evaporated milk
1 (15 ounce) can English
   peas, drained
10 olives, sliced
Salt, pepper and garlic to
   taste
2 cups grated Cheddar
   cheese

Brown ground beef in skillet; boil macaroni until tender, drain and set aside. Add all other ingredients except cheese and macaroni to the skillet. Heat well. Prepare a 13x9x2-inch casserole dish by spraying with non-stick vegetable spray. Layer macaroni and meat mixture alternately in the casserole dish. Sprinkle grated cheese on top. Bake at 350° in oven for 30 minutes.

Note: *This can be made ahead and frozen. You have a meal when you add French bread and green salad or wheat rolls and fruit salad.*

Jane Cunningham (William R.)

"No Peek" Casserole

2 pounds boneless stew
   meat
1 (1.2 ounce) package dry
   onion soup mix
2 (10¾ ounce) cans cream of
   mushroom soup
1 (4 ounce) can mushrooms,
   drained
½ cup red wine (burgundy) or
   ½ cup water

Cut meat into bite-size pieces. Mix with the other ingredients and cover tightly in an ungreased 2½-quart casserole dish. Bake at 300° for 3 hours. Don't peek! Serve over noodles or rice. Serves 6-8.

Note: *This is a good dish to serve for Sunday dinner. It cooks while you're at church!*

Glennis Boutwell (Frank A.)

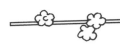

Oodles of Noodles

1 (16 ounce) package egg
noodles
2 medium onions, chopped
3 or 4 cloves of garlic,
crushed or finely chopped
1 green pepper, chopped
2 pounds ground beef

1 teaspoon chili powder
Salt and pepper to taste
2 (15 ounce) cans cream-
style corn
2 (15 ounce) cans tomatoes
Cheddar cheese, grated

Prepare noodles according to package directions; set aside to cool. Sauté onions, garlic and green pepper. Add beef, chili powder, salt and pepper to taste. Cook together until meat is no longer red. Mix together beef mixture, corn, tomatoes and cooled noodles. Place in 13x9x2-inch baking dish and cover with grated cheese. Bake at 350° until cheese melts and is bubbly. This dish can be mixed together in advance and baked at mealtime. Serves 22.

Note: *This is great for a church crowd! This recipe was given to me by Janiece Skinner of St. Paul's UMC in Bay City.*

Jean Haskell (William A.)

Braised Beef Tips Over Rice

2 tablespoons vegetable oil
2 pounds beef tips, cut into
cubes
1 (10½ ounce) can beef
consommé

⅓ cup red Burgundy wine or
cranberry juice
2 tablespoons soy sauce
1 clove garlic, minced
¼ teaspoon onion powder
4 cups hot cooked rice

Heat oil in a large skillet; brown meat and drain. Stir in consommé, wine, soy sauce, garlic and onion powder. Heat to boiling. Reduce heat; cover and simmer for 1 hour or until meat is tender. Serve over rice.

Kathleen Megill (Greg)

Spanish Steak

2 pounds round steak, cut in
　serving size pieces
All-purpose flour
Salt and pepper to taste
Vegetable oil
1 small onion, chopped
½ pound sliced mushrooms
　(optional)

2 (10¾ ounce) cans cream of
　mushroom soup
1 cup cold coffee, water or
　milk
1 (6 ounce) jar Spanish
　olives, sliced

Coat steak with flour seasoned with salt and pepper. Brown quickly in hot oil. Drain on paper towels. Sauté onion and mushrooms in oil and drippings. Remove excess oil. Add soup and enough coffee, water or milk to make a gravy. Add olives and their liquid. Add steak and simmer until tender. May be cooked on stove in large skillet or in a roaster in the oven at 350° for 1 hour. Serve over rice.

Beverly Duree (Sam)

Classic Beef Stroganoff

½ pound fresh mushrooms,
　sliced
½ cup minced onion
2 tablespoons butter or
　margarine
1 pound beef sirloin steak or
　tenderloin (cut diagonally
　into very thin slices)

1 (10½ ounce) can beef
　bouillon, divided
2 tablespoons ketchup
1 small clove garlic, minced
1 teaspoon salt
3 tablespoons flour
1 cup dairy sour cream
3-4 cups hot cooked noodles

Cook and stir mushrooms and onion in butter until onion is tender; remove from skillet. In same skillet, brown meat lightly on both sides. Set aside ⅓ cup bouillon; stir remaining bouillon, ketchup, garlic and salt into the skillet. Cover and simmer 15 minutes. Blend reserved ⅓ cup bouillon and flour; stir into skillet. Add mushrooms and onion. Heat to boiling, stirring constantly. Boil 1 minute. Stir in sour cream; heat through. Serve over hot noodles. Serves 4.

Julia Miller (William A. "Buddy," Sr.)

Shanghai Beef

1 pound round steak, cut into thin strips
2 tablespoons vegetable oil
2 tablespoons cornstarch
1½ cups beef broth
1 (8 ounce) can sliced water chestnuts, drained
1 medium red pepper, coarsely chopped
5 scallions, cut diagonally into 1-inch pieces
3 tablespoons soy sauce
¼ teaspoon pepper
1½ cups dry instant rice

Sauté beef in oil in a large skillet until browned, about 5 minutes. Add cornstarch and stir until blended. Stir in broth, water chestnuts, red pepper, scallions, soy sauce and pepper. Bring to a full boil, stirring frequently. Stir in rice. Cover and remove from heat. Let stand 5 minutes. Fluff with a fork. Serves 4.

Kathleen Megill (Greg)

Sunday Brisket

5 - 6 pound brisket
¼ cup liquid smoke
1 (8 ounce) bottle Italian dressing
1 (12 ounce) can cola-flavored carbonated drink
1 (12 ounce) bottle chili sauce
1 envelope onion soup mix

Using meat fork, poke several holes in brisket (do not trim fat). Sprinkle liquid smoke and Italian dressing over meat. Let meat marinate for 12 hours. Turn meat halfway through marinating time. Pour off marinade. Combine cola, chili sauce and onion soup mix; pour over brisket. Bake brisket, fat side up at 325° for 5-6 hours. Trim off fat and serve.

Sheryl Travis (Harold)

Peppered Brisket

5 pound brisket
¼ cup black pepper
⅔ cup soy sauce
1 tablespoon ketchup

2 cloves garlic, crushed
½ cup vinegar
1 teaspoon paprika

Trim fat from brisket. Sprinkle pepper on waxed paper, press brisket onto pepper, then turn and press, coating evenly. Place in a shallow baking pan. Combine remaining ingredients and pour over brisket. Refrigerate overnight, turning occasionally. When ready to cook, remove meat from marinade and wrap securely in aluminum foil. Bake at 300° for 3-4 hours until tender. Serve hot or cold.

Peggy Renfroe (Rob)

Straw and Hay

1 (8 ounce) package green spinach egg noodles
1 (8 ounce) package medium egg noodles
½ cup butter or margarine, divided
½ cup chopped onion
1 cup sliced fresh mushrooms

1 (10 ounce) package frozen baby peas, thawed
6 ounces cooked ham, cut into 1-inch cubes
2 cups heavy or whipping cream
1 cup grated Parmesan cheese
1½ teaspoons salt
½ teaspoon pepper

In a large sauce pot, cook both noodles in boiling water until tender. Drain and keep warm. Meanwhile in large skillet, melt ¼ cup butter over low heat, add onion and cook until soft. Increase heat to medium and add mushrooms; sauté until tender. Add peas and ham and sauté 2 minutes. Remove from heat and add noodles, toss well and cover. In medium sauce pan, heat cream and remaining ¼ cup butter until hot. Pour over noodles, sprinkle with cheese, salt and pepper. Toss well to combine. DO NOT OVER STIR. Pour into 13x9x2-inch dish. Serves 8-12.

Sylvia R. Blankenship (V. O.)

Quiche Lanore

1 cup chopped onion
⅓ cup chopped bell pepper
2 tablespoons margarine
1 cup milk
6 eggs, slightly beaten

1 cup biscuit mix
1 cup diced cooked ham or turkey ham
1 (8 ounce) package grated cheese

Sauté onions, bell pepper and margarine in microwave on HIGH for 3 minutes. Stir once during cooking time. Pour into 13x9x2-inch baking dish which has been sprayed with non-stick vegetable spray. Mix milk, eggs and biscuit mix by hand until smooth. Pour over vegetables, add ham and cheese and stir together until well mixed. Bake at 350° for 45 minutes. Serves 6-8.

Eleanor Little (Don)

Creamy Ham and Rice for Two

½ (10¾ ounce) can cream of mushroom soup (about ⅔ cup)
⅔ cup water
1 cup cubed cooked ham
⅔ cup instant rice, uncooked

1 (8 ounce) can green beans, drained
1 tablespoon chopped onion
¼ cup fine breadcrumbs
1 teaspoon margarine, melted

Combine all ingredients in a saucepan, except breadcrumbs and margarine. Cook over medium heat until mixture begins to boil. Pour into a greased 1-quart casserole. Toss crumbs with melted butter; sprinkle over casserole. Bake at 400° about 20 minutes. Serves 2.

Note: This is a good way to use leftover ham and can easily be doubled.

Cookbook Committee

Sweet 'N Sour Sausage

½ cup ketchup
½ cup wine vinegar
½ cup brown sugar
1 teaspoon soy sauce
1 teaspoon ginger
1 pound link sausage

1 (16 ounce) can pineapple
  chunks, drained
2 green sweet peppers, cut
  into chunks
1 jar sweet pickled
  cauliflower

Mix ketchup, vinegar, sugar, soy sauce and ginger in a saucepan. Cut sausage into bite size pieces and add to sauce. Add final 3 ingredients and heat through, but don't cook any more. Serve hot with toothpicks or over rice.

Mary Lou Krause (Bruce E.)

Pork Tenderloin in Red Wine

1 (3 - 4 pound) pork
  tenderloin (trim all fat)
Nutmeg, sage, salt and
  pepper to taste
1 clove garlic, crushed

¼ cup chopped parsley
1 bay leaf
2 cups red wine
¼ cup chopped onion
1 cup beef consommé

Mix together nutmeg, sage, salt and pepper to taste and rub into pork roast. In a skillet over medium high heat, brown both sides of roast with garlic added. Place in baking pan and add parsley, bay leaf, red wine and onion. Bake covered at 350° for 2 hours, turning twice. Add beef consommé and bake for another 20 minutes. Place roast on hot serving platter. Drain wine and meat drippings and serve separately with the roast.

Frances Stanton (Leroy)

Crock Pot Pork Bar-B-Q

1 (3 - 4 pound) pork loin roast
   (trim all fat)
Salt and pepper to taste
Crushed black pepper flakes
   to taste

1 cup water
1 cup plus 2 tablespoons
   vinegar
2 tablespoons ketchup

Combine all above ingredients except ketchup and cook 4 - 6 hours in a crock pot until tender. Remove meat and shred. Mix ketchup and small amount of cooking juice with shredded meat. Serve on toasted bun.

Frances Stanton (Leroy)

Baked Spareribs and Sauerkraut

3 - 4 pounds spareribs
1 (32 ounce) jar sauerkraut,
   undrained

Salt and pepper to taste
½ cup hot water

Trim meat; place in greased roasting pan with cover. Bake, uncovered, in hot oven at 400° for 20 minutes. Remove ribs. Put sauerkraut in pan, arrange ribs on top, season with salt and pepper. Pour on hot water, cover and bake at 350° for 1 hour. Serves 6.

Note: We use country spareribs and serve on a bed of mashed potatoes. David's father always said it is an old German custom to eat this for New Year's Day to have good luck. So, in our house we have spareribs, kraut and mashed potatoes for lunch and black-eyed peas and cornbread for supper. We need all the good luck we can get!

Helen Diller (David)

Va.'s Pork Chops and Rice

1 cup uncooked brown rice
1 small onion, diced
1 teaspoon parsley
1 rib celery with leaves, diced
1 teaspoon salt

1 cup hot water
½ teaspoon chili powder
2 apples
4 thick sliced pork chops

A crock pot or slow cooker is used for this recipe. Spray the crockery with non-stick vegetable spray. Combine all ingredients except apples and pork chops in the crockery. Stir well. Core the apples and slice each one making 4 rings. Place on top of the rice mixture. In a skillet, lightly brown the chops on each side to help seal in the flavor. Place on top of the apples. Set temperature on LOW and cook for 6-8 hours. Serves 4.

Virginia Irene Crowe (Thomas W.)

Grandma's Pork Chops and Rice

4 lean pork chops
Salt and pepper to taste
1 cup uncooked rice

½ cup chopped onion
2 cups chicken broth

Season pork chops with salt and pepper. Spray large skillet with non-stick vegetable spray and brown chops on both sides over medium-high heat. Remove to a plate covered with paper towels to absorb grease. Spray an 11x7-inch casserole dish with non-stick vegetable spray and then spread uncooked rice evenly over bottom of dish. Sprinkle chopped onions on top of rice. Place chops on top of rice and onions and then pour the chicken broth over all. Cover tightly with foil. Cook at 350° for about 45 minutes or until all liquid is absorbed. Serves 4.

Note: *After my grandfather died, my grandmother moved from Kentucky to Texas to be near her daughter and grandchildren. All my teen years, she had us over for dinner nearly every Wednesday evening, and this recipe was one of her regular offerings. It is still my favorite way to eat pork chops.*

Laura Neff (Jerry)

Sausage Quiche

1 pound bulk pork sausage
1 pound small whole
 mushrooms
½ cup minced fresh parsley
2 eggs

1 cup light cream or
 evaporated milk
½ cup grated Parmesan
 cheese
¼ teaspoon salt
1 9-inch unbaked pie shell

Crumble sausage in skillet. Add mushrooms. Cook over medium heat for 15 minutes, stirring until meat and mushrooms are slightly brown and all liquid from mushrooms has evaporated. Drain off excess grease. Add parsley to mixture. Beat eggs with cream and cheese. Blend into mixture. Stir in salt. Pour into unbaked pie shell. Bake at 400° for 25-30 minutes or until crust is done. Let stand 10 minutes before serving. Serves 6-8.

Helen Archer (Kenneth)

Breakfast Pizza

1 pie crust, unbaked
½ - ¾ pound sausage
½ cup chopped bell pepper
8 eggs
¾ cup milk

Salt and pepper to taste
1 cup grated Cheddar cheese
1 cup grated Monterey Jack
 cheese

Pat crust into ungreased 13x9x2-inch baking dish until crust is formed around dish. In skillet, brown sausage with bell pepper; drain. Beat eggs. Add milk, salt and pepper; beat well. Crumble sausage evenly over crust. Sprinkle cheeses over sausage. Pour egg mixture over all. Bake in 350° oven for 35-45 minutes, or until you can stick a knife in the center and it comes out clean. Serves 8-12.

Sherri Young (Mark)

Sausage Strata

6 slices of bread, without
  crust
1 pound sausage, browned
  and drained
1 cup grated Cheddar cheese
4 eggs, beaten

1¾ cups milk
1 cup half-and-half
1¼ teaspoons
  Worcestershire sauce
Salt and pepper to taste

Place bread slices in the bottom of a greased 13x9x2-inch casserole dish. Spoon the meat over the bread. Sprinkle the cheese over the meat. Mix eggs, milk, half-and-half, Worcestershire sauce, salt and pepper. Pour over sausage and cheese. Refrigerate overnight. Bake uncovered at 350° for 30-45 minutes, until solid. Serves 8.

Joan White (Dick)

Overnight Breakfast Casserole

8 eggs, beaten
1 cup biscuit baking mix
1 cup grated Cheddar cheese
1 pound of sausage,
  browned, drained and
  crumbled

2 cups milk
1 teaspoon salt
1 teaspoon dry mustard

Mix the above ingredients and pour into a greased 13x9x2-inch baking dish. Refrigerate overnight. Bake at 350° for 30-40 minutes.

Mary Akin (Sidney)

Breakfast Casserole

6 boiled eggs, chopped
8 slices crisply fried bacon,
  crumbled
½ cup milk

½ cup margarine, melted
1 (10¾ ounce) can cream of
  mushroom soup

Combine eggs, bacon, milk, margarine and cream of mushroom soup. Stir well and place in an 8x8x2-inch baking dish. Bake uncovered at 350° for 20 minutes. Serve with toast or English muffins. Serves 8.

Sherri Young (Mark)

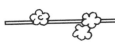

Chicken and Artichokes

12 chicken breast halves, skinned and boned
2 (14 ounce) cans artichoke hearts, drained and cut in half
2 (10¾ ounce) cans cream of chicken soup, undiluted

½ cup water
1 teaspoon salt
¼ teaspoon pepper
½ stick butter
1 cup herb-seasoned stuffing mix

Grease 13x9x2-inch casserole or spray with non-stick vegetable spray. Arrange artichokes in bottom of casserole. Arrange chicken breasts over artichoke hearts. Mix soup, water, salt and pepper. Spoon over chicken. Melt butter and lightly sauté stuffing mix. Spoon over soup mixture. Bake at 350° for 45 minutes, covered, and 30 minutes uncovered. Serves 8-12.

Janet Kennedy (Tom)

Easy Sweet 'N Sour Chicken

8 boneless, skinless chicken breast halves
1 (8 ounce) bottle Russian dressing

1 (12 ounce) jar apricot preserves
1 envelope onion soup mix

Arrange chicken in 13x9x2-inch pan. Mix remaining ingredients well and pour over chicken. Bake at 350° for 1 hour. Cover with foil for at least 20 minutes. Serves 6-8.

Gina Baker (Doug)

Church service was over and my husband, Bob Stepp, raised his hand to say the benediction. Jad, age 3, waved back and called out "Hi, Daddy!"

Mary Ann Stepp (Bob)

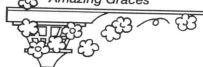

Party Chicken Critters

8 chicken breast halves,
  boned and skinned
8 slices bacon
1 (2¼ ounce) jar dried beef,
  cut up

1 (10¾ ounce) can cream of
  mushroom soup
1 cup sour cream

Wrap each piece of chicken with one strip of bacon. Place "critters" in ungreased 3-quart oblong baking dish, lined with dried beef slices. Mix soup and sour cream together and cover top of chicken with mixture. (Use no salt because of beef and bacon.) Refrigerate overnight or at least several hours before baking. Bake uncovered for 3 hours at 250°. Serves 8.

Glennis Boutwell (Frank A.)

Variation: Omit bacon and add 1 (10¾ ounce) can cream of chicken or cream of celery soup. Continue as above.

Mada Killen (James L., Jr.)

Variation: Pre-fry bacon slices and lay on top of chicken breasts. Spread soup and sour cream mixture on top of meats. Do not refrigerate; bake at 350° for 1 hour.

Virginia Jones (William F.)

No-Fat Yogurt Chicken Bake

6 - 8 chicken breasts
1 teaspoon lemon pepper
1 teaspoon paprika

½ cup chicken bouillon
1 - 2 cups no-fat yogurt

Layer chicken in large baking dish and sprinkle with lemon pepper and paprika. Pour ½ cup bouillon over chicken. Bake 40 minutes at 350°. Remove from oven. Spread yogurt over top of chicken and heat 5 more minutes.

Dorothy Dugger (William E., Jr.)

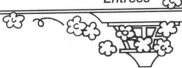

Cranberry Chicken

8 - 10 boneless chicken
  breasts
Salt and pepper to taste
Garlic powder
1 (8 ounce) bottle Catalina
  salad dressing

1 package dry onion soup
  mix
1 (16 ounce) can whole berry
  cranberry sauce

Sprinkle chicken with salt, pepper and garlic powder. Mix dressing, soup mix and cranberry sauce together and pour over chicken. Place in a 14x11-inch dish (do not stack or crowd pieces). Cover and refrigerate overnight. Bake at 350° for 1½ hours, basting every 15 minutes.

Audrey Barfield (John)

Boneless Breasts à la Vineyard

2 whole chicken breasts,
  skinned and boned
Salt and pepper to taste
2 tablespoons butter or
  margarine

1½ cups seedless grapes,
  halved (about ½ pound)
3 tablespoons dry white wine
  or white grape juice

Sprinkle chicken with salt and pepper. Heat butter in large skillet. When bubbly, add chicken and brown on both sides. Add grapes and wine. Cover tightly and cook over medium heat for about 5 minutes. Serve with wild rice.

Kathleen Megill (Greg)

Country Style Chicken Kiev

½ cup breadcrumbs
2 tablespoons Parmesan
  cheese
1 teaspoon basil
1 teaspoon oregano
½ teaspoon garlic salt
¼ teaspoon salt

2 whole chicken breasts,
  split
⅔ cup melted margarine
¼ cup apple juice or white
  wine
¼ cup chopped green onion
¼ cup chopped fresh parsley

Combine first 6 ingredients. Dip chicken pieces in margarine; set remaining margarine aside. Roll in crumbs. Place in 1½-quart shallow casserole. Bake at 375° for 50-60 minutes. To leftover margarine, add juice, onion and parsley. Pour over baked chicken and bake for 2-3 minutes more.

Jane Cambre (Allison)

Easy Chicken Cordon Bleu

2 slices provolone cheese
2 slices honey-baked ham or
  turkey ham
4 boneless skinless chicken
  breasts
½ cup margarine, melted

2 cups Italian breadcrumbs
1 (2½ ounce) jar sliced
  mushrooms, thoroughly
  drained and patted dry
  (optional)
Parmesan cheese

Cut slices of cheese and ham in half, making 4 half-moon shaped slices. Lay chicken breasts on plate and place 1 slice cheese, then ham, on top of each of the breasts. Fold chicken breast combination, roll in margarine and then in breadcrumbs. Top with mushrooms, if desired. Sprinkle with Parmesan cheese. Cook at 350° for 30-45 minutes or until desired doneness is reached.

Note: *Delicious served with a rice dish — plain, wild or seasoned rice. Add a salad and rolls and enjoy your quick gourmet meal.*

Jerrie Reiley (Ben)

Garlic Chicken Parmesan

6 - 8 boneless, skinless
  chicken breasts
½ cup margarine, melted
1 stack round buttery
  crackers, finely crushed

½ cup grated Parmesan
  cheese
2 teaspoons garlic powder

Mix garlic powder, Parmesan cheese and finely crushed cracker crumbs together in a bowl. Pat the chicken dry, then dip in melted margarine, roll in cracker crumbs until thoroughly covered. Bake in 350° oven about 35-40 minutes until golden brown. Serves 6-8.

Joyce Pace (Rudy)

Sour Cream Chicken

6 boneless, skinless chicken
  breast halves
Butter or margarine
1 (10¾ ounce) can cream of
  chicken soup

½ pint carton sour cream
1 stack round buttery
  crackers, crushed
Slivered almonds

Preheat oven to 350°. Place 6 chicken breasts in 12x9x2-inch glass baking dish. Leave uncovered and bake almost done, about 30 minutes. Remove from oven and dot with butter. Combine cream of chicken soup and sour cream and pour over chicken, being sure to cover chicken. Top with crushed crackers and slivered almonds. Return to oven until mixture is hot and bubbles, about 30 minutes. The top will brown slightly and will be tender to fork.

Janna Byrd (Kenneth)

Variation: Replace chicken breasts with 5-6 cups diced cooked chicken. Mix chicken with soup and sour cream, season with paprika or dill weed, and pour into baking dish. Top with crushed crackers and drizzle with ¾ cup melted margarine. Bake as above. Freezes well. Serves 12-15.

Nettie Mae Earls (Grady)

His Majesty's Special

Salt and pepper to taste
2 pounds chicken breasts
(about 4)
2 (10¾ ounce) cans cream of
chicken soup
2 tablespoons
Worcestershire sauce

2 tablespoons lemon juice
½ cup milk
¼ cup chopped onion
¼ cup chopped bell pepper
Butter or margarine

Salt and pepper chicken and place skin side up in pan. Mix all other ingredients except butter and pour over chicken. Bake at 325° for 50-60 minutes. Just before done, dot with butter. Sauce is good over rice or whipped potatoes.

Nancy Lee (Clifford)

Chicken Pasta Shells

1 (12 ounce) package large
pasta shells
2 cups cooked diced chicken
6 tablespoons margarine
6 tablespoons all-purpose
flour
½ teaspoon salt
½ teaspoon celery salt
¼ teaspoon pepper

3 cups chicken stock
1 cup half-and-half
8 ounces drained sliced
mushrooms
3 tablespoons freshly minced
parsley
½ cup grated Parmesan
cheese

Stuff pasta shells with diced cooked chicken and place in a greased 13x9x2-inch glass casserole dish. Make cream sauce by melting margarine; stir in flour, salt, celery salt and pepper. Cook until bubbly. Gradually add chicken stock and half-and-half. Cook until thick, stirring occasionally. Blend in mushrooms and parsley, pour sauce over shells, sprinkle cheese on top and bake at 350° for 45 minutes. Serves 6.

Cindi Cox Woodward (Mark B.)

128

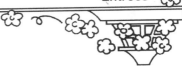

Beggars' Bundles

1 (3 ounce) package cream
  cheese, softened
2 cups cooked chicken, cut
  in small pieces
¼ teaspoon salt
⅛ teaspoon pepper
2 tablespoons milk
1 tablespoon chopped chives

1 tablespoon chopped
  pimiento
1 (8 count) package
  refrigerated crescent rolls
2 tablespoons melted butter
Crushed seasoned croutons
1 (10¾ ounce) can cream of
  mushroom soup
½ cup milk

Mix the first 7 ingredients. Separate the rolls into 4 rectangles on an ungreased cookie sheet, sealing perforations. Spoon ½ cup of the chicken mixture into the center of each rectangle and seal. Brush the tops with butter and dip in croutons. Bake at 350° for 20 minutes. Meanwhile, make sauce by stirring soup and milk into a small saucepan and heating. Remove bundles to serving tray and spoon heated sauce over each bundle. Serves 4.

Note: A friend from Fairfield gave me this recipe for a dinner party. It was such a hit that it has become one of my favorites!

Karen Bagley (Bert)

Easy Chicken Casserole

2 sticks margarine
1 small onion, chopped
1 cup rice, uncooked
6 - 8 pieces boneless chicken
  breasts

1 (10¾ ounce) can chicken
  gumbo soup
1 soup can water

Melt margarine in 13x9x2-inch pan. Add chopped onion. Pour in uncooked rice. Layer chicken pieces over rice. In a small mixing bowl, dilute gumbo soup with 1 soup can full of water; stir well; pour over chicken. Cover tightly with foil and bake at 350° for 1½ hours. No peeking!

Nancy Culbertson (Lawrence)

Chicken Mexican Dressing

2 (6 ounce) packages
  cornbread mix (1 Mexican,
  1 plain)
¼ cup chopped onion
¼ cup chopped green pepper
¼ cup chopped celery
3 tablespoons melted
  margarine
1 chicken, cooked and boned
2 (10¾ ounce) cans cream of
  chicken soup
3 cups chicken broth

Bake cornbread as directed; cool, crumble and set aside. Sauté the vegetables in margarine. Add chicken, vegetables, soup and broth to cornbread; mix well. Put mixture into a greased 13x9x2-inch baking dish. Bake at 350° until bubbly.

Mary Margaret Smith (Lawrence)

Chicken and Dressing Casserole

6 chicken breasts
1 cup sour cream
½ teaspoon poultry
  seasoning
1 (10¾ ounce) can cream of
  mushroom soup
1 cup reserved chicken broth
½ cup melted butter
1 (8 ounce) bag cornbread
  stuffing mix

Boil chicken, remove from bone and break into bite-size pieces. Reserve 1 cup broth. Place chicken in a 13x9x2-inch casserole dish. Blend sour cream, poultry seasoning and soup. Pour over chicken. Stir together reserved broth, butter and stuffing mix. Pour over sour cream mixture. Bake at 350° for 30 minutes.

Peggy Laing (Charles)

Green Chili Chicken Enchiladas

6 large chicken breast
  portions
12 corn tortillas
½ cup vegetable oil
1 large onion, chopped
1½ pounds grated Cheddar
  cheese, divided

1 (7 ounce) can sliced green
  chilies
1 (10¾ ounce) can cream of
  chicken soup
1 (10¾ ounce) can cream of
  mushroom soup

Boil the chicken, remove skin and bones, then cut in small bite-size pieces. Soft fry the tortillas in hot oil, then drain on paper towel to remove excess oil. Be sure the tortillas do not get crisp, but stay soft. It is better to work with 2 or 3 at a time. Place a heaping tablespoon of chicken, onion and cheese in each tortilla, then roll tightly. Place close together in a 13x9x2-inch baking pan. Sprinkle the green chilies over top, then cover with mixture of the soups. You may thin the soup with a small amount of chicken broth to spread more evenly. Top with remaining grated cheese. Bake in 350° oven about 35-40 minutes. Serves 8.

Joyce Pace (Rudy)

Chicken Tortilla Casserole

1 (10¾ ounce) can cream of
  mushroom soup
1 (10¾ ounce) can cream of
  chicken soup
1 (12 ounce) can evaporated
  milk

1 medium onion, chopped
1 chicken, boiled and boned
1 (16 ounce) package tortilla
  chips
1 cup grated Cheddar cheese

Mix all ingredients except chips and cheese. Heat over medium heat until hot. In the bottom of a greased 2-quart casserole, put a layer of chips, then add a layer of soup mixture. Top with cheese. Repeat. Bake in 350° oven for 30 minutes. Serves 6.

Willie Mae Beckendorf (Harvey)

131

 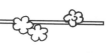

Chicken à la King

½ cup chopped or sliced
  mushrooms
½ cup chopped bell pepper
½ stick margarine
¼ cup all-purpose flour
2-3 cups milk

1 (10¾ ounce) can cream of
  mushroom soup
1 egg, beaten
1 chicken, cooked and boned
1 (2 ounce) jar chopped
  pimiento

Brown mushrooms and bell pepper in margarine until soft. Add flour, blend and add milk. Add soup and cook until thick. Stir some hot mixture into beaten egg and add to mixture. Cook a minute or two, stirring constantly. Add chicken and pimiento. Serve on toast.

Winnie Morris (J. B.)

Three Cheese Chicken Casserole

1 (12 ounce) package egg
  noodles
½ cup chopped onions
½ cup chopped green pepper
½ cup chopped celery
3 tablespoons margarine
1 (10¾ ounce) can cream of
  chicken soup
1 (6 ounce) jar mushrooms,
  drained
1 (2 ounce) jar pimiento,
  drained

⅓ cup milk
1 (8 ounce) jar pasteurized
  process cheese spread
1½ cups cottage cheese
  (jalapeño flavored if
  desired)
½ cup Parmesan cheese
2 cups diced cooked chicken
  breast
Salt and pepper to taste

Cook noodles as directed on package. Sauté onions, pepper and celery in margarine and add to drained noodles. Mix together all ingredients. Place in greased casserole. Bake at 350° for 45 minutes. Serves 12.

Carol Crawford (James)

Chicken Rice Casserole

4 cups cooked, cubed
   chicken
3 cups cooked rice
2 cups cooked French-style
   green beans
1 (10¾ ounce) can cream of
   mushroom soup

1 (10¾ ounce) can creamy
   onion soup
1 (14½ ounce) can chicken
   broth
3 teaspoons pimiento
½ cup slivered almonds
½ cup grated cheese

Combine all ingredients — saving a small portion of almonds and cheese for sprinkling on top. Bake for 30 minutes at 350°.

Mary E. Williamson (Roy)

Easy Curried Chicken

1 (2½-3 pound) hen or fryer
1 (7 ounce) box chicken-
   flavored rice vermicelli mix
1 teaspoon curry powder
1 (10¾ ounce) can cream of
   mushroom soup
1 (16 ounce) can "seasoned"
   green beans

2 (8 ounce) cans sliced water
   chestnuts, drained
4 tablespoons grated onion
½ cup mayonnaise (not salad
   dressing)
1 cup chicken broth (saved
   from boiling chicken)

Boil the chicken; bone it and chop it in bite size pieces, reserving the broth. Preheat oven to 350°. Cook the chicken-flavored rice vermicelli mix according to the directions on the box, adding the curry powder with the dry seasoning package. Mix all the other ingredients with the rice, in the order listed. Pour into a greased 13x9x2-inch baking pan. Bake at 350° for 45 minutes. Let set for at least 15 minutes before serving. Serves 8-10.

Note: *This recipe was given to me by a friend in Houston. I've used it for luncheons, staff dinners and for the family. Very often, when I serve it, someone asks for the recipe.*

Millie Feller (Verlon)

Chicken Pot Pie

1 cup chopped onion
1 cup chopped celery
½ cup margarine
3 - 4 cups chopped chicken
¼ cup all-purpose flour
3 cups chicken stock
1 cup milk
⅓ cup American cheese, grated
1 (10¾ ounce) can cream of mushroom soup
1 (10¾ ounce) can cream of chicken soup
3 cups fresh cooked carrots
16 ounces frozen vegetables
1 (10 ounce) package frozen English peas
1 tablespoon chicken bouillon
Salt to taste
1 unbaked pie crust

Sauté onion and celery in margarine for 2 minutes. Cook chicken with onion and celery, then remove and set aside. Add flour and stir for 1 minute, then add chicken stock, milk and American cheese. Stir to make a cream sauce. Add soups and stir. Add cooked carrots (be sure not to overcook), frozen vegetables, English peas, chicken bouillon and salt. Pour into baking dish. Add chicken. Top with pie crust and bake at 375° until brown.

Helen Walker (Derwin)

Chicken Tettrazini

1 onion, chopped
1 bell pepper, chopped
1 small pimiento, diced
½ chicken, boiled and boned
2 (10¾ ounce) cans cream of mushroom soup
1 cup reserved chicken broth
Parsley flakes to taste
1 (12 ounce) package spaghetti
2 cups grated cheese, divided

Sauté onion and pepper in a small amount of butter. Add pimiento, chicken, soup, broth and parsley flakes. Boil spaghetti, drain and add to chicken mixture. Add 1 cup of grated cheese to chicken and spaghetti mixture. Pour into casserole dish and cover top with remaining cup of grated cheese. Bake at 350° for 15-20 minutes or until bubbly and heated through. Serves 6.

Shirley Williamson (David)

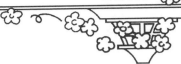

Chicken Spaghetti

2 fryers or 4-5 pounds chicken pieces
1 quart reserved broth
3 ribs celery, chopped
1 green pepper, chopped
2 onions, chopped
2 cloves garlic, crushed
1 (4 ounce) can mushrooms
12 ounces spaghetti, uncooked

1 (14 ounce) can chopped tomatoes
2 tablespoons chopped ripe olives
1 (10¾ ounce) can cream of mushroom soup
Salt, pepper, paprika, few dashes of Worcestershire sauce
1 pound grated pasteurized process cheese spread

Boil chicken in water seasoned with salt and pepper until tender. Remove chicken from bone and chop into bite-size pieces. Save broth. Simmer broth, celery, green pepper, onions, garlic and mushrooms for a few minutes. Add chopped spaghetti to broth mixture and cook until tender. Add tomatoes, olives, soup, seasonings and cheese. Add chopped chicken. Mix well. Heat. May be made early, placed in casserole and heated in oven. Freezes well.

Jean Cragg (Gene)

Perlow

1 chicken
1 pound sausage
1 large onion, chopped

2 cups dry rice
5 cups chicken broth

Boil chicken in salted water. Remove meat from bones, chill broth, skim off fat and add water to make 5 cups. Brown sausage in skillet, add chopped onion and cook slightly. Place rice in large pan, add sausage, onion, chicken and 5 cups broth. Cook until rice is done. Add seasonings to your taste. (I like to add green peas which make it especially good.)

Mary House (Morris)

 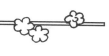

Chicken Broccoli Casserole

½ stick butter or margarine
1 (6 ounce) package herb-seasoned stuffing mix
1 (16 ounce) bag chopped frozen broccoli
4 chicken breasts or 1 fryer, cooked, boned and cut into bite-size pieces
1 egg, beaten

2 (10¾ ounce) cans cream of chicken soup
1 (10¾ ounce) can cream of celery soup
⅔ cup mayonnaise
1 teaspoon lemon juice
1½ cups grated Cheddar cheese

Melt butter and mix with stuffing mix. Cook broccoli and drain; do not salt. Layer broccoli in 13x9x2-inch pan, then chicken on top. Mix egg, soups, mayonnaise and lemon juice; pour over chicken. Sprinkle cheese on top, then dressing. Bake at 350° for 45 minutes to 1 hour.

Sue Gibbs (Walter)

Spectacular Chicken Supreme

1 (6 ounce) package long grain and wild rice mix
1 (10¾ ounce) can cream of celery soup
¾ cup mayonnaise
2 - 4 cups cubed cooked chicken
1 (16 ounce) can French-style green beans, drained

1 (8 ounce) can sliced water chestnuts, drained
1 small onion, chopped
1 (2 ounce) jar diced pimiento, drained
Salt and pepper to taste
1 (2¼ ounce) package slivered almonds (optional)
1 cup grated Cheddar cheese (optional)

Prepare long grain and wild rice according to package directions. In a large bowl, combine all other ingredients, except cheese, with the cooked rice and mix well. Pour into an ungreased 2½-quart casserole dish. Top with grated cheese, if desired. Bake at 350° for 30 minutes. Cover with foil for first 15 minutes of baking. This dish can be frozen before baking. Enjoy! Serves 12-16.

Lesly Haygood (Bill)
Susan Helm (Cy)
Peggy Laing (Charles)
Mary Margaret LeGrand (Leslie P.)
Gerry Millikan (Herman)
Merle Thomas (Clyde)

 ## Santa Fe Chicken "Steam-Fry"

½ cup chicken broth
¼ cup fresh lime juice
1 tablespoon sugar
1 tablespoon chili powder
1 tablespoon vegetable oil
1 teaspoon garlic powder

¼ teaspoon salt
¼ teaspoon pepper
2 teaspoons Dijon mustard
1 pound boned and skinned
  chicken breasts
1 teaspoon cilantro leaves

To prepare marinade combine in a shallow baking dish: chicken broth, lime juice, sugar, chili powder, oil, garlic powder, salt, pepper and mustard. With fork, pierce chicken in several places on both sides. Place in marinade, turning to coat completely. Let stand at room temperature for 15-30 minutes. Place chicken and marinade in a large skillet and bring liquid to a boil. Reduce heat and simmer uncovered, turning once or twice until chicken is no longer pink in center, about 12 minutes. Sprinkle with cilantro.

Lanelle Brown (Bryan)

 ## Chicken Oriental

1 pound boneless, skinless
  chicken breast halves
¼ cup soy sauce
1 tablespoon cornstarch
2 teaspoons sugar
1 teaspoon vinegar
¼ teaspoon ground ginger

¾ cup water
2 green peppers, cut into thin
  strips
1 celery stem, thinly sliced
1 clove garlic, chopped
½ cup toasted nuts (optional)

Cut chicken breasts crosswise into very thin strips. In 3-quart casserole, combine soy sauce and next 4 ingredients, plus ¾ cup water. Add green pepper, celery and garlic. Microwave on HIGH 5 or 6 minutes until mixture boils, stirring once. Add chicken. Cook, covered, on HIGH 4 or 5 minutes just until chicken loses its pink color, stirring twice. Add nuts if desired. Serve over rice. Serves 4.

Martha Hardt (John Wesley)

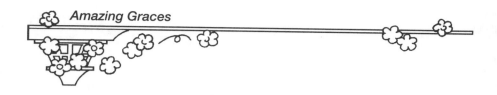

Quick Chick

1 cup rice
1 cup water

1 (10¾ ounce) can cream of
  mushroom soup
5 - 10 pieces chicken

Spread the rice on the bottom of a 13x9x2-inch ungreased casserole dish. Stir in the soup and water. Add the chicken. Cover with aluminum foil and bake at 350° for 1 hour. Serves 6.

Joe Watt (Sharon)

Glorified Chicken and Rice

1 (10¾ ounce) can cream of
  chicken soup
2 cups water
2½ - 3 pounds frying chicken
1 cup rice
1 envelope dry onion soup
  mix

1 tablespoon butter
½ cup chopped green bell
  peppers
½ cup chopped celery
1 (2 ounce) jar pimiento,
  drained and chopped
Paprika (optional)

Combine chicken soup and water and set aside ¾ cup. Cut up chicken. Lightly grease 13x9x2-inch baking pan and pour rice in pan. Sprinkle onion soup mix over rice. Melt butter in small frying pan and sauté peppers, celery and pimiento until tender. Add the peppers and celery to chicken soup and pour over rice. Place chicken pieces on top of rice and add the reserved ¾ cup chicken soup to top. Sprinkle paprika on top, if desired. Bake 1 hour at 350°.

Hazel Hampton (Jed)

Chicken Wings

2 pounds chicken wings
½ cup plain breadcrumbs
¼ cup Parmesan cheese
1 tablespoon chopped
  parsley flakes

1 teaspoon paprika
½ teaspoon oregano
1 teaspoon salt
¼ teaspoon pepper
⅓ cup melted margarine

Disjoint chicken wings and discard tips. Mix breadcrumbs, cheese and seasonings. Dip chicken pieces in margarine, then roll in crumb and cheese mixture. Place on a foil lined cookie sheet. Bake at 350° for 30-35 minutes. This makes a good buffet dish or covered dish for a pot-luck dinner. Serves 10.

Kay Frazier (James)

Chicken in Soy Sauce

2½ pounds chicken pieces
¾ cup soy sauce
¼ cup unsweetened
  pineapple juice

½ teaspoon dry mustard
1 tablespoon dehydrated
  onion flakes
1 clove garlic, minced

Remove all skin from chicken and arrange pieces in a casserole baking dish. Mix other ingredients and pour over chicken. Marinate for at least 2 hours, turning once. (Can be marinated overnight, but turn several times.) Cover and bake at 375° for 1 hour. Serve over hot rice. Serves 4.

Selena Johnson (Ray)

Oven-Fried Chicken

1 cup cornflake crumbs
1 teaspoon paprika
½ teaspoon garlic powder
¼ teaspoon red pepper
¼ teaspoon ground thyme
6 chicken breast halves,
  skinned
¼ cup buttermilk

Combine first 5 ingredients in plastic bag. Shake to mix well. Brush both sides of chicken with buttermilk. Place in bag of crumbs and shake to coat. Place chicken on broiler pan which has been sprayed with vegetable spray. Bake at 400° for 45 minutes or until done. Serves 6.

Joan M. Tanner (Charles R.)

Broccoli Supreme

2 (10 ounce) boxes frozen
  broccoli spears or equal
  amount fresh broccoli
2 packages very thinly sliced
  smoked chicken or turkey
  sandwich meat
2 cups milk
2 tablespoons butter or
  margarine
¼ cup all-purpose flour
Salt and pepper to taste
1 cup grated cheese
Pimiento strips (optional)

Steam broccoli until tender. DO NOT OVERCOOK! Roll each spear in 1 slice of sandwich meat and place crosswise in bottom of slightly greased 13x9x2-inch casserole dish. Make a cream sauce of milk, margarine and flour. Season with salt and pepper. Stir in cheese until melted. Pour over broccoli. A garnish of pimiento strips is attractive. This casserole may be served at once, or kept in the refrigerator and reheated at a later time in the oven. Just heat, do not overcook. Overcooked broccoli is hard to serve and loses its color.

Muryl McCombs (Hal)

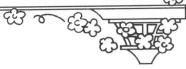

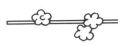

 ## Cornish Hens on Wild Rice

½ package dry onion soup mix
1 (6 ounce) package long grain and wild rice mix

2 Rock Cornish hens, split to make 4 pieces
1 (10¾ ounce) can low-fat cream of mushroom soup
1½ cups chicken broth

Spray 13x9x2-inch glass casserole dish with non-stick vegetable spray. Sprinkle ½ package dry onion soup mix in bottom of dish. Spread uncooked rice over the soup mix. Sprinkle seasoning package from the rice mix over the rice. Place Cornish hen halves, cut side down, on top of rice and seasonings. Stir together mushroom soup and chicken broth and pour over hens and rice. Cover tightly with foil. Bake in preheated 350° oven for 1½ hours, removing foil for last 15 minutes so hens can brown. Serves 4.

Cookbook Committee

 ## Heart-Healthy Turkey & Cabbage

1 pound ground turkey (95-97% fat-free)
1 large head green cabbage, coarsely chopped

1 large onion, chopped
Salt and pepper to taste or low sodium soy sauce

Spray large, deep skillet with non-stick vegetable spray and cook ground turkey until pinkness is gone. Add onion and cook until tender. Add cabbage. Cook covered, stirring frequently, until desired tenderness. Makes 8 100-calorie servings.

Note: Great with Heart-Healthy Cornbread!

Alice A. Dawson (Ferd, III)

141

Cabbage Casserole

1 pound ground turkey or
   ground beef
1 medium onion, chopped
Salt and pepper to taste

1 medium head of cabbage,
   chopped
1 (10¾ ounce) can tomato
   soup

Sauté turkey and onion in a small amount of margarine. Add salt and pepper. In a 2-quart casserole put half of chopped cabbage, all of turkey and onion mixture and top with rest of cabbage. Pour can of undiluted soup over top and spread over cabbage. Bake in covered casserole 1½ hours at 325°.

Shirley Phillips (Richard)
Maxine Stitt (Gerald)

Turkey Tetrazzini

1 medium onion, cubed
1 cup cubed celery
1 cup cubed turkey or
   chicken
1 cup cooked rice
1 (10¾ ounce) can cream of
   mushroom soup

½ teaspoon seasoned salt
½ cup sliced almonds
¾ cup mayonnaise
1 teaspoon lemon juice
Parmesan cheese or
   shredded Cheddar cheese

Sauté onion and celery. Mix all ingredients except cheese together and place in greased 9x9x2-inch pan. Sprinkle cheese on top, with a few more almonds. Bake at 375° for 30 minutes. Freezes well.

Claudia Dvorak (Otto)

Lighthearted Lasagna

1 pound ground turkey
1 (32 ounce) jar spaghetti
   sauce, divided
½ cup red wine
¼ teaspoon garlic powder
16 ounces low-fat cottage
   cheese
⅓ cup Parmesan cheese,
   grated

½ teaspoon dried basil
1 tablespoon chopped fresh
   parsley
8 uncooked lasagna noodles
8 ounces low-fat mozzarella
   cheese, sliced
½ cup sliced ripe olives
   (optional)

Crumble turkey into a 2-quart glass bowl. Stir in ½ cup spaghetti sauce. Stirring midway through cooking, microwave on HIGH 4 - 5 minutes. Stir again and add remaining spaghetti sauce. Pour wine into sauce jar, replace lid and shake to loosen remaining sauce in jar. Pour into turkey mixture along with garlic powder. Cover bowl with plastic wrap and microwave on HIGH 7 - 8 minutes or until bubbly. In a small bowl, combine cottage cheese, Parmesan cheese, basil and parsley; set aside. Pour ⅓ of hot spaghetti sauce mixture into a 2-quart rectangular dish; level. Place 3 lasagna noodles in dish, pressing lightly into sauce. Break off part of another lasagna noodle to fit across end of dish. Spread half of cottage cheese mixture on noodles. Arrange half of mozzarella on top. Pour half of remaining sauce over mozzarella; level. Repeat layers ending with remaining sauce. Distribute olives over top layer. Cover dish with heavy plastic wrap, venting one corner slightly. Microwave on HIGH 6 minutes; then microwave on 70% power for 20 minutes. Let stand covered 20-30 minutes. Serves 8.

Laura Neff (Jerry)

A*t the Annual Conference in Palestine, Texas, in 1942, the Reverend F. D. Mayes, a very influential member of the conference, had told my husband to be sure to be there. As we sat quietly while the appointments were read, no appointment was read for my husband. Suddenly the Bishop and others rushed back into the cabinet meeting. When they returned, they called out Brother Willie Ford, Caldwell. My heart leaped for joy. Our prayers were answered.*

Demmer Ford (Willie)

Shrimp Andrea

1 stick butter
1 (10¾ ounce) can French onion soup
1 (10¾ ounce) can cream of celery soup
1 (10 ounce) can tomatoes with chilies

1 medium onion, chopped
1 bell pepper, chopped
4 tablespoons parsley flakes
1½ pounds cleaned raw shrimp
2 cups raw rice

Melt butter in 13x9x2-inch dish. Mix undiluted soups, tomatoes, onion, bell peppers and parsley. Then add shrimp and rice and place in baking dish. Cover with foil and bake at 350° for 30 minutes. Remove foil and stir, then cover and bake for another 30 minutes.

Lanelle Brown (Bryan)

Shrimp Bisque

¼ cup grated onion
2 tablespoons grated green bell pepper
2 tablespoons butter or margarine
1 (10¾ ounce) can cream of potato soup
¾ cup light cream

½ cup grated sharp Cheddar cheese
2 teaspoons lemon juice
1½ cups shrimp, cooked and peeled or seafood of choice
1 (10 ounce) package frozen puff pastry shells

In a skillet, sauté onion and green pepper in butter. Blend in soup, cream, Cheddar cheese, lemon juice and prepared seafood. Season to taste. This may be stored in refrigerator or frozen until serving. When ready to serve, prepare puff pastry shells according to package directions. Thaw and heat seafood mixture thoroughly; pour into baked pastry shells. Serves 4-6.

Note: I like to prepare a lot of seafood dishes and this is one of my favorites! It is easily doubled or tripled. I usually serve this with Orange - Cranberry Salad, fresh asparagus, homemade bread and Angel Pie.

Nancy Oliphint (Ben)

Shrimp Creole

¼ cup margarine
2 tablespoons minced onion
1 cup chopped celery
½ cup chopped green pepper
2 tablespoons all-purpose
   flour
1 tablespoon seasoned salt
¼ teaspoon cayenne or red
   pepper

½ cup water
3½ cups tomatoes (28 ounce
   can)
1½ pounds cleaned shrimp
1 cup dry rice
2 cups water
1 teaspoon salt

Melt margarine in heavy pot. Sauté onions, celery and green pepper until tender. Blend in flour. Add the next 4 ingredients. Cover and cook for 30 minutes on low heat. Add shrimp and cook for 10 more minutes. Cook the rice separately in salted water. Serve over hot rice. Serves 6-8.

Mary Thompson (James)

Shrimp and Rice

1 cup dry rice
2 cups water
1 teaspoon salt
1 cup of chopped onions
1 cup of chopped bell
   peppers
1 cup of chopped celery

½ cup corn oil
2 cups chopped shrimp
3 cups of water
1 (10¾ ounce) can cream of
   chicken soup
½ teaspoon salt
1 teaspoon garlic powder

Cook the rice in salted water. Keep warm. Sauté onions, bell peppers and celery in oil. Stir in shrimp and let simmer for 10 minutes. Add water, soup, salt and garlic powder. Simmer 20 minutes more. Serve over hot rice.

Elodie Breaux (Clarence)

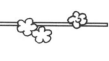

Hot Shrimp Casserole

½ stick margarine
10 slices day-old bread
1 medium onion, chopped
1 green pepper, chopped
2 ribs celery, chopped
Salt and pepper to taste
1 cup mayonnaise

2 (10¾ ounce) cans cream of
  mushroom soup
1 cup milk
2 cups cooked shrimp
8 ounces Cheddar cheese,
  grated

Generously grease bottom of rectangular casserole dish with butter. Break up 5 slices of bread into small pieces and lay on bottom of casserole dish. Layer onion, green pepper and celery over bread. Combine salt, pepper, mayonnaise, soup and milk with shrimp and pour over vegetable layer. Break other 5 slices of bread into small pieces and layer over shrimp mixture. Sprinkle Cheddar cheese over second bread layer. Cover and refrigerate overnight. Cook uncovered for 1 hour at 325°.

Hint: This recipe can be expanded to feed 200 people. Follow the same directions as above, using the following amounts of each ingredient: 10 sticks margarine, 10 (1½ pound) loaves of bread, 20 medium onions, 20 green peppers, 3 large stalks of celery, 5 quarts mayonnaise, 40 (10¾ ounce) cans of cream of mushroom soup, 5 quarts milk, 20 pounds shrimp, and 10 pounds Cheddar cheese.

Dorothy McClure (Jewel)

Green Bean Shrimp

2 (16 ounce) cans whole
  green beans, drained
1 clove garlic, crushed
¼ teaspoon dill, crushed
2 teaspoons seasoned salt
½ teaspoon seasoned pepper
1 teaspoon grated lemon rind

¼ cup lemon juice
¾ cup vegetable oil
2 tablespoons pimiento,
  chopped
1 (4 ounce) can broiled-in-
  butter mushrooms
1 pound shrimp, boiled

Combine all ingredients and refrigerate overnight. Serves 8.

Violet Waters (Bob E.)

Cheese Shrimp or Chicken

1 stick margarine, melted
¼ cup chopped celery
¼ cup chopped onion or
  green onion and tops
¼ cup chopped bell pepper
1 (10¾ ounce) can golden
  mushroom soup

1 (8 ounce) package
  pasteurized process
  cheese spread
2 cups shrimp, shelled and
  deveined or chicken, boned
Prepared rice

Sauté the vegetables in margarine. Add undiluted soup. Add cheese and melt slowly. Stir in shrimp or chicken. Serve over rice or inside a rice circle. Best made a day ahead. Make rice the day it is to be served. All can be heated in microwave.

Note: A good recipe for a ladies luncheon!

Shirley Williamson (David)

Creamed Tuna

1 medium potato, diced
2 carrots, diced
½ cup diced celery
1 small onion, diced
1½ tablespoons melted
  margarine
2 tablespoons all-purpose
  flour

1 cup milk
¼ teaspoon salt
Pepper to taste
1 (6⅛ ounce) can tuna,
  drained
Dried parsley and/or other
  herbs as desired
Grated cheese of choice

Cook vegetables in salted boiling water until tender. Start with the potatoes and carrots, then add celery and onion a few minutes later. Drain; set aside. In a skillet over medium heat, make white sauce by combining margarine, flour, milk, salt and pepper; cook and stir until thick and bubbly. Fold in tuna and vegetables; season to taste. Simmer carefully for a few minutes. Then serve on dry toast or rice. Serves 4.

Note: We like our toast very dry — I usually put it in the oven to crisp, then serve it warm. Grated cheese on top makes it even better!

Ann Fancher (Carroll)

Zesty Crab Cakes

1 pound fresh crabmeat,
  drained and flaked
¾ cup shredded carrot
½ cup fine, dry breadcrumbs
½ cup frozen egg substitute,
  thawed
2 teaspoons chopped fresh
  parsley
½ teaspoon dried Italian
  seasoning
½ teaspoon dry mustard
¼ teaspoon pepper
⅛ teaspoon garlic powder
2 teaspoons fat-free
  mayonnaise
1½ teaspoons low-sodium
  Worcestershire sauce
Creamy Seafood Sauce
  (recipe below)

Combine all ingredients in a medium bowl; stir well. Shape mixture into 6 patties. Cover and chill 1 hour. Coat a large non-stick skillet with non-stick vegetable spray; place over medium heat until hot. Add patties; cook 4-5 minutes on each side or until golden. Serve with Creamy Seafood Sauce. Serves 6.

Creamy Seafood Sauce:
¼ cup fat-free mayonnaise
¼ cup nonfat sour cream
¼ cup reduced-calorie
  ketchup
1½ tablespoons finely
  chopped green onions
2 tablespoons prepared
  horseradish
1 teaspoon chopped fresh
  parsley
1½ teaspoons lemon juice

Combine all ingredients in a small bowl, stirring well. Cover and chill at least 3 hours.

Cookbook Committee

It was 1940. We were living in Livingston, our third appointment. We were very fortunate to have a loving young lady, Ida Mae, to help with household duties, including helping with our two small children. One day, Ida Mae walked into the kitchen to find that 1-year-old Warren had climbed up on the counter and was reaching for the cabinet shelves above. Ida Mae grabbed him and said, "As the Master said to Zacchaeus, 'Little man, come down out of that tree!'"

Hazel Conerly (W. W.)

 *Halibut Lemon Sauté*

1 pound halibut, cut into
  1-inch cubes
Salt and pepper to taste
3 tablespoons vegetable oil,
  divided
1 cup thinly sliced carrots
1 cup sliced celery
1 cup sliced green onions
1 cup broccoli flowerets
¼ teaspoon salt
¼ teaspoon grated ginger
  root
¾ cup chicken stock
6 teaspoons cornstarch
3 teaspoons grated lemon or
  lime peel

Season halibut with salt and pepper. Sauté fish in 2 tablespoons of the vegetable oil until barely cooked. (Barely cooked means it is just barely whiter than translucent — opaque is overdone.) Remove halibut from skillet. Sauté vegetables in the remaining 1 tablespoon oil until tender. Return halibut to skillet. Add salt and ginger root. Combine chicken stock, cornstarch and lemon peel. Add to fish mixture. Cook and stir until thickened and halibut flakes easily when tested with a fork. Serve with rice.

Sandra Lambert (Steve)

 *Lemon - Broiled Orange Roughy*

4 (4-ounce) orange roughy
  fillets
3 tablespoons lemon juice
1 tablespoon Dijon mustard
1 tablespoon reduced-calorie
  margarine, melted
¼ teaspoon coarsely ground
  pepper
Coarsely ground pepper
  (optional)
Lemon slices (optional)

Place fillets on rack of a broiler pan coated with non-stick vegetable spray. Combine lemon juice, Dijon mustard, margarine and pepper; stir well. Brush half of lemon juice mixture over fillets. Broil fillets 5½ inches from heat 8-10 minutes or until fish flakes when tested with a fork. Drizzle remaining lemon juice mixture over fillets; transfer to a serving platter. If desired, sprinkle with ground pepper, and garnish with lemon slices. Serves 4.

Cookbook Committee

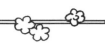

Mushroom - Stuffed Fish Rolls

4 (4 ounce) fresh or frozen
fish fillets
1 cup sliced fresh
mushrooms
1 tablespoon butter or
margarine
2 cups fresh spinach,
chopped
1 cup shredded lettuce

Scant ½ teaspoon dried
marjoram, crushed
¼ teaspoon salt
⅛ teaspoon pepper
1 teaspoon cornstarch
¼ teaspoon chicken bouillon
granules
½ cup water
1 beaten egg yolk
1 tablespoon lemon juice

Thaw fish if frozen; separate fillets. In a 1-quart casserole combine mushrooms and butter or margarine. Micro-cook, covered, on 100% power (HIGH) for 2 minutes. Add spinach and cook, covered, 1 minute more. Stir in lettuce, marjoram, salt and pepper. Spoon about ¼ cup mushroom mixture down the center of each fillet. Roll the fillet around filling (if necessary, secure with wooden picks). Place rolls seam side down in 10x6x2-inch baking dish. Cook, covered, with vented plastic wrap on HIGH for 5 - 7 minutes or until the fish flakes easily when tested, turning dish once. Remove rolls to platter. In a 2-cup glass measure, combine cornstarch, bouillon granules and ½ cup of water. Cook on HIGH for 1½ - 2 minutes or until thickened and bubbly, stirring every 30 seconds. Stir half of the mixture into egg, return to hot mixture. Cook 15 seconds. Stir in lemon juice. Spoon over fish rolls. Serves 4.

Merryl James (Roy)

One day when all 5 of our boys were still at home, Jim came in from work and announced that we needed to spend more time praying together as a family. He decided that before we could eat our supper, we would go around the table and let each member of the family offer a short prayer. Jim began by asking forgiveness for not being a better husband and father. I chimed in by confessing that I had not been the kind of mother and wife I should be. The boys picked up the tone of the prayer, and each in turn asked forgiveness for their various shortcomings, until the prayer reached Mark, the youngest. "Father," he said, "please help all these poor people."

Bobbie Neff (Jim)

Spinach Lasagna

1 (8 ounce) package regular or whole wheat lasagna noodles, uncooked
32 ounces tomato sauce
2 teaspoons dried oregano, divided
1½ teaspoons dried basil, divided
½ teaspoon plus ⅛ teaspoon garlic powder, divided
1½ cups water
1 (14 ounce) package soft or medium tofu
1 (10 ounce) package frozen chopped spinach, thawed and drained

In large bowl, combine tomato sauce, 1 teaspoon oregano, 1 teaspoon basil, ½ teaspoon garlic powder and water. Mix well and set aside. Drain tofu slightly. Place in blender and blend until smooth. Spoon tofu into bowl and add spinach and remaining spices, mixing well. In 13x9x2-inch pan spread 1 cup of tomato sauce. Top with ⅓ of noodles, then ½ cup of sauce. Next spread ½ of spinach mixture over noodles, and top with ½ cup of sauce. Top with ⅓ of noodles and press down firmly. Repeat layers, adding ½ cup sauce, remaining spinach mixture, ½ cup sauce and remaining noodles. Press down firmly. Spoon remaining sauce over noodles and make sure noodles are covered entirely by the sauce. Bake at 350°, covered, for 40 minutes. Uncover and bake 20 more minutes. Serves 6.

Note: No cholesterol and great for you!

Lea Bynum (Jonathan)

Wouldn't you know it — it was Sunday afternoon and the bishop was coming to our home, for the first time ever. I had cleaned and cooked and carefully admonished our 4 children about good behavior. Bob left to pick up the bishop. I said emphatically, "And don't drive him to the back; bring him through the front door." So when they drove up to the front of the house, what should they see? An entire window completely gone, lying in pieces and splinters on the ground. A shocked husband seated the bishop in the living room, then quickly found our 3 "well-behaved" boys waiting in the front bedroom. At first, all claimed innocence, but the truth finally emerged that one had pushed another into the window. Fortunately, there were no injuries and a good meal cures many ills!

Violet Waters (Bob)

Tofu Cheddar Enchiladas

1 (14 ounce) package firm
  tofu, drained and broken
⅓ cup chopped chilies
⅓ cup sliced green onion
2 cups shredded Cheddar
  cheese
2 (10 ounce) cans enchilada
  sauce

8 tortillas, corn or flour
½ - 1 cup shredded
  mozzarella cheese
1 medium tomato, finely
  chopped
2 tablespoons chopped
  cilantro

Put tofu, chilies and onion in blender; mix until smooth. Stir in Cheddar cheese. Grease a 17x11-inch dish with shortening. In non-stick skillet, heat ½ - 1 cup of enchilada sauce. Dip each tortilla in sauce to coat only one side. Put in dish and spoon 2 heaping tablespoonsful of tofu mixture onto coated side of each tortilla; roll up and place in dish seam side down. Spoon remaining enchilada sauce over tortillas; sprinkle on mozzarella. Cover and bake at 350° for 25 minutes or until hot. Sprinkle with tomato and cilantro and bake 5 minutes more. Serves 4.

Note: For less spicy enchiladas, decrease or omit chilies accordingly.

Lea Bynum (Jonathan)

The first time Clarence told me about going into the ministry, I was very glad. I thought after he finished his theological training, we would be on a "high-roll," and all of our problems would be over. We would move to different locations, serving people and the church. I saw ourselves on a missionary journey, sowing and reaping. The District Superintendent offered a charge to us, and according to him, this 3-point circuit had a lovely parsonage. At the time, we were living in our own home. We answered the call, packed up and left. Wow! What a surprise! The house was in very bad condition. From the inside you were able to see the outside during the day and count the stars at night. When it rained you had no place to stay dry. I told Clarence that we needed to go back home, that the house was only fit for rats, roaches and other creepy insects. In 32 years, we have moved only 3 times. We retired at Annual Conference in May, 1993, and on September 29, 1993, we celebrated 50 years of marriage.

Elodie Breaux (Clarence)

Together We Serve

Side Dishes

Dear Lord, we humans are all made in Thy image. When we at table "break bread," we may be eating rice, or nan, or pita, or noodles, or matzos, or tortillas, or poi, or white bread. We are all God's race and God's color. We are, together, God's family.

Amen.

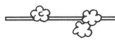

Asparagus / Pea Casserole

2 (15 ounce) cans asparagus
   spears, drained
1 (15 ounce) can small, early
   green peas, drained
1 (4 ounce) can sliced
   mushrooms, drained

1 (8 ounce) can water
   chestnuts, sliced and
   drained
1 (10¾ ounce) can cream of
   mushroom soup
1½ cups grated cheese
Seasoned breadcrumbs
1¾ sticks butter or margarine

Grease a 13x9x2-inch casserole dish with butter. Place drained asparagus in the bottom. Layer with peas, mushrooms, water chestnuts and soup. Top with grated cheese. Cover with breadcrumbs. Melt remaining butter and pour over all. Bake at 350° for 30 minutes.

Cookbook Committee

Escalloped Asparagus

4 tablespoons butter or
   margarine
¼ cup all-purpose flour
1 teaspoon salt
¼ teaspoon pepper
2 (16 ounce) cans asparagus
   spears, undrained
Milk

1 (2 ounce) jar chopped
   pimiento
4 hardboiled eggs
½ cup grated American
   cheese
½ cup breadcrumbs
½ tablespoon butter or
   margarine, melted

Melt 4 tablespoons butter in a small saucepan and stir in flour, salt and pepper to make a smooth paste. Drain and save liquid from asparagus. Add enough milk to the reserved liquid to make 2 cups liquid. Add to flour paste and cook slowly, stirring constantly until thickened. Stir in pimiento. Cover bottom of greased casserole with half the asparagus. Slice eggs and layer half of eggs over the asparagus. Sprinkle half of cheese over the eggs. Repeat layers. Pour sauce over all. Top with breadcrumbs and drizzle ½ tablespoon of melted butter over all. Bake at 425° for 20-30 minutes or until browned.

Martha Wells (Joe B.)

Herbed Green Beans

1 pound fresh green beans	½ teaspoon basil leaves
⅓ cup pine nuts	½ teaspoon garlic salt
¼ cup olive oil	¼ cup grated Parmesan
¼ cup vinegar	cheese
1 teaspoon oregano leaves	Salt and pepper to taste

Wash and snip end of beans. Cut all beans in half. Cook beans uncovered in large amount of boiling salted water until barely tender, about 5-8 minutes. Drain, plunge in cold water and drain again. Cover and chill. Spread pine nuts in shallow baking pan. Toast until lightly brown for about 15 minutes in a 350° oven. In another pan, combine oil, vinegar, oregano, basil, garlic salt and toasted pine nuts. Add beans and place over medium-low heat until heated thoroughly, turning several times so beans are well-coated. Season to taste with salt and pepper. Transfer to serving dish and sprinkle with Parmesan cheese. May be served warm or as a chilled vegetable.

Pat Nicholas (Martin)

Bean Bundles

2 (16 ounce) cans whole green beans, drained	8 - 10 slices bacon, cut in half
1 cup commercial Italian dressing	

Combine beans and dressing, tossing gently. Cover and chill overnight. Drain beans; arrange in bundles of 10-12. Wrap a half slice of bacon around each bundle and secure with a toothpick. Broil bundles 5 inches from heat about 7 minutes until bacon is cooked.

Shirley Williamson (David)

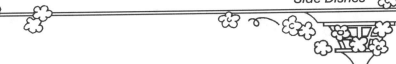

Dutch Beans

3 slices bacon
1 large onion, chopped
2 tablespoons brown sugar
2 tablespoons vinegar

1 teaspoon prepared mustard
2 (16 ounce) cans whole
green beans

Fry bacon until crisp. Drain and set aside. Sauté onion in drippings. Add sugar, vinegar and mustard, then simmer for about 10 minutes. Drain most of the liquid from beans. Stir beans into sauce and crumble bacon on top. Cook slowly, covered, for 1 hour.

Doris Davis (E. J., Jr.)

Christmas Beans

¾ - 1 pound bacon
1 onion, chopped
1 cup sugar
½ cup water
⅓ cup vinegar
Pepper to taste
1 (16 ounce) can butter
beans, drained

1 (16 ounce) can green
beans, drained
1 (16 ounce) can pinto beans,
drained
1 (16 ounce) can pork and
beans

Cut bacon into small pieces and fry in skillet. Pour off half the grease and sauté onion in remaining half. Add sugar, water, vinegar and pepper to the mixture. Simmer for 5 minutes. Place all beans in large casserole dish. Add bacon mixture and stir. Bake at 350° for 1 hour.

Dorothy Faulk (C. W.)

Baked Beans

2 - 3 (16 ounce) cans pork
and beans
¾ cup light brown sugar,
packed

1 teaspoon dry mustard
½ cup ketchup
3 slices bacon, cut in 1-inch
pieces

Spray 2-quart casserole dish with non-stick vegetable spray. Combine all ingredients except bacon in dish. Top with bacon and bake uncovered at 325° for 2 to 2½ hours.

Joan M. Tanner (Charles R.)
Sheryl Travis (Harold)

Fancy Ranch-Style Beans

½ pound bacon
1½ large onions, chopped
1 bell pepper, chopped
1 (4¼ ounce) can diced ripe
olives, drained

2 jalapeños, diced
½ pound fresh mushrooms,
sliced
2 (16 ounce) cans ranch-style
beans

In a skillet, fry bacon until crisp. Remove from skillet and set aside. Sauté onion and bell pepper in bacon grease. In a large saucepan, combine sautéed ingredients with remaining ingredients and simmer until hot. Serve. Serves 10.

Wanda Andrews (Andy)

O*n the day we moved to Matagorda, it was dark by the time we got there. Forrest put me out at the parsonage, while he went downtown to find the church member with the key. I sat on the screened-in porch in the dark and waited. After a long time, someone came and found me. I wasn't at the Methodist parsonage! Forrest had left me at the Episcopal manse!*

Elva Dorine Dyson (Forrest)

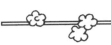

Hoppin' John (New Year's Day Special)

1 pound dried black-eyed
  peas
8 slices bacon
1 large onion, chopped
2 ribs celery, chopped

1 (15 ounce) can tomatoes,
  undrained
1 (10 ounce) can tomatoes
  with chilies, undrained
Salt and pepper to taste
⅔ cup uncooked rice

First soak and cook peas for several hours. Fry bacon until crisp; set aside. While cooking peas, sauté onion and celery in bacon drippings. Stir in slightly chopped tomatoes. You may add only half the can of tomatoes with chilies if you do not want the peas so spicy. Crumble bacon and add. Season with salt and pepper. Add cooked peas and uncooked rice. Combine in casserole. Bake covered about 30 minutes at 350°. May be frozen. Serves 10-12.

Betsy Stutes (Robert)

Broccoli and Rice Casserole

½ cup chopped celery
½ cup chopped green onions
1 stick margarine
1 (8 ounce) jar pasteurized
  processed cheese spread
2 cups cooked rice

1 (10 ounce) box frozen
  chopped broccoli, thawed
  and drained
1 (10½ ounce) can cream of
  mushroom soup

Sauté celery and onions in margarine. Combine cheese spread, rice, broccoli and soup in a greased casserole dish. Add the rest of ingredients and mix well. Bake for 30-45 minutes at 350° or until bubbly.

June Moore (Jim)

Variation: Add 1 (6 ounce) can mushroom pieces, drained.

Jane Decelle (Claude)

Variation: Omit green onions and replace with one package dry onion soup mix.

Tammy Gilts (Kip)

159

Chilled Sesame Broccoli

1 pound fresh broccoli
2 tablespoons vinegar
1 tablespoon soy sauce
1 teaspoon sugar

¼ teaspoon vegetable oil
1 tablespoon sesame seeds, toasted

Cut off broccoli flowerets and set aside. Bias-slice the broccoli stems into ½-inch thick pieces. Cook stems, covered, in small amount of boiling salted water for 5 minutes. Add broccoli flowerets and cook about 5 more minutes or until crisp-tender. Drain well. Transfer to serving bowl, cover and chill. Meanwhile, combine vinegar, soy sauce, sugar and oil in a jar. Cover and shake well to mix. Refrigerate until ready to serve. Just before serving, shake dressing again and drizzle over chilled broccoli; toss gently. Sprinkle with toasted sesame seeds. Serves 4.

Cookbook Committee

Carrots In Orange Sauce

1 pound of carrots, pared and sliced
½ teaspoon salt
¼ cup margarine
¼ cup brown sugar, packed

½ cup orange juice
1 tablespoon grated orange peel
⅛ teaspoon mace (optional)
2 teaspoons cornstarch

Cook carrots for 10 minutes in small amount of water. Drain and add remaining ingredients, except cornstarch. Bring again to a boil and simmer, covered, for 20 minutes or until tender. Blend cornstarch with small amount of cold water and stir into mixture. Omit cornstarch if liquid has almost evaporated. Cook, stirring gently until clear and thickened.

Nancy Culbertson (Lawrence)

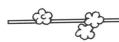

Glazed Carrots

12 medium carrots, pared
and halved lengthwise
½ cup tomato ketchup
3 tablespoons brown sugar

2 tablespoons bacon
drippings or melted
margarine
¼ teaspoon allspice

Cook carrots in boiling salted water until tender. (Don't overcook.)
Combine ketchup and remaining ingredients. Pour this over carrots.
Simmer 15 minutes on top of stove. Stir occasionally until well glazed.
Serves 6.

Mary Reed (Eldon)

Cheesy Mushroom Cauliflower

1 medium head cauliflower
1½ cups sliced fresh
mushrooms or 1 (4 ounce)
can sliced mushrooms,
drained
2 tablespoons butter or
margarine
2 tablespoons all-purpose
flour

Dash of pepper
¼ teaspoon salt
1 cup milk
1 cup shredded Cheddar
cheese
1 teaspoon prepared mustard
1 tablespoon snipped parsley
(optional)

Break cauliflower into flowerets. In a covered saucepan, cook cauliflower in a small amount of boiling salted water until just tender, about
10-15 minutes. Do not overcook, as cauliflower will become bitter.
Drain thoroughly and keep warm. Meanwhile, cook fresh mushrooms
in butter until tender, about 4 minutes. (If using canned mushrooms, set
aside and just melt butter.) Blend flour, pepper and salt into butter. Add
milk all at once. Cook, stirring constantly, until thick and bubbly. Stir in
cheese and mustard (if using canned mushrooms, add these as well).
Heat until cheese melts. Place flowerets in serving bowl and pour
sauce over cauliflower. Sprinkle with parsley, if desired.

Cookbook Committee

Cheesy Corn Casserole

1 (16 ounce) can cream-style
  corn
1 cup evaporated milk
½ cup finely crushed cracker
  crumbs
3 eggs, beaten

1 medium onion, finely
  chopped
½ teaspoon salt
⅛ teaspoon pepper
1½ cups (6 ounces) grated
  sharp Cheddar cheese

Combine corn, milk, cracker crumbs, eggs, onion, salt and pepper in a bowl. Stir until blended. Place half of the mixture in a well greased 8x8x2-inch baking pan and sprinkle with half of the grated cheese. Pour the remaining mixture in the pan and sprinkle the rest of the cheese on top. Bake, uncovered, in a 350° oven for 35 minutes or until the mixture is set and the cheese is golden in color. Serves 6-8.

Virginia Harris (Jesse)

Corn Casserole

1 small onion or ¾ cup green
  onions, chopped
1 green bell pepper, chopped
1 stick margarine
1 (14½ ounce) can cream-
  style corn
1 (12 ounce) can whole corn,
  drained

1 (6 ounce) package
  cornbread mix
1 egg
1 cup shredded cheese (any
  kind)
2 packets sugar substitute or
  3 tablespoons sugar
1 (2 ounce) jar pimiento (or
  chopped red bell pepper)

Cook onion, bell pepper and margarine in microwave for 3 minutes. Combine all other ingredients mixing by hand; do not use an electric mixer. Bake in a greased 2-quart casserole dish at 350° for 45 minutes.

Note: *This recipe can be easily doubled with good results.*

Beth West (Ned)

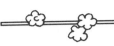

Easy Corn Pudding

2 (16 ounce) cans cream-style corn
1 tablespoon all-purpose flour
2 tablespoons sugar
½ teaspoon salt
1 cup milk
4 eggs, beaten
1 stick margarine, melted

Mix all ingredients together. Pour into a 13x9x2-inch casserole dish. Bake at 350° for 60 minutes.

Betty Pry (Guy)

Avalon Inn Corn Pudding

4 tablespoons butter or margarine
1⅓ tablespoons all-purpose flour
1⅓ tablespoons sugar
1 teaspoon salt
3 eggs, well beaten
1½ cups fresh corn
1¼ cups milk or half-and-half

Blend butter or margarine with flour, sugar and salt. Add eggs, beating well. Stir in corn and milk. Pour into buttered 1½-quart casserole. Bake at 325° for 45 minutes. Stir only once during baking, just after mixture is heated through and before it becomes set.

Ava Porterfield (David)

Creamed Corn

32 ounces frozen corn
½ pint whipping cream
½ pint milk
6 teaspoons sugar
1 teaspoon salt
¼ teaspoon MSG
½ teaspoon pepper
2 tablespoons butter
2 tablespoons all-purpose flour

Over medium heat, combine all ingredients except butter and flour. Bring to a boil. Melt butter and stir in flour. Add to corn mixture, blending well. Reduce heat and simmer until thickened to desired consistency.

Gina Baker (Doug)

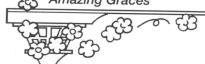

Christmas Corn

1 medium onion, chopped
1 bell pepper, chopped
½ cup margarine, melted
3 eggs, slightly beaten
3 (14½ ounce) cans cream-
style corn

1 (2 ounce) jar sliced
pimiento
1 (3½ ounce) package instant
rice, uncooked
3 tablespoons sugar
Salt and pepper to taste
2 ounces grated cheese

Sauté onion and bell pepper in melted margarine until tender. Mix together in large mixing bowl with eggs, corn, pimiento and rice. Add sugar, salt and pepper. Pour into lightly greased casserole dish. Sprinkle top with grated cheese. Cover and bake at 350° for 45 minutes.

Helen Langham (Robert B., Jr.)

Linda's Corn Pudding

1 (16 ounce) can whole corn,
undrained
1 (16 ounce) can cream-style
corn
4 eggs, beaten

¼ cup butter or margarine
2 cups shredded Cheddar
cheese
1 (6 ounce) package
cornbread mix

Mix ingredients together and bake in dish 45-50 minutes at 350°. Serves 12.

Nettie Mae Earls (Grady)

Variation: Add 1 (4 ounce) can chopped green chilies and decrease cheese to 1 cup.

Joan White (Dick)

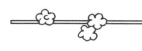

Shoepeg Corn / Green Bean Casserole

½ cup chopped onion
½ cup chopped celery
½ cup grated sharp cheese
1 (11 ounce) can Shoepeg
  corn, drained
1 (16 ounce) can French-style
  green beans, drained

1 (10¾ ounce) can cream of
  celery soup
½ pint sour cream
Salt and pepper
1 stick margarine
1 stack round buttery
  crackers, crushed

Mix together all ingredients except margarine and crackers. Place mixture in a 13x9x2-inch pan. Melt margarine and mix with crushed crackers and sprinkle on top of mixture. Bake in a 350° oven for 45 minutes.

Lynn Luton (Robert)

Hominy Casserole

1 cup chopped onions
1 cup chopped celery
½ stick margarine
1 (8 ounce) jar pasteurized
  processed cheese spread

1 (10¾ ounce) can cream of
  mushroom soup
2 (15 ounce) cans hominy,
  drained

In a skillet, sauté onions and celery with margarine. Add cheese spread and melt. Add mushroom soup and hominy. Pour into a 1½-quart casserole dish. Bake at 350° for about 30 minutes.

Margaret Downs Moore (Rubal)

Monterey Hominy

2 (30 ounce) cans hominy,
  drained
3 tablespoons chopped
  onion

1½ cups Monterey Jack
  cheese, shredded
2 (4 ounce) cans chopped
  green chilies
1½ cups sour cream

Mix together into greased casserole. Bake at 350° for 30 minutes.

Fran Richardson (Frank M., Jr.)

Eggplant Casserole

2 cups peeled and diced
  eggplant
1 teaspoon sugar
½ cup chopped onion
½ cup grated cheese

¼ cup mayonnaise-type
  salad dressing
1 egg
2 tablespoons butter
Cracker crumbs

Cook eggplant until tender in water. Drain and mash. Add ingredients in order listed. Mix well and pour into a 2-quart casserole dish, sprayed with non-stick vegetable spray. Top with cracker crumbs. Bake for 35-40 minutes at 350°.

Louzell Snowden (Bonner)

Roman Eggplant

1 large eggplant
1 (16 ounce) can tomatoes,
  drained
1 medium onion, chopped
1 bell pepper, chopped
1 teaspoon basil

1 teaspoon oregano
Salt and pepper to taste
Ground beef, cooked
  (optional)
Grated Cheddar cheese
  (optional)

Cut eggplant into cubes; you do not need to peel eggplant. Chop other vegetables and sprinkle with spices. Place in covered container in microwave for 10 minutes on High power. Stir and you may add more spices if you desire. Microwave another 10 minutes or until done. If desired, add ground beef and top with grated cheese.

Note: *This recipe was given to me by a woman I met in Italy. It can be cooked on top of the range, but you have to stir it - a lot!*

Barbara Gant (Louis R., Jr.)

166

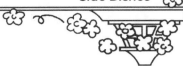

Onion Pie Casserole

30 crushed saltine crackers
½ cup melted margarine
¼ cup margarine
3 cups thinly sliced onions
2 cups (8 ounces) shredded
  sharp Cheddar cheese

1½ cups scalded milk
3 beaten eggs
½ teaspoon salt
¼ teaspoon pepper

Make a crust out of the crushed saltines and ½ cup melted margarine in a 9-inch pie pan. Sauté onions in ¼ cup margarine until golden brown. Place onions on top of crust. Sprinkle cheese on top of onions. (This may be made ahead of time.) When ready to cook, add milk to eggs, salt and pepper. Pour over onions and cheese. Bake at 350° for 30 minutes.

Edith Tate (Chris)

Party Potatoes

24 ounces frozen hash brown
  potatoes, thawed
¾ cup butter or margarine,
  melted, divided
½ cup chopped onion
1 teaspoon salt
¼ teaspoon pepper

1 pint sour cream
1 (10¾ ounce) can cream of
  chicken soup
1 cup grated sharp Cheddar
  cheese
2 cups corn flakes

Combine potatoes, ½ cup of the butter, onion, salt, pepper, sour cream, soup and cheese. Stir well. Pour into a greased 13x9x2-inch casserole dish and top with corn flakes mixed with the remaining ¼ cup butter. Bake for 45 minutes at 350°.

Janie McPhail (James)
Patti Meadows (David)

Variation: Add ½ pound ground beef, cooked and drained, to make this a main dish.

Doris Carlisle (Nick)

Sweet Potato Casserole

**3 cups boiled sweet potatoes
 (2-3 large)**
2 eggs, slightly beaten
½ cup melted margarine
⅓ cup milk
1 teaspoon vanilla

½ cup sugar
**1¼ cups brown sugar,
 packed**
⅓ cup margarine
½ cup all-purpose flour
1 cup pecans, chopped

Mash sweet potatoes in a large mixing bowl. Add eggs, melted margarine, milk, vanilla and sugar. Mix together well. Place in 8x8-inch buttered dish. Mix together brown sugar, ⅓ cup of margarine, flour and pecans; sprinkle over potatoes. Bake at 350° for 25 minutes.

Tena Spitsberg (Scott)

Sensational Spinach

**3 (10 ounce) packages frozen
 chopped spinach**
1 pint sour cream

1 envelope onion soup mix
Bacon bits

Cook and drain the spinach well. Combine all ingredients and bake 25 minutes at 350°. May top with bacon bits. Also good with chopped broccoli. Serves 6.

Note: *Frances Garrett, one of my favorite people and a Texas Conference minister's wife, gave this recipe to me in June of 1989. Frances died within the year of cancer. This recipe remains one of my favorites, because it is simple and delicious, and it came from her.*

Susan Hageman (Randy)

Spinach Dressing

1 pound bacon
1 pound spinach, fresh or
  frozen
8 cups cooked rice, cold
1 (16 ounce) can mushrooms,
  drained
4 stalks celery, diced
2 (8 ounce) cans water
  chestnuts, drained and
  diced
1 (14 ounce) can chicken
  broth

½ pound margarine, softened
¼ cup finely chopped parsley
2 cups minced green onions,
  including tops
1½ tablespoons dry mustard
1 tablespoon dried chives
Dry rosemary to taste
Garlic salt to taste
Dry tarragon to taste
Pepper to taste

Dice bacon in medium pieces; cook slowly in frying pan over medium heat. Remove bacon, leaving enough bacon grease in frying pan to cook spinach gently. Slice spinach in ¼-inch strips. Cook spinach until it wilts; remove from heat. In a 13x9x2-inch casserole dish, stir rice and spinach together. Add bacon, mushrooms, diced celery, water chestnuts; mix together with rice and spinach. Add chicken broth and blend together. Set aside. In a large bowl, beat margarine until fluffy. Blend in ¼ cup of finely chopped parsley and add finely minced green onions; add dry mustard and dried chives. Add rosemary, garlic salt, tarragon and pepper to taste. Blend mixture into spinach rice dressing. Bake at 325° for 1 hour.

Cheryl Papp (Patrick)

During the Depression Kenneth was pastor of a very small church in Wichita Falls, Texas. The men who had jobs at all worked for an oil field equipment manufacturing company at meager salaries. The Women's Society of Christian Service at a meeting with about 8 members decided a new kitchen stove was needed for the parsonage. I said to them, "The stove we have is all right. It is as good as the stove any one of you has." The reply was, "We cannot all have a new stove, but all of us together can have one for the parsonage." Needless to say, their sacrificial spirit brought tears to my eyes — and in reflection still does.

Catherine Copeland (Kenneth)

Spinach Kitty

2 (10 ounce) packages frozen
 chopped spinach, thawed
1 teaspoon salt
¼ teaspoon pepper
¼ teaspoon nutmeg

1 (8 ounce) package fat-free
 cream cheese
1 (8 ounce) container fat-free
 sour cream
Paprika

Slightly cook and drain spinach. Mix cream cheese into spinach, along with salt, pepper and nutmeg. Put in buttered 2-quart casserole. Cover top completely with sour cream and paprika. Bake at 300° for 30-45 minutes. This can be prepared ahead of time and then baked. Serves 6-8.

Beulah Lenox (Asbury)

Crunchy Squash Casserole

2 - 3 pounds yellow squash,
 sliced
Salt and pepper to taste
½ cup butter or margarine,
 melted
1 cup sour cream
1 (10¾ ounce) can cream of
 chicken soup, undiluted

2 onions, finely chopped
1 (8 ounce) can sliced water
 chestnuts, drained
1 (2 ounce) jar pimientos,
 drained
1 (8 ounce) package herb-
 seasoned stuffing mix

Cook squash in boiling water until tender. Drain, reserving 1½ cups of the liquid. Season to taste with salt and pepper; mash. Combine reserved liquid and remaining ingredients except ½ cup of the stuffing mix. Stir in squash. Pour mixture into ungreased 2½-quart casserole dish. Top with reserved stuffing mix. Bake at 350° for 30 minutes. Serves 12.

Mary Ann Stepp (Robert)

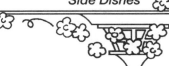

Baked Squash

5 or 6 yellow squash
1 teaspoon seasoned salt
1 teaspoon pepper
2 tablespoons chopped
  onion
2 eggs, beaten

1 cup milk
½ cup grated American
  cheese
1 cup crushed seasoned
  croutons

Slice, cook and mash squash. Mix with the other ingredients except croutons. Put into a 2-quart casserole and top with croutons. Bake at 400° for about 30 minutes until center is firm.

Gussie Vance (Nolan)

Squash Casserole Ole

4 cups diced, raw yellow
  squash
4 eggs, beaten or equivalent
  egg substitute
½ cup vegetable oil
1 cup grated Cheddar cheese

1 cup biscuit mix
1 small onion, chopped
1 clove garlic, minced
1 (4 ounce) can chopped
  green chili peppers
Salt and pepper to taste

Mix all ingredients and pour into a 13x9x2-inch greased casserole. Add extra grated cheese to top of mixture. Bake at 350° for 45 minutes. Serves 8-12.

Laura Winborn (Conrad)

171

Squash Creole

1 large onion, chopped
1 large bell pepper, chopped
3 ribs celery, chopped
½ cup margarine
3 tomatoes, peeled and
chopped
4 or 5 zucchini or yellow
squash, sliced

3 tablespoons uncooked rice
1 tablespoon sugar
1 teaspoon salt
¼ teaspoon freshly ground
black pepper
½ jalapeño pepper, finely
chopped (optional)

Combine onion, bell pepper and celery. Sauté in margarine for about 5 minutes. Add tomatoes, squash, rice, sugar, salt, pepper and jalapeño. Stir well. Bake in ungreased 8x8x2-inch casserole dish at 350° for 30 minutes. Stir and bake for 30 minutes more. Serves 8.

Merryl James (Roy)

Cream Cheese - Corn Squash Casserole

6 large yellow squash (add
some zucchini for color), 3
pounds total
1 large white onion, chopped
1 (8 ounce) package light
cream cheese, softened
1 (16½ ounce) can cream-
style corn

Salt and pepper to taste
Round buttery crackers,
crumbled
1½ cups (6 ounces) grated
mozzarella cheese (or
Cheddar cheese)

Steam cut up squash and onion until tender, about 6-8 minutes. Press softened cream cheese over bottom of ungreased 2-quart casserole. Pour squash into casserole. Top with cream style corn. Sprinkle top with round buttery crackers and cheese. Bake at 350° for 20-25 minutes or until cheese is melted and bubbly. Serves 6-8.

Note: *This casserole may be prepared in advance and refrigerated. Leave cheese off until squash and cream cheese are warm, then add cheese.*

Lucille Broach (L. B., III)

Squash Medley

¼ cup sweet cream butter
1½ cups peeled and cubed
  butternut squash
1½ cups unpeeled yellow
  crookneck squash, sliced
  ½-inch thick and quartered

1½ cups unpeeled zucchini,
  sliced ⅛-inch thick
1 heaping tablespoon brown
  sugar
⅛ teaspoon nutmeg

In a 10-inch skillet melt butter; stir in all other ingredients. Cook over medium heat, stirring occasionally. Cook about 8-10 minutes until tender. Serves 6.

Juanita Giles (Lloyd)

Fried Green Tomatoes

1 medium green tomato (per
  person)
1 teaspoon salt
½ teaspoon pepper

1 cup white cornmeal
Bacon drippings from about
  6 pieces bacon

Slice tomatoes about ¼ inch thick, season with salt and pepper and then coat both sides with cornmeal. Set aside for a few minutes. In a large skillet, heat enough bacon drippings to coat the bottom of the pan and fry tomatoes until lightly browned on both sides.

Note: *I decided to try this recipe after seeing the movie "Fried Green Tomatoes." I still get tears thinking about the movie. Hope you enjoy the tomatoes as much as Idgie did!*

Carolyn Lanagan (David)

Vegetable Casserole

1 (16 ounce) package frozen mixed vegetables
¼ teaspoon garlic powder or to taste
1 cup mayonnaise
8 ounces grated Cheddar cheese
½ cup chopped onion
1 (8 ounce) can water chestnuts, sliced and drained
Pinch of garlic powder
½ cup margarine
1 roll of round buttery crackers, crushed

Cook mixed vegetables according to package directions with ¼ teaspoon garlic powder and drain. Spread in an ungreased 1½-quart Pyrex casserole dish. Combine mayonnaise, cheese, onion, water chestnuts and a pinch of garlic powder; mix well and spread over vegetables. Melt margarine and mix with crushed crackers. Spread over vegetables and cheese mixture. Bake at 350° for 25-30 minutes. Serves 6-8.

Sue Gilpin (Clayton)

Rice - Vegetable Casserole

½ cup uncooked rice (not instant)
1 large onion, chopped
1 bell pepper, chopped
2 (16 ounce) cans cut green beans, drained
2 pounds yellow squash, cut in thick slices
2 (16 ounce) cans whole tomatoes, drained, cut in large pieces
Salt and pepper to taste
½ cup margarine, melted

Layer rice in bottom of ungreased 2-quart casserole dish; add onion and bell pepper. Place vegetables on top. Season to taste. Pour melted margarine over all. Cover tightly and bake at 350° for 1 hour or until rice is cooked. Best if left standing covered for about 15 minutes so rice can soften.

Note: This is a great dish for fellowship meals.

Marjorie Willis (Don)

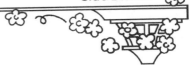

Scalloped Pineapple

6 slices of bread broken into
   pieces
1 (8 ounce) can crushed
   pineapple, drained
1 (8 ounce) can pineapple
   tidbits, drained
1 cup sugar
1½ sticks margarine, melted
3 eggs, beaten

Combine all ingredients. Pour into a 2-quart casserole dish and bake at 325° for 50 minutes.

Doris Smith (Lamar)

Baked Fruit

1 (16 ounce) can peaches
1 (16 ounce) can pears
1 (16 ounce) can apricots
1 (16 ounce) can sliced
   pineapple
1 (6 ounce) jar cherries
½ cup butter
½ cup brown sugar
½ teaspoon curry powder
2 tablespoons cornstarch
1 cup dry sherry

Drain fruits and place in a 13x9x2-inch casserole dish. Melt butter and add dry ingredients. Add sherry. Cook until thick. Pour over fruit. Bake 30-45 minutes at 350°.

Joye Chamness (Ben)

Cowboy Rice

1 cup rice (not instant rice)
1 (10¾ ounce) can French
   onion soup
1 (10¾ ounce) can beef
   consommé
1 stick margarine (optional,
   but it tastes better with it)

Preheat oven to 350°. Put all ingredients into a casserole dish and place in the oven, uncovered. Bake for 1 hour. This dish goes well with beef, poultry and fish.

Judy Barnes (Jay)

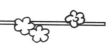
Green Rice Casserole

2 cups cooked rice
1 cup grated sharp cheese
¼ cup melted butter
2 tablespoons chopped
onion

1 cup chopped parsley
3 well-beaten egg yolks
Salt and pepper to taste
3 stiff-beaten egg whites

Combine all ingredients, except egg whites. Blend and fold in egg whites. Bake for 25 minutes at 350° in a greased baking dish. Serves 6-8.

Blanche Roberts (William F.)

Great Seasoned Rice

2 cups white rice
1 stick margarine
2 cups chopped celery
2 cups chopped white onion
6 cups chicken broth

3 cubes bouillon
2 cups sliced almonds
1 (10 ounce) package frozen
green peas and carrots,
thawed (optional)

Brown white rice in melted margarine until light brown. Heat on medium to medium high heat stirring often to avoid burning. Add celery and onion while continuing to cook until lightly browned. Heat chicken broth strengthened with 3 cubes of bouillon. Pour over rice and vegetables. Simmer, covered, for 20 minutes or more. Stir lightly with fork. Add sliced almonds. Add green peas and carrots, if desired. Cover and let sit 10 minutes.

Virginia Vodicka (Stanley A., Jr.)

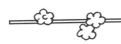

Mexican Rice

2 cups cooked rice
1 (10¾ ounce) can cream of
  celery soup, undiluted
1 (4 ounce) can chopped
  green chilies, drained
½ cup (2 ounces) shredded
  sharp Cheddar cheese

½ cup (2 ounces) shredded
  Monterey Jack cheese
½ cup sour cream
¾ teaspoon garlic powder
½ teaspoon ground cumin
Additional shredded sharp
  Cheddar cheese

Combine all ingredients except final addition of Cheddar cheese. Mix well. Spoon into greased 1½-quart baking dish. Bake, uncovered, at 325° for 20 minutes. Top with the additional cheese. Bake an additional 5 minutes.

Janet Scales (Roland)

Texas Gumbo Rice

4 slices bacon
1 large onion, chopped
1 green pepper, chopped
½ cup rice, uncooked
6 medium tomatoes or 1 pint
  canned tomatoes

1 cup sliced fresh or frozen
  okra
1½ teaspoons salt
¼ teaspoon pepper
½ teaspoon chili powder

Cook bacon until crisp, then crumble. Add onion, green pepper and rice. Cook until onion and green pepper are done. Add remaining ingredients and cook until rice is done.

Janie Newsome (John)

177

 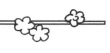

Baked Grits and Cheese

1 cup grits
4 cups boiling water
½ teaspoon salt
1 pound rat cheese, grated
1 stick margarine

3 teaspoons hot pepper
  sauce, according to taste
1 - 3 teaspoons seasoned
  salt, according to taste
3 eggs, beaten

Boil grits and salt in water until thickened. Add cheese and margarine and stir until melted. Add hot pepper sauce, seasoned salt and eggs and mix well. Pour into greased casserole dish and bake at 350° for 35-40 minutes. Sprinkle a few caraway seeds on top before cooking, if desired.

Nora Beth Morton (Weldon)

Methodist Grits

6 cups boiling water
1 teaspoon salt
1½ cups quick-cooking grits
1 stick butter or margarine

1 pound American
  pasteurized process
  cheese, grated
4 eggs, whipped

Cook grits in salted boiling water for about 5 minutes. Add butter and grated cheese. Let cool and add eggs. Bake in greased casserole dish 40-50 minutes at 300°. Serves 12.

Hint: Add a little bit of cooked and cooled grits to eggs as they are whipped and before they are added to rest of grits. Goes well with ham and makes a good supper dish.

Mary Goodell (Kenneth W.)

178

Cheese Fondue Casserole

1 cup scalded milk
1⅓ cups breadcrumbs
1½ cups grated cheese
½ teaspoon salt

⅛ teaspoon paprika
4 eggs, separated (yolks beaten, whites beaten stiff)

Pour scalded milk over the breadcrumbs and cheese. Add the seasonings and the yolks of the eggs well beaten. Fold stiffened egg whites into the mixture. Turn into a greased 1-quart baking dish. Bake for 30 minutes at 350°.

Note: *Another recipe from my mother. She often fixed this when my father would be out of town on business. It was a favorite of mine and my sister. It's a fun recipe to make and to see how it rises during baking. Unfortunately, it's not for those of us with high cholesterol!*

Linda Jordan (Clinton)

Hot Deviled Eggs

12 eggs
3 tablespoons salad dressing
½ cup real bacon bits (not imitation bits)
¼ cup butter or margarine
1 heaping tablespoon all-purpose flour

1 teaspoon salt
½ teaspoon dry mustard
Dash of red pepper
2 cups milk
1 (8 ounce) jar pasteurized processed cheese spread

Boil eggs in 2 quarts of water over medium heat for 20 minutes. Remove from heat and when cool, peel eggs. Slice eggs in half lengthwise and remove yolks. Mash yolks with salad dressing and mix in bacon bits. Stuff eggs with yolk mixture and place in buttered 13x9x2-inch baking dish. To make cheese sauce, melt ¼ cup butter over medium heat; add flour and mix well. Add salt, mustard, pepper, milk and cheese spread. Cook mixture over low heat until it bubbles, stirring frequently. Cover eggs with cheese sauce and bake in 350° oven until bubbly. Serves 6.

Sue Shuemate (Roger)

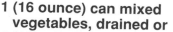

Corn Relish

1 (16 ounce) can mixed
  vegetables, drained or
1 (10 ounce) package frozen
  mixed vegetables
2 (16 ounce) cans whole
  kernel corn, drained
½ cup chopped celery
½ green bell pepper, sliced
  or chopped

1 cup sugar (½ cup may be
  used)
1 teaspoon salt
2 tablespoons mustard or ½
  teaspoon mustard seed
1 cup vinegar
1 teaspoon celery seed

Combine all ingredients in a saucepan. Heat to boiling, lower heat and simmer for 20 minutes. Chill overnight. Serve chilled.

Blanche Roberts (William F.)

Cranberry Chutney

1 pound fresh cranberries
1 cup granulated sugar
½ cup brown sugar, packed
2 teaspoons cinnamon
1½ teaspoons ginger
½ teaspoon ground cloves

¼ teaspoon ground allspice
1 cup water
1 cup chopped onion
1 cup chopped apple
½ cup chopped celery

Simmer cranberries, sugars, spices and water uncovered in a 2-quart saucepan over medium heat, stirring frequently, until juice is released from berries (about 15 minutes). Mash cranberries a little to speed up this process. Reduce heat and stir in remaining ingredients. Simmer uncovered until thick (about 15 more minutes). Cover and refrigerate. Will last about 2-3 weeks. Can be frozen.

Bette Jo Smale (Bill)

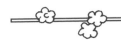

Apple-Ring Pickles

16 - 18 large cucumbers (the ones that get too big to use, or if buying them, get the largest salad cucumbers you can find)
2 gallons plus 3 cups water, divided
2 cups pickling lime
4 cups vinegar, divided
1 tablespoon alum
1 ounce red food coloring
5 pounds sugar
12 sticks cinnamon
30 ounces cinnamon red-hot candy

Peel, slice and seed cucumbers; cut in rounds ½-inch thick. (Use a doughnut-hole cutter and/or a syrup bottle plastic cap with a couple of holes melted or punched in it to cut the seed center out of each slice. This works best on a cutting board.) Cut enough slices to make 2 gallons (I cut the top off a plastic gallon milk jug to use for measuring.) Put slices in large crock or plastic container. Combine 2 gallons of water and lime, stir well, then pour over cucumbers. Soak for 24 hours, then drain off lime water. Wash several times and drain, being sure to wash lime sediment out of bottom of container. Soak 3 hours in tap water. Drain. Make solution of 1 cup vinegar, alum, food coloring and enough water to cover cucumber slices. Pour over cucumbers and simmer for 3 hours. Drain and throw away liquid. Make solution of sugar, 3 cups vinegar, cinnamon sticks, candy and 3 cups of water. Stir with wooden spoon. Bring almost to a boil and pour over cucumber slices. Let stand 24 hours. Each day for 3 days, pour off liquid, bring almost to boil, and pour back over cucumber slices. On the fifth day from beginning, heat pickles in liquid bringing almost to a boil. Put pickles in hot, sterile jars, fill with liquid leaving ½-inch head space. Seal while hot. Complete process takes 5 days.

Note: *I got this recipe from my mother, Viola Wieting, who was also a minister's spouse. Daddy, Wilson H. Wieting, and mother served in rural ministry of the Texas Conference for many years. Mother and I have had many, many compliments on these wonderful pickles through the years. I even won first place in a July 4th Pickling Contest in Baytown, Texas, with these pickles!*

Vivian White (Donald)

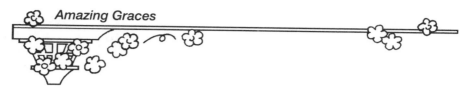

Jalapeño Jelly

1 cup chopped jalapeño
  peppers
1 cup chopped bell peppers
1½ cups cider vinegar

5½ cups sugar
1 (16 ounce) bottle liquid fruit
  pectin
Food color (red or green)

Wash peppers and chill; remove seeds, cut up and measure. In blender, add peppers, vinegar and sugar and chop. Simmer in medium saucepan until tender. Add pectin and boil for 1 minute. Reduce heat and cook 15 minutes. Add food color and pour into sterile jars and seal. Serve over cream cheese with crackers. CAUTION! Be extremely careful handling jalapeño peppers. The juice burns sensitive skin and eyes. Use rubber gloves.

Carolyn Curry (Gary)

Strawberry Preserves

1 (16 ounce) package frozen
  strawberries, unsweetened
3 tablespoons powdered fruit
  pectin

2 cups sugar
1 tablespoon lemon juice

Cook strawberries in microwave on full power for 2 minutes. Stir in pectin and cook on full power for approximately 2 minutes or until bubbles appear on top. Stir in sugar and lemon juice. Cook on full power for 6 minutes, stirring 2 or 3 times during cooking time. Watch carefully to prevent from boiling over. Pour into glass jars; cover and refrigerate.

Note: *Any kind of frozen fruit may be used.*

Sue Shuemate (Roger)

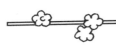

Virginia's Better Butter

1 (24 ounce) container low-
  fat cottage cheese
10 drops yellow food
  coloring (optional)

2 single packets Butter Buds
¼ cup water

Pour into a blender all the ingredients. Blend on low speed and increase speed until ingredients pull a suction. Use a small spatula to assist in blending. Scrape into containers and store in refrigerator. Use to season vegetables and great on baked potatoes. Only 7 calories per tablespoon serving.

Note: *This recipe was given to me by my friend Virginia Barnes.*

Fussy Heflin (James)

A*s the wife of a Methodist minister, I found that life can be abundant and fulfilling in every place and at every age. One of my personal joys is physical activity—movement, acceleration (though I do prefer "cruise control" to traffic tickets). For my 70th birthday I chose to SKY DIVE, something I had long wanted to experience. The 15 minute flight up to the 10,500 foot altitude was delightful. Already in my protective suit, my instructor had me pull on my goggles and helmet just before the jump. The excitement grew as I moved to the door of the plane and stepped out on the brace of the wing. Just before jumping, I experienced an instant of terror! A brief moment later this was replaced by sheer exhilaration during a 60-second "free fall." When the chute opened, the sound of rushing wind was replaced by utter silence, peacefulness and a feeling of being light as a butterfly. I was then able to maneuver in spirals and curves. The indescribable beauty of the earth far below was like a "taste of heaven." Though friends waited below, I did not want it to end. It was a very special birthday!*

Margaret Hall (Sherrill)

Did you ever have a special occasion fall apart? That happened to us when Monroe Vivian, our District Superintendent, called a Charge Conference. We invited the Vivians to dinner that Sunday. Excellent plans were in the making, when we learned of a family illness 300 miles away. We left quickly, to return on Saturday night to a "messed up" house. We agreed that Eldon should bathe, feed and put the 3 children to bed (ages 1-5), and then do what he could to make the house presentable. I concentrated on the kitchen, food preparation and dining area. Sunday after church, our son Ralph said to Mrs. Rowena Vivian, "You ought to see my room." Then he took her by the hand and led her to the room all 3 children shared. Expecting to see a newly decorated room, Rowena gasped when she saw opened suitcases, toys helter-skelter, unmade beds and piles of dirty clothes—the result of Eldon's "cleaning!" Laughingly, she replied, "Oh, this reminds me so of days gone by." I have always remembered the Vivians with love.

Mary Reed (Eldon)

Many years ago, we lived in a parsonage next door to the church. One Sunday evening, I decided to skip church, using as my excuse that the children were tired and fussy! I decided to give them a bath and prepare them for bed. When the bath was over, I dried off our oldest son and sent him to get his pajamas. I then dried off the youngest son and left him standing next to the tub. "Stay here while I get your pajamas," I told him. When I returned to the bathroom, he was not there. I asked the older boy if he had seen his brother. "Yes. He just went out the front door." I raced to the door in time to see him going into the back door of the church. Remember, he was completely nude! I hurried after him, but he was halfway down the center aisle amid a startled congregation. My husband was in the middle of his sermon. Our son explained, as I scooped him up: "Daddy, I come to church. Mommie didn't want to come!" With that, we rushed out of the church. Shortly, my husband came home. "Why are you home so soon?" He explained: "I couldn't remember where I was in the sermon, so we sang a hymn and had the benediction."

Mary Goodell (Kenneth)

Sweet Benedictions

Desserts

Thank you for the world so sweet,
Thank you for the food we eat,
Thank you for the birds that sing.
Thank you, God, for everything.
                    Amen.

Strawberry Cinnamon Chiffon Cake

2¼ cups cake flour
2 cups sugar, divided
1 tablespoon baking powder
1 teaspoon cinnamon
¾ teaspoon salt
6 eggs, room temperature
½ cup vegetable oil

¾ cup water
1½ teaspoons vanilla extract, divided
½ teaspoon cream of tartar
1 quart fresh strawberries
2½ cups heavy cream

Combine flour, 1 cup of the sugar, baking powder, cinnamon and salt in a large mixing bowl. Separate eggs, and combine yolks, oil, water and 1 teaspoon of vanilla in a small bowl. Beat yolk mixture into flour mixture until smooth. Beat egg whites in a separate bowl with cream of tartar until whites hold soft peaks. Beat in ½ cup of the remaining sugar, adding it gradually. Continue beating until whites hold stiff peaks. Carefully fold egg whites into cake batter. Pour into an ungreased 10-inch angel food cake pan. Bake at 325° for 60-70 minutes. Cool. Slice off top ½ inch of cake and set aside. Cut a tunnel about 1½ inches deep in the cake. The cuts should be about ¾-inch from the center and from the outside. Remove cake with a fork to form the tunnel. Hull and cut strawberries in half. Beat heavy cream with remaining ½ cup of sugar and ½ teaspoon vanilla until cream holds stiff peaks. Combine 1½ cups of whipped cream with half the strawberries. Fill the tunnel with the strawberry and whipped cream mixture. Replace the top of the cake. Frost the cake with the remaining whipped cream. Decorate the cake with the other half of the strawberries.

Susan Helm (Cy)

 Stewart and Charlse Bell had been our friends since college days, so it was natural that whenever we could find a mutual "day off" our families would get together. On one such occasion as our families sat down to dinner, James asked Stewart to say our blessing. Our 5-year-old son Tommy interrupted, saying, "Daddy, let me pray! I want to say grace!" Of course, Stewart insisted that Tommy be allowed to pray. Tommy bowed his head and prayed, "God, bless this food. Amen." Then he added, "STEWART PRAYS TOO LONG!"

Mary Thompson (James)

187

Banana Nut Cake

¾ cup shortening
1¼ cups sugar
2 eggs
¾ cup mashed, ripe banana
1¾ cups all-purpose flour
1 teaspoon baking soda

1 teaspoon baking powder
½ teaspoon salt
⅔ cup buttermilk
½ cup chopped pecans
Filling & Frosting (recipes below)

In a large mixing bowl, beat shortening and sugar on high speed of electric mixer until light and fluffy. Add eggs; beat 2 minutes at medium speed. Add mashed banana and vanilla; beat 2 minutes more. In another small bowl, stir together flour, baking soda, baking powder and salt; add to creamed mixture alternately with buttermilk, beating well after each addition. Stir in the chopped nuts. Pour batter into 2 greased and floured 9-inch round cake pans. Bake at 375° for 25 minutes or until toothpick inserted just off center comes out clean. Cool layers in pans 10 minutes; invert onto wire racks to cool completely. Meanwhile, prepare filling and frosting (recipes below).

Filling:
½ cup brown sugar, firmly packed
2 tablespoons all-purpose flour
½ cup evaporated milk

2 tablespoons butter or margarine
⅓ cup finely chopped pecans
½ teaspoon vanilla
Dash of salt

In a medium saucepan, stir together brown sugar and flour; stir in evaporated milk. Add butter; cook, stirring constantly, until mixture thickens and bubbles. Remove from heat; stir in pecans, vanilla and salt. Spread between layers of cooled cake.

Frosting:
1 egg white
½ cup shortening
¼ cup butter or margarine, softened

1 teaspoon vanilla
2 cups sifted confectioners' sugar

In a medium mixer bowl, beat together egg white, shortening, butter and vanilla on medium speed of electric mixer until well blended. Gradually add confectioners' sugar, beating until light and fluffy. Frost whole cake with frosting. Garnish top with pecan halves, if desired.

Kathy Danheim (Dan)

Apple Butter Cake

½ cup shortening
1 cup sugar
3 eggs
1½ cups apple butter, divided
2½ cups sifted cake flour
3 teaspoons baking powder

½ teaspoon baking soda
½ teaspoon salt
½ teaspoon cinnamon
¼ teaspoon nutmeg
1 cup milk
White frosting of your choice

Cream together shortening and sugar in a large mixing bowl. Beat in eggs one at a time. Beat until light and fluffy. Stir in 1 cup of the apple butter. In a separate bowl, sift together the flour, baking powder, baking soda, salt, cinnamon and nutmeg. Add flour mixture to creamed mixture alternately with milk. Pour batter into 2 greased and lightly floured 9-inch round cake pans. Bake at 350° for 30-35 minutes. Cool 10 minutes in pans. Remove from pans and cool completely. Spread frosting on bottom layer of cake and then spread ¼ cup of apple butter on top of frosting. Put other layer of cake on top and frost the whole cake. Spread remaining ¼ cup of apple butter on top of frosted cake.

Anne McKay (Scott)

Three-Day Coconut Cake

1 box butter cake mix
1¾ cups sugar
1 (16 ounce) carton sour
  cream

1 (12 ounce) package flaked
  coconut
1 (8 ounce) carton frozen
  whipped topping, thawed

Prepare cake mix according to package directions, making two 8-inch or 9-inch layers. When layers are completely cool, split each in half, making 4 thin layers. While cake is cooling, combine sugar, sour cream and coconut, blending well; chill. Before putting cake together reserve one cup of sour cream mixture. Spread remainder between layers of cake, making a layer cake 4 stacks high. Combine reserved sour cream mixture with whipped topping, blending until smooth. Spread on top and side of cake. Seal cake in an airtight container and refrigerate for 3 days before serving. This will keep in the refrigerator for several more days, if it has the chance.

Lynn Luton (Robert)

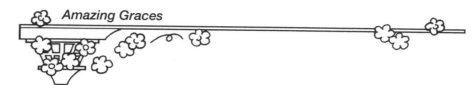

Eggless Raisin Cake — 1910

1 cup raisins
2 cups water
½ cup butter or margarine
1¾ cups all-purpose flour
1 teaspoon baking soda
½ teaspoon salt

1 cup sugar
½ teaspoon cinnamon
½ teaspoon nutmeg
1 cup chopped walnuts
(optional)

Boil raisins in water in a 2½-quart saucepan for 10 minutes. Add butter and stir until melted. Let cool. Preheat oven to 350°. Add flour, baking soda, salt, sugar, cinnamon and nutmeg to the raisins in the saucepan. (Do not sift dry ingredients). Add walnuts, if desired. Mix well. Pour into a greased and floured 10-inch square baking pan and bake at 350° for 35 minutes.

Note: *This was a favorite at church functions at the Chapel Street Church of Christ in Waukeegan, Illinois, in the early 1900's. The lady who made this cake refused to give out the recipe because she didn't want anyone to know she couldn't afford eggs. However, when my family left Waukeegan and moved to Michigan, she agreed to give the recipe to my mother as long as my mother promised not to share it with anyone in Waukeegan.*

Shirley Stultz (Hugh)

Apple Cake Quickie

1 stick margarine, softened
1 box yellow cake mix
½ cup flaked coconut
2 cups canned apples

½ cup sugar
1 teaspoon cinnamon
1 cup sour cream
1 egg

Mix margarine and cake mix in blender or food processor. Stir in coconut. Pat mixture into an 11x7-inch baking pan. Bake 10 minutes at 350°. Remove from oven and spread apples over cake. Mix sugar and cinnamon and sprinkle over cake. Mix sour cream and egg thoroughly and spoon over apples. Bake 25 minutes at 350°. Serves 9.

Zoe Wilson (Joe A.)

Oatmeal Cake

1 cup quick-cooking oats	1½ cups flour
1½ cups boiling water	¼ teaspoon salt
½ cup shortening or	1 teaspoon baking soda
margarine, softened	1 teaspoon cinnamon
1 cup granulated sugar	1 teaspoon vanilla
1 cup brown sugar, firmly	½ cup chopped pecans
packed	(optional)
2 eggs	Praline Icing (recipe below)

Combine oats and boiling water in a small bowl and let cool. Cream together margarine, sugars and eggs in a large bowl. Add cooled oat mixture to this and mix. Sift together dry ingredients and add to creamed mixture. Stir in vanilla and pecans, if desired. Pour in a greased 13x9x2-inch cake pan and bake at 350° for 35-40 minutes or until cake tests done. Meanwhile prepare Praline Icing (recipe below).

Praline Icing:

1 cup brown sugar, firmly	1 cup coconut
packed	1 teaspoon vanilla
1 stick margarine	1 cup chopped pecans
⅓ cup milk	(optional)

Mix all icing ingredients together in a medium saucepan and boil for 5 minutes, stirring constantly. Spread on warm cake and place cake under broiler until icing gurgles, watching it carefully.

Patricia K. Eifert (Richard)
Ginger Hood (T. Mac)
Karen Munn (Michael)

W hen my husband, Bob, had a heart attack, we took out a year from the ministry and moved to a quiet neighborhood in Palestine. All the neighbors knew Bob's condition. We had become good friends with the funeral director and one day he decided to come to see us. He was driving the hearse, which he parked out front. When he was ready to leave we followed him out to his hearse. The neighbors were all standing outside to see what was happening and were relieved to see both of us smiling and talking and able to walk out to the hearse.

Mary Ann Stepp (Bob)

Apple Harvest Cake

2¼ cups all-purpose flour
1 cup sugar
¾ cup brown sugar, firmly
  packed
1 tablespoon cinnamon
2 teaspoons baking powder
1 teaspoon salt
½ teaspoon baking soda

¾ cup vegetable oil
1 teaspoon vanilla
3 eggs
2 cups peeled, finely
  chopped apples (about 2
  medium apples)
¾ cup to 1 cup chopped nuts
Glaze (recipe below)

Preheat oven to 325°. Using 1 tablespoon solid shortening, generously grease and flour Bundt pan (even if using a non-stick pan). Lightly spoon flour into measuring cup and level off. Pour into a large mixing bowl and add all other ingredients except apples and nuts. Blend until moistened and then beat 3 minutes at medium speed. Stir in apples and nuts by hand. Pour batter into prepared pan and bake at 325° for 50-65 minutes or until toothpick inserted into cake comes out clean. Remove from pan and cool. Spoon glaze (recipe below) over cooled cake.

Glaze:
½ cup confectioners' sugar
¼ teaspoon vanilla

2-3 teaspoons milk

In a small bowl blend all ingredients until smooth.

Mary Lou Krause (Bruce E.)

Sam's Cake

1 package German chocolate
  cake mix with pudding
1 package pecan frosting mix
1 envelope whipped topping
  mix

1¼ cups vegetable oil
1¼ cups water
3 eggs
1 tablespoon vanilla

Mix all ingredients well. Pour into a well greased and floured tube pan. Bake at 350° for 45 minutes or until done. Cool cake before removing from pan.

Note: *This recipe was originated by my sister, Sammie Ruth Murdock.*

Bonnie Cannon (Wayne)

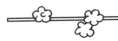
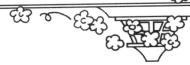

Fudge Cake

2 sticks margarine
4 tablespoons cocoa
4 eggs
2 cups sugar
1½ cups flour

Pinch salt
1 cup chopped nuts
2 teaspoons vanilla
1 (10½ ounce) bag miniature marshmallows

In a medium saucepan, melt margarine and cocoa. Set aside. In large mixing bowl, beat eggs; add sugar and mix well. Add margarine and cocoa. Then, mix in flour and salt. Add nuts and vanilla. Bake in a greased and floured 15x11-inch sheet pan at 350° for 30-35 minutes. Remove and cover with miniature marshmallows immediately.

Karen Munn (Michael)

Cocoa Party Cake

1 cup butter or margarine, softened
2¼ cups sugar
2 eggs
1 teaspoon vanilla

2¾ cups unsifted cake flour
½ cup cocoa
2 teaspoons baking soda
1 teaspoon salt
2 cups buttermilk

Cream butter and sugar together in large mixing bowl. Add eggs and vanilla and blend well. Combine flour, cocoa, baking soda and salt in a separate bowl; add alternately with buttermilk to creamed mixture. Pour into 3 greased and floured 8-inch round cake pans or a greased and floured 13x9x2-inch pan. Bake at 350° for 30-35 minutes for layers or 55-60 minutes for oblong cake, or until toothpick inserted in center comes out clean. Cool 10 minutes, then remove from pans. Cool completely, then frost with icing of your choice. Serves 16.

Mada Killen (James L., Jr.)

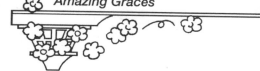 

Penny's Special Chocolate Chip Cake

1 cup dates, chopped
1¼ cups boiling water
1¾ teaspoons baking soda, divided
¾ cup shortening or margarine, softened
1 cup sugar
3 eggs

1 teaspoon vanilla
1¾ cups all-purpose flour
1 teaspoon salt
¾ cup brown sugar, firmly packed
¾ cup chopped nuts
¾ cup chocolate chips

In a small bowl, mix together the dates, boiling water and 1 teaspoon baking soda; cool. In another bowl, cream together the margarine and sugar. Add eggs and vanilla to the creamed mixture and mix well. Sift together the flour, remaining ¾ teaspoon baking soda and salt. Add flour mixture to the creamed mixture alternately with the date mixture. Pour into a greased 13x9x2-inch pan. Combine the brown sugar, nuts and chocolate chips and sprinkle on top of cake. Bake in preheated 350° oven 40-45 minutes. This can be served hot or cold; no frosting is needed.

Note: *When I received this recipe from my sister-in-law, it was called "Date Cake." I was afraid that the foster children we had just received would not eat it with that name, and I knew they liked chocolate chips, so I renamed it!*

Penny Johnson (Ken)

The Leon Mathises were serving Williams Memorial in Texarkana. I was involved in the WSCS, and for our mission study we were putting on a PLAY! Naturally I was in the play! Someone got the idea of asking the actresses' children to help. Our middle son, Bob, had been asked to hand out programs. He was some 5 or 6 at the time. He was proudly stationed at the door of the Fellowship Hall, dressed in his Sunday suit. One of the patrons asked Bob if he were going to be in the play. "Oh, no," replied Bob. "They asked me to stand out here and hand out pilgrims."

Martha Mathis (Leon)

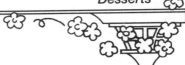

Chocolate Chip Cake

2¾ cups sugar, divided
5 eggs
2 sticks margarine, softened
2 cups all-purpose flour

1 teaspoon vanilla
1 cup chocolate chips
¾ cup water

Mix all ingredients, except ¾ cup of sugar and water, in a large bowl and pour into a greased and floured 12x9-inch glass pan. Bake at 325° for 20 minutes. While cake is baking, boil the reserved ¾ cup sugar with the water for several minutes until sugar is completely dissolved. Set aside. When cake is done, prick all over with a toothpick and pour sugar-water over it.

Lorrie Beasley (E. B.)

Five-Flavor Cake

2 sticks butter, softened
½ cup shortening
3 cups sugar
5 eggs, well beaten
3 cups all-purpose flour
½ teaspoon baking powder
1 cup milk

1 teaspoon coconut extract
1 teaspoon rum extract
1 teaspoon butter extract
1 teaspoon lemon extract
1 teaspoon vanilla extract
Glaze (recipe below)

Cream together the butter and shortening; then add sugar and beat until light and fluffy. Add eggs and beat well. Combine flour and baking powder; add to creamed mixture alternately with milk. Stir in flavorings and spoon batter into a greased and floured 10-inch tube pan. Bake at 350° for 1½ hours. With fork make holes in top of cake and pour glaze (recipe below) over hot cake.

Glaze:
1 cup sugar
½ cup water
1 teaspoon coconut extract
1 teaspoon rum extract

1 teaspoon butter extract
1 teaspoon lemon extract
1 teaspoon vanilla extract

Combine all ingredients in a saucepan and bring to a boil, stirring until sugar melts. Glaze is good over sliced cake, too.

Juanita Giles (Lloyd)

195

Pineapple Pound Cake

1 cup shortening
2 sticks butter, softened
2¾ cups sugar
6 eggs
3 cups all-purpose flour
1 teaspoon baking powder

¼ cup milk
1 teaspoon vanilla
¾ cup crushed pineapple, drained
Glaze (recipe below)

Cream shortening, butter and sugar in a large mixing bowl. Add eggs one at a time, beating well after each addition. Sift together the flour and baking powder; add to mixture alternately with milk, mixing well. Add vanilla and pineapple. Pour into a greased 10-inch tube pan. Place in cold oven and set oven at 325°. Bake for 1½ hours. Let stand for a few minutes before turning out. Pour glaze (recipe below) over hot cake.

Glaze:
¼ cup butter, softened
1 cup crushed pineapple, drained

1½ cups confectioners' sugar

Combine above ingredients in a bowl and stir until well mixed.

Judy Barnes (Jay)

Million Dollar Pound Cake

3 cups sugar
2 cups margarine, softened
6 eggs
4 cups all-purpose flour

¾ cup milk
1 teaspoon butter flavoring
1 teaspoon vanilla flavoring

Combine sugar and margarine and cream until light and fluffy. Add eggs one at a time, beating well after each addition. Add flour to creamed mixture alternately with milk, beating well after each addition. Add flavorings to mixture. Pour batter into a well greased and floured 10x4-inch tube pan. Bake at 300° for 1 hour and 40 minutes, or until toothpick inserted in center comes out clean. Serves 20.

Frances Prickett (Joe)

Coconut Pound Cake

5 eggs
2 cups sugar
1 cup vegetable oil
2 cups all-purpose flour
½ teaspoon salt
1½ teaspoons baking powder

½ cup milk
1 teaspoon coconut flavoring
1 teaspoon vanilla flavoring
1 cup shredded coconut
Sauce (recipe below)

In a large mixing bowl, beat the eggs and then add the sugar and oil. Beat well. Sift together the flour, salt and baking powder. Add alternately to creamed mixture with milk, mixing well. Add flavorings and mix well. Stir in coconut. Pour into a greased and floured tube pan. Bake at 350° for 1 hour. Meanwhile, prepare sauce (recipe below) and pour over hot cake while still in pan. Remove cake from pan after it is completely cooled.

Sauce:
1 cup sugar
½ cup water

1 teaspoon coconut flavoring
¼ cup margarine

Combine ingredients in a saucepan and boil one minute.

Sue Cantrelle (Earl)

My Cream-Cheese Pound Cake

2 sticks margarine, softened
1 (8 ounce) package cream
  cheese, softened
2¾ cups sugar
4 large eggs
½ teaspoon vanilla
½ teaspoon almond flavoring

½ teaspoon orange flavoring
½ teaspoon lemon flavoring
3½ cups sifted cake flour
1 teaspoon baking powder
¼ teaspoon salt
¼ - ⅓ cup milk

Cream together margarine, cream cheese and sugar in a large mixing bowl. Add eggs one at a time, beating well after each addition. Add flavorings and mix. Sift together dry ingredients and then add to creamed mixture alternately with milk. Pour into a greased and floured Bundt pan and bake at 300° for 1½ hours.

Virginia Vodicka (Stanley A., Jr.)

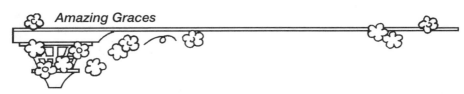

Grandmother's Orange Cake Ministry

1 box yellow cake mix	⅔ cup water
1 (3 ounce) box orange gelatin	4 eggs
⅔ cup vegetable oil	2 cups sugar
	1 cup orange juice

Mix cake mix and orange gelatin together. Add oil and water. Beat until well mixed. Add eggs one at a time, beating after each addition. Pour batter into a greased 13x9x2-inch pan. Bake for 1 hour at 300°. While baking, dissolve sugar in orange juice. When done, remove cake from oven and punch holes in the cake with a fork. Dribble orange juice mixture over hot cake.

Note: *My grandfather, the Rev. Jack Sparling, has been a minister in the Texas Conference since the 1930's. He says he would often go to visit someone who was ill or in sorrow and find that my grandmother, Vera Sparling, had already been there. She often left her orange cake—she does kind things quietly.*

Susan Hageman (Randall)

Pear Cake

3 cups sifted all-purpose flour	1½ cups butter or margarine, softened
1 teaspoon baking soda	2 cups sugar
1 teaspoon cinnamon	4 eggs
1 teaspoon allspice	1 cup buttermilk
1 teaspoon nutmeg	1 cup pear preserves
	1 cup chopped pecans

Sift flour and measure out 3 cups. Add baking soda and spices and sift 3 more times and set aside. Cream together the butter and sugar. Add eggs one at a time, beating well after each addition. Add flour in 3 portions alternately with buttermilk. Beat well. Stir in preserves and nuts. Pour into a greased and floured 10-inch Bundt pan and bake for 1 hour at 350°. Remove from pan and cool.

Dorothye Polk (Floyd J., Sr.)

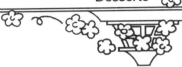

Earthquake Cake

1 cup shredded coconut
1 cup chopped pecans
1 box German chocolate or
  Swiss chocolate cake mix
½ cup margarine, softened

1 (8 ounce) package cream
  cheese, softened
1 (16 ounce) box
  confectioners' sugar
1 teaspoon vanilla

Preheat oven to 350°. Spread coconut on bottom of greased 13x11-inch pan. Sprinkle chopped nuts on top of coconut. Prepare cake mix as directed on box. Pour over coconut and pecans. Combine margarine, cream cheese, sugar and vanilla in a bowl and mix well. Drop this mixture by teaspoonsful on top of cake batter. Do not stir. Bake at 350° for 40-45 minutes.

Kathy Reiter (James)

Turtle Cake

1 (18½ ounce) package
  German chocolate cake mix
1 (12 ounce) can evaporated
  milk, divided
¾ cup margarine, melted
3 eggs

1 (14 ounce) package
  caramels
1 tablespoon margarine
¼ teaspoon vanilla
1 cup milk chocolate chips
1 cup chopped pecans

Mix cake mix, ⅔ cup evaporated milk, melted margarine and eggs. Divide this mixture in half. Pour ½ of mixture into a greased and floured 13x9x2-inch pan. Bake for 15 minutes at 350°. Remove from oven and set aside. Melt caramels in a saucepan with ½ cup evaporated milk, 1 tablespoon margarine and vanilla. Pour this evenly over baked layer. Sprinkle with milk chocolate chips and pecans. Pour remaining batter over chips and nuts. Bake for an additional 20 minutes at 350°. Cool before cutting.

Doris Smith (Lamar)

Crème de Menthe Cake

1 box white cake mix
1 (8 ounce) bottle crème de
menthe topping

1 (10 ounce) bottle fudge
topping
1 (8 ounce) carton frozen
whipped topping, thawed

Prepare cake mix according to package directions, adding ½ cup crème de menthe topping to batter. Bake in a greased 13x9x2-inch baking pan according to directions on box; cool. Spread all of fudge topping on the cooled cake. Fold the remaining crème de menthe topping into the thawed whipped topping; spread over the cake. Store in the refrigerator.

Janell Edwards (Timothy)

Snowball Cake

2 (¼ ounce) packages
unflavored gelatin
2 tablespoons cold water
1 cup boiling water
1 cup sugar
1 (16 ounce) can crushed
pineapple with juice
1 cup chopped nuts

3 packages whipped topping
mix, prepared according to
package directions •
Large, store-bought angel
food cake
1 (7 ounce) package angel
flake coconut

Dissolve gelatin in cold water in a medium bowl. Add boiling water and mix well. Stir in sugar, pineapple with juice and nuts. Fold in about ⅔ of prepared whipped topping. Trim brown crust from angel food cake and break cake into small pieces. Line a large (approximately 3-quart) mixing bowl with waxed paper. Put a layer of the gelatin mixture in bowl, then a layer of angel food cake pieces and continue layering until all the gelatin mixture and all the cake have been used. Cover and refrigerate overnight. Next day, turn out onto a cake plate and frost with remaining whipped topping mix. Cover with coconut. Keep refrigerated. A 13x9x2-inch pan may be used, if large mixing bowl is not available. Serves 12-15.

Charlse Bell (J. Stewart)

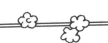
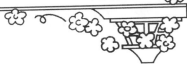

Red Velvet Cake

1 cup margarine, softened
1½ cups sugar
2 eggs
1 (1½ ounce) bottle red food coloring
3 tablespoons cocoa
2½ cups cake flour

1 teaspoon salt
1 cup buttermilk
1 teaspoon vanilla
1 teaspoon baking soda
1 tablespoon vinegar
Cream Cheese Icing (recipe below)

Cream margarine, sugar and eggs in a large mixing bowl. In a separate bowl, make a paste of food coloring and cocoa, then add to creamed mixture. Sift together the flour and salt; add alternately with buttermilk to the creamed mixture and mix well after each addition. Add vanilla. Mix baking soda and vinegar in another small bowl; add to batter and blend well. Pour batter into 2 greased and floured 9-inch round baking pans. Bake at 350° for 30 minutes. Remove from pans and cool completely; frost with Cream Cheese Icing (recipe below).

Cream Cheese Icing:
1 (8 ounce) package cream cheese, softened
1 stick margarine, softened

3 cups confectioners' sugar
1 teaspoon vanilla

In a medium bowl, cream together the cheese and margarine; blend in the remaining ingredients.

Kay Frazier (James)

As a young and inexperienced minister's wife, who was quite frankly "afraid about my responsibilities," I was called upon to host one of our conference's most beloved ministers for an overnight visit. His evening meal was to be with the Methodist Men, but breakfast would be in the parsonage. In preparation, I spent nearly a week's food money on breakfast foods—hot and cold cereal, juices, fruits, bacon, sausage, eggs, breads, etc. Before going to bed that night, I asked our guest what he'd like to have for breakfast the next day, letting him know his many and varied options. He replied, "Honey, if I could just have some coffee and hot water til I have my action, I'll get on the road for home."

Frances Stanton (Leroy)

 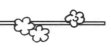

Chop Suey Cake

2 cups all-purpose flour
2 cups sugar
2 eggs
2 teaspoons baking soda
½ teaspoon salt
1 (15 ounce) can crushed
  pineapple, undrained
1 stick margarine, melted

1 (8 ounce) package cream
  cheese, softened
1 (16 ounce) box
  confectioners' sugar
1 teaspoon vanilla
½ cup shredded coconut
  and/or
½ cup chopped pecans

Mix flour, sugar, eggs, baking soda, salt and pineapple in a large mixing bowl. Pour into a 13x9x2-inch baking pan. Bake 30-40 minutes at 350°. Meanwhile, combine margarine, cream cheese, confectioners' sugar and vanilla and mix well. Pour over cake immediately upon removing from oven. Sprinkle coconut and/or pecans on top. Serves 16.

Mamie Shelton (B. R.)

Punch Bowl Cake

1 box Pineapple Supreme
  cake mix
2 (5¼ ounce) packages
  instant vanilla pudding
5 cups milk
1 (21 ounce) can cherry pie
  filling

2 (8 ounce) cans crushed
  pineapple, well drained
4 - 5 bananas, sliced
1 (12 ounce) carton frozen
  whipped topping, thawed
1 cup chopped pecans
1 (6 ounce) jar maraschino
  cherries

Prepare and bake cake as directed on box and cool. Meanwhile, prepare pudding as directed on package, using 5 cups of milk. Crumble ⅓ of cake in a punch bowl. Cover cake in punch bowl with ⅓ of pudding mixture. Add ⅓ of each of the following ingredients in the order listed: cherry pie filling, pineapples, sliced bananas, whipped topping and pecans. Repeat layers two more times in the same order. Garnish with cherries. Prepare a day ahead and store, covered, in refrigerator until ready to serve.

Audrey Jones (Harold)

Pumpkin Cake

2 cups sugar
1 cup vegetable oil
4 eggs
1 (16 ounce) can pumpkin
1 cup drained crushed
   pineapple
½ cup raisins
½ cup flaked coconut
2 cups all-purpose flour

2 teaspoons baking powder
1½ teaspoons baking soda
1 teaspoon salt
1 teaspoon cinnamon
½ teaspoon nutmeg
½ cup chopped nuts
Cream Cheese Icing (recipe
   below)

Cream together the sugar, oil and eggs. Add next 4 ingredients and mix well. In a separate bowl, stir together the dry ingredients and nuts. Add to pumpkin mixture and mix well. Pour into 3 greased and floured 9-inch round cake pans. Bake at 350° until done about 35-40 minutes. When cool, frost with Cream Cheese Icing (recipe below).

Cream Cheese Icing:
1 stick butter or margarine,
   softened
1 (8 ounce) package cream
   cheese, softened

1 (16 ounce) box
   confectioners' sugar
1 teaspoon vanilla
½ cup chopped nuts

Cream together butter, cream cheese and sugar. Add vanilla and nuts and mix until of spreading consistency. Makes enough for 1 cake.

Toni Steele (Jimmy)

My husband Don likes to boast about his first "pounding" while serving a circuit as a student at Vanderbilt. The gift box included 6 1-gallon jars of homemade pickles. However, I can top that with the story of my first years in the ministry with my late husband, Ferris Norton. We were serving the 4-point Pittsburg Circuit and Ferris decided to have a 10-day revival at each of the 4 churches. During those 40 days of revival, we were given 32 dozen eggs, so we bought a freezer on time and froze all those eggs in paper cups. On top of that, for 39 of those 40 days, we were served fried chicken in the homes of various parishioners. Finally, Ferris had had enough—he got up on a chair and crowed like a rooster. Lo and behold, on the last night of the last revival, we were served roast beef!

Constance Waddell (Don)

Carrot Cake

2 cups all-purpose flour
2 cups sugar
2 teaspoons baking powder
2 teaspoons baking soda
1 - 2 teaspoons cinnamon
1 teaspoon salt
4 eggs

1½ cups vegetable oil
3 cups grated carrots
½ cup chopped nuts,
    optional
Cream Cheese Frosting
    (recipe below)

In a medium bowl, mix together all dry ingredients. In a separate large bowl, beat eggs and then add oil. Add dry ingredients and mix. Add carrots and nuts. Pour into 3 greased 9-inch round cake pans or 1 greased 13x9x2-inch pan. Bake at 300° for 45 minutes or at 350° for 25-30 minutes. When cool, frost lightly between layers with Cream Cheese Frosting (recipe below), then ice the sides and top for the layer cake or frost the top for the oblong cake. Serves 20.

Cream Cheese Frosting:
1 (8 ounce) package cream
    cheese, softened
½ stick margarine, softened
1 (16 ounce) box
    confectioners' sugar

½ cup chopped nuts,
    optional
2 teaspoons vanilla, optional

Cream together the cheese and margarine. Add sugar and beat well. Stir in nuts and vanilla, if desired. Icing can be thinned with a little milk, if necessary.

Janet Kennedy (Tom)
Ollie Phifer (Ernest)

Leslie and Lutie Beth Griffin entered the ministry as a second career, after many years in the field of education. When Lutie Beth learned of Leslie's decision to enter the ministry, she told her mother that she couldn't be a minister's wife. When her mother inquired as to why she could not, Lutie Beth's response was, "I don't know how to play the organ!" Her mother said, "But you can be sweet!" Years later, Lutie Beth stated, "Many times, it would have been easier to have taken organ lessons."

Anonymous

Deluxe Gingerbread

1 (16 ounce) box dark brown sugar	2 eggs
2 cups all-purpose flour	1 cup buttermilk
1½ sticks margarine, softened	1 teaspoon ginger
	2 teaspoons cinnamon

Blend brown sugar, flour and margarine with a pastry blender or 2 knives until small granules are formed. Set aside 1 cup of this mixture to be used for topping. In a separate bowl, mix eggs, buttermilk, ginger and cinnamon; add to first mixture, beating until free of lumps. Pour into a greased and floured 13x9x2-inch pan; sprinkle with the reserved topping. Bake at 350° for 25-30 minutes or until cake tests done. Serves 16.

Note: *This is delicious served plain or with applesauce. It is festive served with a dollop (about 1 tablespoon) of whipped cream and a red cherry on top.*

Elizabeth R. Summers (Edwin T.)

Light-As-A-Feather Gingerbread

½ cup boiling water	1½ cups all-purpose flour
½ cup shortening	½ teaspoon salt
½ cup brown sugar, firmly packed	½ teaspoon baking powder
½ cup light molasses	¾ teaspoon ginger
1 egg, beaten	¾ teaspoon cinnamon
	½ teaspoon baking soda

Pour water over shortening in a medium mixing bowl. Add sugar and molasses and mix well. Cool mixture, then add beaten egg. Beat well. Sift together all the dry ingredients. Add to creamed mixture and beat until smooth. Pour into a greased 8-inch square pan and bake at 350° for 35 minutes. Cool in pan.

Note: *This is an old recipe of my mother's. When I was a girl, I made it as part of my 4-H project for the county fair in western Montana and won a blue ribbon!*

Anne Jordan (Milton, Jr.)

Swirl Coffee Cake

1½ cups sugar
½ cup margarine, softened
½ cup shortening
1½ teaspoons baking powder
1 teaspoon vanilla
1 teaspoon almond extract
4 eggs

3 cups all-purpose flour
1 (21 ounce) can cherry,
  apricot, blueberry or apple
  pie filling
1 cup confectioners' sugar
1 - 2 tablespoons milk

Preheat oven to 350°. Generously grease a 15½x10½x1-inch jelly roll pan or two 9-inch square cake pans. Blend sugar, margarine, shortening, baking powder, vanilla, almond extract and eggs in large mixing bowl on low speed, scraping bowl constantly. Beat on high speed, scraping bowl occasionally, 3 minutes. Stir in flour. Spread ⅔ of the batter in jelly roll pan or ⅓ in each square pan. Spread pie filling over batter. Drop remaining batter by tablespoonsful onto pie filling. Bake until light golden brown, 40-45 minutes. Cover with foil and store at room temperature. When ready to serve, heat, covered, in 325° oven until warm, about 10 minutes. Prepare glaze by mixing confectioners' sugar and milk until mixture is smooth and drizzly in consistency; drizzle over warm coffee cake. Cut cake in jelly roll pan into 3-inch pieces; cut cake in square pans into 2¾-inch squares. Serves 15.

Note: *Draws squeals of delight at any type of breakfast, brunch or morning gathering! The best part is that most of the work is done the day before it is actually served.*

Virginia Irene Crowe (Thomas W.)

On the way to preach the first sermon at a new church, *Jack and Vera Sparling's Model-T got stuck in the mud. Grandmother would not let Granddaddy push the car, because he would get dirty. She took off her shoes, waded into the mud puddle and pushed the sputtering vehicle onto dry ground. The congregation was quite impressed with their new minister, but had a few questions about his mud-splattered bride!*

Susan Hageman (Randy)
Granddaughter

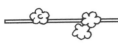
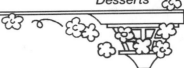

Individual Cheesecakes

12 vanilla wafers
2 (8 ounce) packages cream
  cheese, softened

1 teaspoon vanilla
½ cup sugar
2 eggs

Line 12 muffin cups with foil liners. Place one vanilla wafer in each liner. Combine cream cheese, vanilla and sugar in a medium bowl. Beat together on medium speed until well mixed. Add eggs and beat until smooth. Pour over wafers, filling ¾ full. Bake 25 minutes at 325°. Makes 12 cheesecakes.

Caroline Boyett (Mike)

Blueberry Cheesecake

1¼ cups graham cracker
  crumbs
¼ cup margarine, softened
1½ cups sugar, divided
2 (8 ounce) packages cream
  cheese, softened
4 eggs
2 teaspoons vanilla

1 (16 ounce) can blueberries
  or 1 pound frozen
  blueberries, thawed
½ cup water or reserved juice
½ cup sugar
2 tablespoons cornstarch
Whipped cream

Combine graham cracker crumbs, margarine and ½ cup sugar. Press into a 13x9x2-inch pan to form a crust. In a medium bowl, blend cream cheese, eggs, vanilla and 1 cup sugar. Pour cream cheese mixture over crust and bake at 350° for 12-15 minutes. Cool. Drain blueberries and reserve juice. Mix reserved juice or water with sugar and cornstarch in a small saucepan. Cook on medium heat, stirring until thickened. Add berries and cool. Pour mixture over cheesecake and refrigerate 1-2 hours. Serve with whipped cream.

Note: *This is a favorite with all the grandchildren.*

Bobbie Neff (Jim)

Pecan Praline Cheesecake

1½ cups graham cracker
   crumbs
1 stick butter or margarine,
   melted
½ cup granulated sugar
1 teaspoon cinnamon
4 (8 ounce) packages cream
   cheese, softened

3 eggs
1 teaspoon vanilla
2 cups brown sugar, firmly
   packed
1 cup chopped pecans
3 tablespoons all-purpose
   flour

Preheat oven to 350°. Combine graham cracker crumbs, melted margarine, granulated sugar and cinnamon. Press mixture into bottom and sides of a 9-inch springform pan. Set aside. Beat cream cheese until smooth. Add eggs and vanilla, and beat until fluffy. Stir in brown sugar, nuts and flour, stirring just to combine (do not use mixer for this step). Pour filling into crust, smoothing flat with spatula. Bake for 1 hour and 10 minutes or until toothpick comes out clean. Cool well and then refrigerate.

Lesly Haygood (Bill)

Easy Icing

1 (14 ounce) can sweetened
   condensed milk

1 (12 ounce) package sweet
   chocolate chips (not semi-
   sweet)

Combine ingredients in top of double boiler; cook over hot water, stirring until chocolate is melted and mixture is well blended. Spread on chocolate or plain cake.

Note: *This is very easy and so good.*

Emma Jo Thomas (Billie)

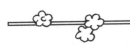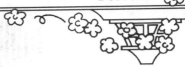

Frosting

1 (16 ounce) box
  confectioners' sugar
½ cup shortening
2 unbeaten egg whites
Dash of salt

1 teaspoon vanilla
½ teaspoon lemon extract
½ teaspoon almond extract
Pinch of cream of tartar

Combine sugar and shortening in a bowl and beat until well blended. Add all remaining ingredients except cream of tartar. Beat well. Add cream of tartar to whiten or, if desired, tint with your choice of food coloring.

Kathy Bagley (Gary)

Four-Minute Butter Frosting

⅓ cup butter or margarine,
  softened
Pinch of salt

3 cups sifted confectioners'
  sugar, divided
¼ cup milk or cream
1½ tablespoons vanilla

Thoroughly cream butter, salt and 1 cup of sugar and beat until light and fluffy. Add remaining sugar and milk, alternately, beating until smooth and of spreading consistency. Add vanilla. Makes enough to frost 1 sheet cake or the tops of three 9-inch layers.

Variations: For Chocolate Butter Frosting, melt 3 (1 ounce) squares of chocolate and add to the butter. For Lemon Butter Frosting, replace milk with ¼ cup lemon juice and omit vanilla. For Orange Butter Frosting, add 1 unbeaten egg yolk to butter, substitute ¼ cup orange juice for milk and 1½ tablespoons lemon juice for vanilla and then add 2 tablespoons grated orange rind. Continue as above.

Evelyn Waddleton (Joe S.)

Fresh Strawberry Pie

1 (14 ounce) can sweetened
condensed milk
1 (12 ounce) carton frozen
whipped topping, thawed

½ cup lemon juice
1 pint fresh strawberries,
sliced
1 baked 9-inch pie shell

Mix by hand the condensed milk, whipped topping, lemon juice and strawberries. Pour into pie shell and refrigerate for 2 hours before serving.

Caroline Boyett (Mike)

Diet Strawberry Pie

2 pints fresh strawberries
1 prepared 9-inch butter
crumb crust
1½ cups water
2 tablespoons cornstarch

1 (0.3 ounce) package sugar-
free strawberry gelatin
4 packages diet sugar
substitute

Clean strawberries, slice in half and arrange in prepared crust. Bring water and cornstarch to boil in a medium saucepan, stirring constantly until mixture is clear and thick. Stir in gelatin and sugar substitute until dissolved. Cool slightly in refrigerator for 5 minutes. Pour evenly over strawberries and chill until set, about 4-6 hours.

Laura Millikan (Charles)

W hen Ed and Liz Summers were serving at DeKalb, Texas, a man in the church had a small airplane. For the city Christmas celebration, it was decided that Ed would be Santa, and they would fly him in and land on the highway near town where the people would be waiting. The plane had to circle several times before landing. When Santa disembarked, he rode on a fire truck through town, holding on with one hand, and waving with the other. At the end of the parade, Ed said, "That was one Santa who had the ho, ho, ho scared out of him!"

Julia Miller (William A. "Buddy," Sr.)

Angel Pie

2 egg whites
⅛ teaspoon salt
⅛ teaspoon cream of tartar
½ cup sugar
1½ teaspoons vanilla,
  divided

½ cup finely chopped pecans
Margarine
1 (4 ounce) package German
  sweet chocolate
3 tablespoons hot water
1 cup whipping cream

In a large mixing bowl, beat egg whites until foamy; add salt and cream of tartar. Beat until stiff peaks form. Fold in sugar, ½ teaspoon of the vanilla and chopped pecans. Grease an 8-inch pie plate with margarine. Turn meringue mixture into pie plate, making a nest-like shell and building sides up above edge of plate. Bake in a slow oven at 300° for 1 hour 15 minutes or until shell seems crunchy. Cool. Melt chocolate in top of double boiler. Add 3 tablespoons hot water, blend and set aside to cool. Meanwhile, beat whipping cream until stiff peaks form in a medium mixing bowl. Add the remaining 1 teaspoon of vanilla to cooled chocolate mixture; fold into whipped cream. Turn into meringue shell. Chill. Makes 8 small or 6 medium slices.

Nancy Oliphint (Ben)

Fudge Pie

1 stick Promise margarine
2 tablespoons cocoa
1 cup sugar

½ cup all-purpose flour
2 eggs
1 teaspoon vanilla

Melt margarine in medium saucepan. Stir in cocoa, sugar and flour. Add unbeaten eggs and vanilla and mix. Pour into a greased 9-inch pie pan (or one that has been sprayed with non-stick vegetable spray). Bake at 350° for 30-35 minutes.

Note: My family likes this warm with peppermint or coffee ice cream.

Anne Hearn (J. Woodrow)

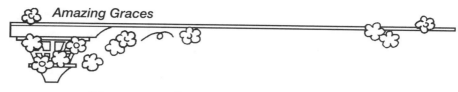

Chocolate Pie with Magic Meringue

1½ cups sugar
3 tablespoons all-purpose
flour
1½ tablespoons cocoa
3 egg yolks
2 cups milk

1½ tablespoons margarine
½ teaspoon vanilla
1 baked 9-inch pie shell
Magic Meringue (recipe
below)

In a large saucepan, blend together the sugar, flour, cocoa, egg yolks and milk. Cook over medium heat until thick, stirring constantly. Remove from heat and add margarine and vanilla. Stir until blended. Pour into baked pie shell. Cool. Prepare meringue.

Magic Meringue:
8 tablespoons sugar, divided
2 tablespoons cornstarch
½ cup water

3 egg whites
⅛ teaspoon salt
½ teaspoon vanilla

Combine 2 tablespoons of the sugar with the cornstarch in a small saucepan. Add water. Cook over medium heat, stirring constantly, until mixture is thick and clear. Cool. In a large mixing bowl, beat egg whites, salt and vanilla. Add 6 tablespoons sugar one at a time to egg whites, beating well after each tablespoon. Add cornstarch mixture and beat to soft peaks. Pile meringue on top of cooled chocolate mixture in pie shell. Bake in 350° oven about 15 minutes or until meringue is light golden brown. Cool before cutting.

Mary House (Morris)

Not-So-Sweet Pecan Pie

¼ cup butter
½ cup sugar
1 cup dark corn syrup
⅛ teaspoon salt

3 eggs
1 cup pecans
1 unbaked 9-inch pie shell

Cream butter. Add sugar and beat until fluffy. Add syrup and salt and beat well. Add eggs one at a time, beating after each addition. Put pecans in bottom of pie shell. Pour sugar and egg mixture over pecans. Bake 50 minutes at 350° or until pie is firm.

Ann Cady (Frank C.)

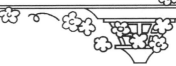

Pecan Pie

¾ cup brown sugar
¾ cup corn syrup
1 teaspoon vinegar
⅛ teaspoon salt

3 eggs
1 cup pecans
1 unbaked pie shell (recipe below)

Blend sugar and syrup. Add vinegar and salt and mix well. Add eggs and beat well. Stir in pecans. Pour into unbaked pie shell (recipe below) and bake at 350° for 45 minutes.

Pie Crust:
1 cup all-purpose flour
½ teaspoon salt

⅓ cup shortening
⅓ tablespoon cold water

In a medium mixing bowl, stir together the flour and salt. Cut in the shortening. Add cold water and mix just until all the flour is moistened. Roll out dough on floured board to fit your pie pan. Place dough in pie pan and trim off edges.

Renna Williamson (W. J.)

Tiny Pecan Tarts

1 cup all-purpose flour
1 stick plus 1 tablespoon margarine, softened
1 (3 ounce) package cream cheese, softened

1 egg, beaten
¾ cup brown sugar, firmly packed
1 teaspoon vanilla
⅔ cup chopped pecans

Combine flour, 1 stick margarine and cream cheese in a mixing bowl and mix until well blended. Form into 36 ½-inch balls. Place one ball in each cup of a miniature muffin pan. Press and mold pastry to line cup. Bake for 5 minutes at 325°. Now beat together the egg, 1 tablespoon margarine, brown sugar, vanilla and pecans until well blended. Pour into each pastry-lined muffin cup. Bake at 325° for 25 minutes. Makes 36 tarts.

Hint: To make 36 tarts in regular size muffin tins, just double the ingredients.

Harriet Willis (Edwin)

Peach Icebox Pie

1½ cups sugar, divided
1 cup water
2 tablespoons cornstarch
1 (3 ounce) box peach gelatin
1 teaspoon almond extract,
  divided
2 cups sliced fresh peaches

1 (8 ounce) package cream
  cheese, softened
1 baked 9-inch pie shell,
  cooled
Whipped cream or frozen
  whipped topping, thawed

Stir together 1 cup of the sugar, 1 cup water and cornstarch in a large saucepan. Cook and stir over medium heat until thickened. Add the dry gelatin and stir until dissolved. Cool and add ½ teaspoon of the almond extract. Gently fold peaches into the gelatin mixture and set aside. Next beat together the cream cheese, ½ cup of the sugar and ½ teaspoon of the almond extract until fluffy. Spread cream cheese mixture in bottom of the baked pie shell, then top with the peach and gelatin mixture. Top with whipped cream or frozen whipped topping. Chill well. Serves 8.

Note: *This can be "stretched" to fill 2 pie shells by using more sliced peaches.*

Ann Fancher (Carroll)

Sugarless Sweetened Deep-Dish Pie

5 cups peeled and thinly
  sliced apples, pears or
  peaches
Juice and grated rind of 1
  lemon
2 tablespoons cornstarch

1 (6 ounce) can frozen apple
  juice concentrate, thawed
½ cup golden raisins
1 teaspoon cinnamon
½ teaspoon nutmeg
¼ teaspoon ground ginger
1 unbaked pie crust

Mix the fruit, lemon juice, grated peel, cornstarch, apple juice concentrate, raisins and spices in a bowl and blend well. Spray a 9-inch square baking dish with non-stick vegetable spray and pour fruit mixture into dish. Cover fruit mixture with pie crust and trim edges to fit pan. Bake for 45 minutes at 425°. Serves 8 at 139 calories per serving.

Marie Beckendorf (Calvin)

Peach Cream Pie

1 unbaked 9-inch pie shell,
 chilled
3 tablespoons all-purpose
 flour, divided
½ cup plus 1 tablespoon
 sugar, divided

½ teaspoon nutmeg
¾ cup light cream
3½ cups peeled, sliced firm
 ripe peaches

Prick bottom of pie shell with fork. Mix 1 tablespoon of flour with 1 tablespoon of sugar and spread over bottom of pie shell. Bake at 375° for about 6 minutes. Meanwhile, mix ½ cup sugar, remaining 2 tablespoons flour, nutmeg and cream. Spread sliced peaches in pie shell after removing from oven. Pour sugar and cream mixture over peaches. Bake at 400° for 40 minutes or until set. Cool before serving.

Doris Davis (E. J., Jr.)

Cherry Ice Box Pie

1 (14 ounce) can sweetened
 condensed milk
⅓ cup lemon juice
1 (16 ounce) can tart pitted
 cherries, drained
½ cup chopped pecans
1 cup whipping cream

Dash of salt
¼ teaspoon almond extract,
 or to taste
¼ teaspoon vanilla extract, or
 to taste
1 prepared graham cracker
 pie crust

Mix first 8 ingredients in a large mixing bowl until well blended. Pour into graham cracker crust. Refrigerate before serving.

Anne Barrow (Emmitt C.)

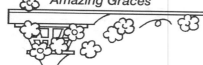

Methodist Pie

18 graham crackers
2 tablespoons sugar
½ cup or ¼ pound butter, melted
1½ pounds Philadelphia cream cheese, softened
3 eggs, well-beaten
¾ cup sugar
1 teaspoon lemon juice
Pinch of salt
1 pint sour cream
2 tablespoons sugar
1 scant teaspoon vanilla

Roll crackers to crush; mix sugar and butter together. Add cracker crumbs and mix well. Line a 10-inch pie pan with graham cracker crumb mixture. In a large mixing bowl, beat cream cheese thoroughly until fluffy. Add well-beaten eggs, ¾ cup sugar, lemon juice and salt; mix well. Pour into crust. Bake exactly 20 minutes in a preheated oven at 375°. While pie is baking, mix together the sour cream, 2 tablespoons sugar and vanilla. Remove pie from the oven. Spoon mixture carefully over the baked pie. Glaze in oven at 475° for 5 minutes more; watch carefully. Chill before serving.

Note: This recipe was found in an issue of "Shepherdess Magazine" in 1955 by Mrs. Forrest King of the North Georgia Annual Conference. It has traveled many miles. I thought you might enjoy this one!

Bonita Calhoun (Ken)

Sweet Potato Pie

2 cups cooked, mashed sweet potatoes
¼ cup melted margarine
¾ cup milk
1 cup sugar
3 eggs
¼ teaspoon salt
1 teaspoon vanilla
1 teaspoon cinnamon
1 teaspoon nutmeg
½ teaspoon allspice (optional)
1 unbaked 9-inch pie shell

Mix all ingredients, except pie shell, in a large bowl and then pour into unbaked pie shell. Bake at 350° for 1 hour or until toothpick comes out clean.

Evelyn Waddleton (Joe S.)

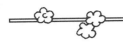
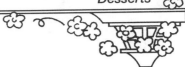

Lime Angel Pie

4 eggs, separated
1 cup sugar, divided
⅓ cup plus 1 teaspoon lime
  juice, divided

1 tablespoon butter
1 baked 9-inch pie shell

Combine 4 egg yolks, ¾ cup sugar and ⅓ cup lime juice in the top of a double boiler and cook over boiling water until thickened. Add butter and stir until melted. Remove from heat. Beat 4 egg whites until stiff. Fold half of the beaten egg whites into the custard mixture. To the other half of the egg whites, beat in ¼ cup sugar and 1 teaspoon lime juice. Continue beating until stiff peaks form. Pour the custard into the baked pie shell. Top with meringue and bake at 325° until meringue is brown, about 10-15 minutes.

Mary Margaret LeGrand (Leslie P.)

Impossible Pie

½ cup margarine, softened
2 cups milk
2 teaspoons vanilla
1 cup sugar

4 eggs
½ cup all-purpose flour
¼ teaspoon salt
1 cup shredded coconut

Combine all ingredients in blender or food processor and mix thoroughly. Grease and flour a 10-inch pie pan and pour mixture into pan. Bake at 350° for 30-40 minutes or until set. Pie will make its own crust as it cools.

Sue Hutchins (David)

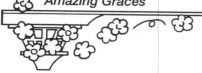

Butterfinger Pie

6 Butterfinger candy bars
1 (12 ounce) carton frozen
whipped topping, thawed

1 9-inch graham cracker pie
crust

Crush 5 of the candy bars by placing them in a plastic bag and rolling over the bag with a rolling pin. Combine candy bar crumbs and whipped topping in a bowl and mix well. Pour into the graham cracker pie crust. Crush remaining candy bar and sprinkle over pie. Refrigerate. Serves 6-10.

Note: *This is still delicious the next day, if you can keep it that long!*

Frances Fagan (Harold)

Blueberry Cream Pie

2 baked 9-inch pie shells,
cooled
3 bananas, sliced
2 (3 ounce) packages cream
cheese, softened

¾ cup sugar
1 (8 ounce) carton frozen
whipped topping, thawed
1 (21 ounce) can blueberry
pie filling

Place banana slices in bottom of pie shells. Cream together the cream cheese and sugar with electric mixer. Stir in the whipped topping. Spoon the cream cheese mixture over the bananas. Top this with the blueberry pie filling. Refrigerate until ready to serve.

Margie Holt (Bill)

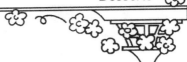

Chocolate Chip Pie

2 eggs
½ cup all-purpose flour
½ cup brown sugar, firmly
  packed
1 cup butter or margarine,
  melted

1 (6 ounce) bag chocolate
  chips
1 cup pecans
1 unbaked deep-dish 9-inch
  pie shell
Whipped cream

Preheat oven to 325°. In large bowl, beat eggs; add flour and brown sugar and beat well. Blend in butter. Stir in chips and nuts. Pour into pie shell. Bake for 1 hour at 325°. Serve warm with whipped cream.

Tana Neel (Jerry)

Chocolate Chess Pie

1 stick margarine, melted
3½ tablespoons cocoa
1½ cups sugar
2 tablespoons all-purpose
  flour

2 eggs
1 teaspoon vanilla
1 (6 ounce) can evaporated
  milk
1 unbaked 9-inch pie shell

Combine margarine, cocoa, sugar and flour in a large bowl and mix well. Add eggs, vanilla and milk and beat until well blended. Pour into unbaked pie shell. Bake at 350° for 45 minutes or until set.

Florence Holcomb (Tom)

The church busybody came for a visit with the pastor's wife. The pastor, knowing of her visit, had retired to the upstairs, prior to her arrival. After a couple of hours, the pastor hollered to his wife, "Has that old battleaxe left yet?" She had not, but the pastor's wife's quick response saved the day! "Oh, she left hours ago. Mrs. _____ is here now!"

Anonymous

219

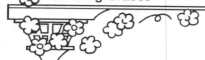 
Old-Fashioned Egg Custard Pie

2 tablespoons butter or
  margarine, softened
1 cup sugar
2 tablespoons all-purpose
  flour

4 eggs
2 cups milk
1 teaspoon vanilla
1 unbaked 9-inch or 10-inch
  pie shell

Preheat oven to 350°. Cream butter with sugar. Add flour and stir well. Add the eggs and beat well. Add milk and vanilla. Stir mixture well and pour into pie shell. Bake for about 50 minutes at 350°. Pie is done when set all over and slightly brown. Serves 8.

Note: *This is delicious!*

Viola Lambert (Alex)

Old Time Buttermilk Pie

½ cup margarine, softened
1½ cups sugar
3 rounded tablespoons all-
  purpose flour
3 eggs, beaten

1 cup buttermilk
1 teaspoon vanilla
Juice of 1 lemon (optional)
⅛ teaspoon nutmeg
1 unbaked 9-inch pie shell

Cream together margarine and sugar; add flour and mix well. Add eggs and beat well. Stir in buttermilk, vanilla and lemon juice. Pour into pie shell and sprinkle nutmeg over top. Bake 45-50 minutes at 350°. Serves 6-8.

Helen Lowe (Robert B.)

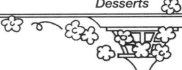

Buttermilk Coconut Pie

1½ cups sugar
2 tablespoons all-purpose
 flour
3 eggs, beaten
¼ cup butter or margarine,
 melted

½ cup buttermilk
1 teaspoon vanilla
1 (3½ ounce) can coconut
1 unbaked 9-inch pie shell

Combine sugar and flour; set aside. Combine eggs, butter, buttermilk and vanilla and mix well. Add sugar mixture, stirring well. Stir in ⅔ cup of the coconut. Pour into pie shell. Bake at 325° for 30 minutes. Then sprinkle remaining coconut over pie. Return to oven and continue baking an additional 30 minutes.

Sheila Crabbe (James)

Coconut Pie

3 tablespoons all-purpose
 flour
1 tablespoon cornstarch
Pinch of salt
1 cup cold water, divided
1 (14 ounce) can sweetened
 condensed milk
4 eggs, separated

½ stick butter or margarine
1 cup shredded coconut
1 teaspoon coconut extract
1 baked 9-inch or 10-inch pie
 shell
¼ teaspoon cream of tartar
3 tablespoons sugar

Sift flour, cornstarch and salt into a medium bowl; add ½ cup of the cold water and mix well. Stir in the remaining water and the milk and stir. Cook in the top of a double boiler until thick, stirring constantly. Beat egg yolks slightly and add to double boiler, stirring constantly. When mixture is thick and custard-like, stir in butter, coconut and extract. Cook and stir for 2 more minutes. Pour custard into baked pie shell. Combine egg whites and cream of tartar in a medium bowl and beat until stiff. When stiff peaks form, add 3 tablespoons of sugar and continue beating until very stiff but not dry. Pile meringue on top of pie and spread to the edges. Bake at 300° for 15-20 minutes. Cool completely before cutting. Serves 8.

Helen President Thomas (Darnell)

Old-Fashioned Pineapple Pie

½ cup butter, softened
1¾ cups sugar
Pinch of salt
3 eggs

1 (16 ounce) can crushed
  pineapple, drained
1 teaspoon vanilla
1 unbaked 9-inch pie shell

Cream together butter, sugar and salt, beating until mixture is well blended. Add eggs and mix well. Stir in well-drained pineapple. Add vanilla and mix. Pour into unbaked 9-inch pie shell and bake at 350° for 40-50 minutes.

Joye Eckols (Glen)
Shirley McIntyre (Earl)

Variation: Decrease sugar to 1½ cups and add 1 tablespoon vinegar when adding vanilla. Continue as above. May need about 10 more minutes in oven.

Bonnie Cannon (Wayne)

Pumpkin Chiffon Pie

5 eggs, separated
1 cup canned pumpkin
1 cup sugar
½ teaspoon salt
¼ - ½ teaspoon nutmeg,
  according to taste

¼ - ½ teaspoon cinnamon,
  according to taste
1 cup rich milk (can use part
  light cream)
1 unbaked 9-inch pie shell
Whipped cream

Beat egg whites until fairly stiff; set aside. Beat egg yolks until creamy; add pumpkin, sugar, salt and spices and mix well. Add milk and mix. Fold in beaten egg whites. Bake in unbaked pie shell at 425° for 10 minutes, then reduce heat to 350° and bake 30 minutes longer. Cool. Spread whipped cream on top.

Note: May be kept out of refrigerator for 3 or 4 hours, but once you put whipped cream on top, it must be refrigerated.

Mary Lou Krause (Bruce E.)

Blackberry Cobbler

2 cups all-purpose flour
½ teaspoon salt
1 teaspoon baking powder

⅔ cup butter or margarine,
softened
5 tablespoons ice cold water

Combine dry ingredients and sift together into bowl. Cut in the butter. Add water and blend. Roll out dough to ⅛-inch thickness on floured board. Cut into 1-inch or 2-inch squares. Let pastry squares rest while you prepare filling, as they will handle better this way.

Filling:
2 - 3 cups sugar, depending
on sweetness of berries
5 tablespoons cornstarch
½ teaspoon cinnamon
2 cups boiling water

5 - 6 cups blackberries (fresh
or frozen)
½ cup butter or margarine
Evaporated milk

Mix sugar, cornstarch and cinnamon in a large saucepan. Stir in 2 cups boiling water. Cook until thickened, stirring constantly. Add berries and butter. Stir until butter is melted. Remove from heat. Pour a third of the berry mixture into a 13x9x2-inch baking dish and top with one third of the pastry squares. Repeat layers, until you have three layers each of berries and pastry squares. Brush top squares with evaporated milk and sprinkle with sugar. Bake at 325° for 30-40 minutes or until squares are golden brown. Put a cookie sheet under the baking dish, as this will bubble over while cooking. May serve hot with ice cream, evaporated milk or cream.

Note: *Other fruit may be substituted for the berries. This recipe is easily doubled.*

Selena Johnson (Ray)

Church Cobbler

½ cup margarine
1 cup sugar
1 cup all-purpose flour
⅔ cup milk
2 teaspoons baking powder

1 teaspoon vanilla
Pinch of salt
1 (29 ounce) can fruit with
 juice, your choice

Melt margarine in 13x9x2-inch baking pan. Combine sugar, flour, milk, baking powder, vanilla and salt in a large mixing bowl and mix until batter is formed. Pour over melted margarine. Spread fruit and juice over batter. Bake at 375° for 45 minutes. The batter will rise to the top as it cooks.

Note: *This is good with canned peaches, canned blackberries, etc. This recipe goes back to one of the first appointments we served— Pineland. We still enjoy it!*

Barbara Gant (Louis R., Jr.)

Peach Cobbler

5 - 6 slices white bread
2 - 3 cups sliced fresh
 peaches
1⅔ cups sugar

2 tablespoons all-purpose
 flour
1 egg, beaten
1 stick margarine, melted

Trim crusts from bread and cut each slice into 5 strips. Place peach slices in bottom of greased 2-quart baking dish. Lay strips of bread across peaches to form crust. Combine remaining ingredients in a medium bowl and mix well. Drizzle over peaches and bread strips. Bake at 325 - 350° for 45 minutes.

Gerry Reeves (Garland)

Cream Cheese Drops

1 (3 ounce) package cream
cheese, softened
¾ cup butter or margarine,
softened
1 cup sugar
2 cups all-purpose flour
3 tablespoons milk

1 teaspoon vanilla
½ cup chopped pecans or
walnuts
¼ cup sweet chocolate
pieces, pecan halves or
candied fruit

Beat cream cheese, butter and sugar until fluffy. Add flour, milk, vanilla and chopped nuts. Beat until well mixed. Grease a large cookie sheet. Drop dough by teaspoonsful about 2 inches apart on cookie sheet. Press a chocolate piece, pecan half or candied fruit into center of each cookie. Bake about 10 minutes at 375°. Remove cookies to wire rack to cool. Store in tightly covered container to use within one week. May be frozen. Makes about 5 dozen cookies.

Margaret Downs Moore (Rubal)

Quick Cookies

1 package good quality cake
mix (chocolate is best)
1 egg

½ cup shortening
2 teaspoons water

Mix all ingredients together and let chill. Roll into small balls and place on ungreased cookie sheet. Cook about 10 minutes at 350°. Do not overcook.

Variation: Roll cookie balls in a mixture of cinnamon and sugar before cooking.

Bonita Calhoun (Ken)

Old-Fashioned Sugar Cookies

½ cup shortening
1 cup sugar
2 eggs
1¼ teaspoons butter
  flavoring

1 teaspoon vanilla
2½ cups sifted all-purpose
  flour
½ teaspoon salt
2 teaspoons baking powder

Cream together shortening and sugar. Add eggs, butter flavoring and vanilla. Mix well. Sift together the flour, salt and baking powder; beat into creamed mixture. Chill. Shape into ¾-inch balls and place on a greased cookie sheet 2 inches apart. Flatten with bottom of glass dipped in sugar. Bake in 375° oven for 8 minutes or until edges begin to brown. Makes 4 dozen.

Demmer G. Ford (Willie)

Sugar Cookies

1 cup margarine, softened
1 cup brown sugar
1 cup granulated sugar
2 eggs
2 teaspoons vanilla

3 cups all-purpose flour
½ teaspoon salt
½ teaspoon baking soda
½ teaspoon baking powder

Cream together the margarine, sugars and eggs. Add vanilla and stir. Add the dry ingredients and mix well. Roll dough into the shape of a log about 2 inches in diameter. Wrap in waxed paper and refrigerate for 2 hours. Cut into ½-inch slices and bake on lightly greased cookie sheet at 300° for about 12 minutes or until lightly browned. Makes about 3½ dozen cookies.

Note: For Christmas, sprinkle with red sugar before baking.

Marie Zenor (Hugh)

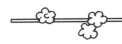

Sour Cream Sugar Cookies

2 cups sugar
1 cup shortening
2 eggs
1 cup sour cream

½ teaspoon baking soda
1 teaspoon vanilla
4 - 5 cups all-purpose flour
¼ teaspoon salt

Cream the sugar and shortening. Add the eggs and continue to mix until smooth. Add sour cream, baking soda and vanilla and mix well. In a separate bowl, mix flour and salt together. Add to creamed mixture. Chill. When ready to bake cookies, preheat oven to 425°. Flour your counter. Take a small portion of the dough and roll out on counter until about ⅛-inch thick. Keep remainder of dough in freezer wrapped in waxed paper until ready to use. Cut dough with favorite cookie cutter. Transfer to ungreased cookie sheet and bake at 425° for 5-7 minutes. Makes 3 dozen cookies.

Kathy Bagley (Gary)

Aunt Selma's Spritz Cookies

2 cups butter
2 cups sugar
2 eggs

1 teaspoon almond extract
4 cups all-purpose flour

Preheat oven to 400°. Cream together butter, sugar and eggs. Add almond flavoring and flour. Mix well. Press the dough through the star shape of a cookie press and form "S"-shaped cookies on an ungreased cookie sheet. Bake at 400° for 8-10 minutes. Makes 6 dozen cookies.

Note: This recipe was given to my mother in 1931 by a neighbor who brought it over from Sweden. It had been in her family for more than 100 years. My daughters and I start baking these Spritz Cookies right after Thanksgiving and keep plenty in the freezer. It wouldn't be Christmas without them.

Shirley Stultz (Hugh)

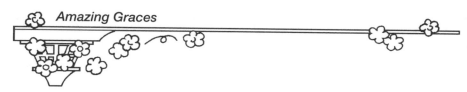

Scotch Shortbread

1 cup butter or margarine	**2½ cups sifted all-purpose**
½ cup sugar	**flour**

Preheat oven to 300°. Cream butter and sugar until light and fluffy. Stir in flour. Chill. Roll out dough on a floured surface to about ⅛-inch thickness. Cut with cookie cutters and place on ungreased cookie sheet. Or drop dough by teaspoonsful onto ungreased cookie sheet and score with a knife. Bake at 300° for 25 minutes. Remove from pan to cool. Makes 24 cookies.

Note: *This is a shortcake base or teacake.*

Beverly Gray (Tom)

Tansy Cookies

1 cup shortening	**¼ teaspoon ground cloves**
1 cup sugar	**1 teaspoon ginger**
3 eggs	**½ teaspoon salt**
½ teaspoon almond extract	**1 egg white, slightly beaten**
3 cups flour	**Confectioners' sugar and**
¼ teaspoon cinnamon	**cinnamon to taste**

Cream thoroughly the shortening and sugar. Add eggs one at a time, beating well after each addition. Add almond extract. Sift flour with cinnamon, cloves, ginger and salt. Add to creamed mixture and mix thoroughly. Turn dough onto waxed paper and wrap closely. Store in refrigerator overnight. Next day, roll out dough on a floured board and cut with floured cookie cutters. Brush with egg white and sprinkle with equal parts confectioners' sugar and cinnamon. Place on greased baking sheet and bake for about 6 minutes at 350°. Makes 5-6 dozen.

Note: *This is an old family recipe made at Christmas.*

Jean Waldman (Bob)

Peanut Butter Cookies

1 cup all-purpose flour
½ teaspoon salt
½ teaspoon baking soda
½ teaspoon baking powder
½ cup peanut butter, at room
   temperature

½ cup shortening, at room
   temperature
½ cup brown sugar, firmly
   packed
½ cup granulated sugar
1 egg
½ teaspoon vanilla

Preheat oven to 350°. Sift together in a bowl the flour, salt, baking soda and baking powder. Set aside. In large mixing bowl, beat peanut butter and shortening together until well blended. Add sugars and beat until smooth. Add egg and vanilla and continue beating until fluffy. Add dry ingredients and mix well. Drop dough by teaspoonsful onto lightly greased cookie sheets about 2 inches apart. Flatten in crisscross pattern with fork dipped in sugar. Bake at 350° for 10-12 minutes or until golden brown. Makes about 3 dozen.

Gene Shoultz (Jack)

Variation: Replace all-purpose flour with 1¼ cups whole wheat flour, replace shortening with butter or margarine and omit the salt. If dough is not stiff enough to make into balls, cover and refrigerate one hour. Form dough into 1-inch balls and roll in granulated sugar. Continue as above. For softer cookies, bake 8-10 minutes. Makes about 45 cookies.

Joyce Morris (Tom)

Wheat-Free Peanut Butter Cookies

1 cup sugar
1 egg

1 cup peanut butter

Cream together sugar and egg. Add peanut butter and mix thoroughly. Drop by teaspoonsful on ungreased cookie sheet. Press with tines of fork. Bake 10-15 minutes at 350°.

Zoe Wilson (Joe A.)

Overnight Ginger Cookies

1 cup molasses
½ cup sugar
½ cup butter or margarine,
  softened
3 cups all-purpose flour

1 teaspoon baking soda
1 teaspoon ground ginger
½ teaspoon cinnamon
½ teaspoon ground cloves

Put all ingredients in a large bowl and mix thoroughly. Shape dough into logs about 2 inches in diameter. Wrap with waxed paper and refrigerate overnight. Slice into ½-inch thick pieces and place on a lightly greased cookie sheet. Bake 10-12 minutes at 350°.

Erna Sherman (H. L.)

Grandma's Pumpkin Cookies

½ cup shortening
1½ cups sugar
1 egg
1⅓ cups canned pumpkin
2¼ cups all-purpose flour
4 teaspoons baking powder

¼ teaspoon nutmeg
½ teaspoon cinnamon
¼ teaspoon ground cloves
½ teaspoon ginger
1 cup chopped pecans

Cream shortening and sugar together, mixing well. Add egg and beat until light and fluffy. Add pumpkin, blending well. Sift flour with baking powder and spices; add to creamed mixture gradually, mixing well after each addition. Fold in the pecans. Drop by rounded teaspoonsful about 2 inches apart on a greased cookie sheet. Bake at 375° for 15 minutes or until lightly browned.

Note: *These are soft cake-like cookies. You may substitute raisins for the pecans, if you prefer.*

Anita Vickers (Jerry)

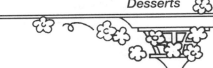

Chocolate Chip Cookies

2¼ cups all-purpose flour
1 teaspoon baking soda
1 teaspoon salt
¾ cup granulated sugar
¾ cup brown sugar, firmly
  packed

1 teaspoon vanilla
1 cup vegetable oil
2 eggs
1 (12 ounce) package semi-
  sweet chocolate chips

Preheat oven to 325°. Sift together flour, baking soda and salt. Set aside. Place sugars in mixing bowl. Add vanilla and vegetable oil to sugars and beat until creamy. Add eggs and beat well. Gradually beat flour mixture into creamed mixture. Stir in chocolate chips. Drop by teaspoonsful onto lightly greased cookie sheets. Bake in 325° oven about 10 minutes or until lightly brown.

Nina Conrad (Mark)

Pink Snowballs

½ - 1 cup butter or
  margarine, softened
1 cup confectioners' sugar,
  divided
1 teaspoon vanilla

2 cups all-purpose flour
1 teaspoon cold water
1 cup chopped nuts
Red food coloring

Cream together the butter and ½ cup of the sugar until fluffy. Add vanilla and mix. Add flour, water and nuts alternately. Add a few drops of red food coloring and mix well. Drop by teaspoonsful onto a greased cookie sheet and bake at 300° for 35 minutes. While still hot, roll in remaining confectioners' sugar.

Erna Sherman (H. L.)

Colorful Cookies

2 cups confectioners' sugar
1 cup margarine, softened
1 egg
1 teaspoon vanilla
½ teaspoon lemon (or other) flavoring

2½ cups all-purpose flour
1 teaspoon baking soda
1 teaspoon cream of tartar
Paste food coloring, as desired

Cream together sugar and margarine. Add egg and flavorings to creamed mixture and mix well. Sift together the dry ingredients and mix into dough. Divide dough into as many portions as colors desired. Add food coloring (paste food coloring works best) to each portion. Wrap individual portions in plastic wrap, put in plastic bag, close tightly and refrigerate. This keeps well in refrigerator, so you can bake only as much as desired at one time. Roll dough out to ⅛-inch thickness on pastry cloth, if available, or on a floured surface, using a knit-covered rolling pin. Cut to desired shapes with cookie cutters and put on ungreased cookie sheets. Bake 4-6 minutes in 375° oven until cookies lose their gloss, but are not brown. Store cooled cookies in airtight containers.

Note: I use an ⅛-inch dowel, cut in half, like "railroad tracks" on which to roll the knit-covered rolling pin. This makes it so easy to get all the cookies the same thickness. This is a fun recipe to use with kids.

Penny Johnson (Ken)

Corn Flake Cookies

2 sticks margarine, softened
½ cup sugar
1 teaspoon cinnamon
2 cups all-purpose flour

2 teaspoons vanilla
2 cups corn flake cereal
1 cup chopped pecans
Confectioners' sugar

Cream together margarine and sugar. Mix cinnamon with flour and add to sugar mixture. Add vanilla; blend well. Stir in corn flakes and nuts and mix well. Form into walnut-sized balls, place on a greased cookie sheet and press down with a fork. Bake for 15 minutes at 350° until lightly browned. Roll in confectioners' sugar while still warm. Makes about 3 dozen.

Kathryn R. Blackwell (Derwood)

Buffalo Chip Cookies

1 cup butter or margarine, softened
1 cup shortening
2 cups granulated sugar
2 cups brown sugar, firmly packed
1 teaspoon vanilla
4 eggs
4 cups all-purpose flour

2 teaspoons baking powder
1 teaspoon baking soda
1 teaspoon salt
1 (3½ ounce) can coconut
4 cups corn flakes
2 cups oatmeal
2 cups chopped nuts
1 (6 ounce) package chocolate chips

Cream together butter and shortening. Add sugars, vanilla and eggs. Beat well. Combine flour, baking powder, baking soda and salt and add to creamed mixture. Add remaining ingredients and mix gently. Drop by teaspoonsful onto lightly greased cookie sheets. Bake at 350° until light brown, about 10-12 minutes.

Paula Huckeba (Don)

Oatmeal Haystacks

2 egg whites
¾ cup sugar
½ cup vegetable oil
1½ teaspoons vanilla
¼ cup all-purpose flour
¼ teaspoon salt
¼ teaspoon baking powder

1½ cups cooking oats (if flakes are not small, roll with rolling pin to make small)
½ cup all-bran
1 cup chopped pecans or walnuts, toasted
1 cup white raisins (optional)

Mix egg whites, sugar, oil and vanilla in large bowl and beat until smooth. Add dry ingredients and mix well. Add nuts and raisins, if desired, and mix. Drop, quarter size, on a foil-lined cookie sheet. Bake at 350° for 18-25 minutes or until lightly browned. Cool and remove. Makes 3 or 4 dozen.

Beulah Lenox (Asbury)

Praline Cookies

½ cup butter or margarine, melted
1 cup brown sugar, firmly packed
1 egg, lightly beaten

1¼ cups sifted all-purpose flour
1 teaspoon vanilla
1 cup chopped pecans

Preheat oven to 375°. Mix melted butter and sugar until blended. Beat in egg, flour, vanilla and pecans. Drop by teaspoonsful 2 inches apart on ungreased baking sheet. Bake 8-10 minutes in 375° oven until lightly browned. Remove immediately from baking sheet and let cool. Makes 3 dozen.

Diane Harberson (Wayne)

Forgotten Cookies

2 egg whites
Pinch of salt
Pinch of cream of tartar

¾ cup sugar
1 cup chocolate chips
1 cup chopped nuts (optional)

Combine egg whites, salt and cream of tartar and beat until soft peaks form. Slowly add sugar, beating until hard peaks form. Add chocolate chips and nuts, if desired. Cover a cookie sheet with foil or a flattened brown paper sack. Spoon 1-inch dollops onto covered cookie sheet. Place in an oven preheated to 350° and immediately turn oven off. Leave for 3-4 hours or overnight. Do not open oven while cooking. If in a hurry, you may turn oven down to 200° as soon as you place cookies in the oven. Cookies will be ready in 2 hours.

Variation: Add a few drops of your choice of food coloring to tint cookies for special occasions.

Jane Cambre (Allison)
Vivian Toland (Michael)

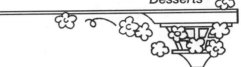

Butterscotch Brownies

1 stick margarine
2 cups light brown sugar
2 eggs, lightly beaten
2 teaspoons vanilla

1 cup all-purpose flour
2 teaspoons baking powder
¾ teaspoon salt
1 cup chopped pecans

Preheat oven to 350°. Grease and flour a 13x9x2-inch pan. In large saucepan over low heat, melt margarine and brown sugar. Remove from heat and stir in lightly beaten eggs and vanilla. Measure flour, baking powder and salt together and stir into mixture. Add pecans and stir. Pour into baking pan and bake at 350° for 20-25 minutes. Do not overcook. Cool and cut into 24 pieces.

Kathy Sinclair (Don)

Caramel Ribbon Brownies

30 caramels
⅔ cup evaporated milk,
  divided
1 2-layer size chocolate cake
  mix

1 cup chopped walnuts
6 tablespoons margarine,
  melted
½ cup semi-sweet chocolate
  pieces

In a double boiler, cook caramels and 3 tablespoons of the evaporated milk over low heat. In mixing bowl, combine remaining milk, cake mix, walnuts and margarine and mix well. Spread half of batter in greased 12x8x2-inch baking pan. Bake at 350° for 10 minutes. Remove from oven, sprinkle chocolate pieces over the hot crust, then drizzle the caramel mixture on top. Now drop the remainder of the raw dough by spoonsful over all. Bake at 350° for 20 minutes. Will be moist when done. Cut into bars while warm. Cool in pan.

Carolyn Curry (Gary)

Cream Cheese Dessert Bars

1 (18¼ ounce) box cake mix, any flavor (lemon, chocolate and butter are good choices)
½ cup butter or margarine, softened
4 eggs

1 (8 ounce) package cream cheese, regular or light, softened
1 (16 ounce) package confectioners' sugar
½ teaspoon vanilla

Preheat oven to 350°. Mix together in a food processor or with an electric mixer the cake mix, margarine and 1 egg. Press mixture into a lightly greased 13x9x2-inch pan. Cream together the cream cheese, 3 eggs, sugar and vanilla until well mixed. Pour over cake mix crust. Bake at 350° for 45 minutes. Makes 32 squares.

Note: *This will fall as it cools—don't despair.*

Beverly Gray (Tom)
Doris Smith (Lamar)

Easy Time Holiday Squares

1½ cups sugar
1 cup margarine, softened
4 eggs
2 cups all-purpose flour
1 teaspoon lemon extract

1 (21 ounce) can cherry pie filling
1 tablespoon confectioners' sugar

Preheat oven to 350°. Gradually add sugar to margarine in large mixer bowl, creaming at medium speed of mixer until light and fluffy. At medium speed, add eggs, one at a time, beating well after each addition. At low speed, add flour and lemon extract. Pour batter into well greased 15x10x1-inch jelly roll pan. Mark off 24 squares. Place one heaping tablespoon of pie filling in the center of each square. Bake at 350° for 45-50 minutes. While warm, sift confectioners' sugar over cake. Cool and cut into squares. Makes 24 squares.

Glennis Boutwell (Frank A.)

Eagle Brand Cookie Bars

½ cup margarine
1½ cups graham cracker
  crumbs
1 (14 ounce) can sweetened
  condensed milk

1 (6 ounce) package semi-
  sweet chocolate chips
1 (3½ ounce) can flaked
  coconut (1⅓ cups)
1 cup chopped nuts

In a 13x9x2-inch baking pan, melt margarine. Remove from heat. Sprinkle crumbs over the margarine. Pour sweetened condensed milk evenly over the crumbs. Top with chocolate chips, coconut and nuts. Press down gently. Bake at 350° for 25 minutes or until golden brown. Cool. Cut into 3x1½-inch bars.

Anne Barrow (Emmitt C.)

Millionaires

1 (14 ounce) package
  caramels
3 cups pecans

1 chocolate candy bar
¼ piece paraffin

Melt caramels in a saucepan over low heat. Stir in pecans. Drop by teaspoonsful onto waxed paper. Refrigerate overnight. Next day, melt chocolate candy and paraffin in top of double boiler. Dip candies in melted chocolate and place on waxed paper to cool.

Merle Williams (Charles)

Candied Pecan Snacks

1 cup sugar
4 tablespoons margarine

2 cups pecans
1 teaspoon vanilla

In a heavy skillet put sugar, margarine and pecans. Cook over low heat, stirring constantly, for about 15 minutes or until pecans are coated and sugar is golden brown. Stir in vanilla. Mold into clusters and sprinkle with salt.

Millie Koch (Robert)

Salted Peanut Chews

1½ cups all-purpose flour
⅔ cup brown sugar, firmly
  packed
½ teaspoon baking powder
½ teaspoon salt
¼ teaspoon baking soda

½ cup margarine or butter,
  softened
1 teaspoon vanilla
2 egg yolks
4 cups miniature
  marshmallows
Topping (recipe below)

Heat oven to 350°. In large bowl, combine first 8 ingredients. Beat with electric mixer on low speed until crumbly. Press mixture firmly in bottom of ungreased 13x9x2-inch pan. Bake at 350° for 12-15 minutes or until light golden brown. Immediately sprinkle with marshmallows. Return to oven for 1-2 minutes or until marshmallows begin to puff. Cool while preparing topping (recipe below). Spoon warm topping over marshmallows and spread to cover. Refrigerate until firm. Cut into bars.

Topping:
⅔ cup corn syrup
¼ cup margarine or butter
2 teaspoons vanilla
1 (12 ounce) package peanut
  butter chips

2 cups crispy rice cereal
2 cups salted peanuts or
  cocktail nuts

In large saucepan, heat corn syrup, margarine, vanilla and peanut butter chips just until chips are melted and mixture is smooth, stirring constantly. Remove from heat, stir in cereal and nuts.

Nancy Boswell (Jimmy)

Crispy Rice Bits

½ cup sugar
½ cup light corn syrup

1 cup peanut butter
2 cups crispy rice cereal

In a 2½-quart saucepan, combine sugar and syrup. Bring to a rolling boil, stirring constantly. Add peanut butter and stir well. Remove from heat. Stir in rice cereal. Drop by tablespoonsful onto waxed paper. Makes 2 dozen.

Ethyl Stafford (Sam)

238

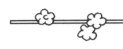

Peanut Butter Squares

1 (14 ounce) jar smooth
  peanut butter
1 stick margarine, softened

1 (1 pound) box
  confectioners' sugar
1 (12 ounce) package
  chocolate chips

Mix together peanut butter, margarine and confectioners' sugar. Spread mixture into 15x10x1-inch jelly roll pan. Melt chocolate chips in top of double boiler over hot water. Spread over peanut butter layer. Chill in refrigerator. Cut into squares.

Julia Miller (William A. "Buddy," Sr.)

Peanut Butter Fudge

¾ cup crunchy peanut butter
¼ cup margarine, softened
½ cup light corn syrup

1 teaspoon vanilla
4 cups sifted confectioners'
  sugar

Put peanut butter and margarine in a bowl. Mix with wooden spoon. Stir in corn syrup and vanilla. Add sugar to peanut butter mixture, stirring after each addition until well blended. Knead fudge until creamy. Pour fudge into a greased 8x8x2-inch square pan. Pat down evenly. Chill about 1 hour. Cut into squares.

Jean Waldman (Bob)

Velveeta Fudge

1 pound Velveeta cheese
1 pound margarine
1 cup cocoa
1 teaspoon vanilla

2 (32 ounce) packages
  confectioners' sugar
2 cups chopped pecans

Butter a 13x9x2-inch pan. In a large, heavy pot melt cheese and margarine over low heat. Add cocoa and vanilla and stir well. Continue to cook over low heat while stirring in the confectioners' sugar. Add pecans and quickly pour out into buttered pan.

Penny Smith (Donald)

Fudge

3 tablespoons marshmallow
  creme
2 teaspoons vanilla
2 cups chopped walnuts
3 cups chocolate chips

4½ cups sugar
1 (13 ounce) can evaporated
  milk
2 sticks margarine

Combine marshmallow creme, vanilla, walnuts and chocolate chips in a large bowl and set aside. In a dutch oven, combine the sugar, evaporated milk and margarine. Bring to a rolling boil, then lower heat and cook to 240° on candy thermometer (soft ball stage), about 10 minutes. Pour hot mixture over the marshmallow creme mixture and stir until very thick. Pour into a 15x10-inch pan. Allow to cool and cut into squares. Freezes well. Makes about 5 pounds.

Mary Hicks (David)

Divinity

2 cups sugar
2 tablespoons white corn
  syrup
1 cup water

1 (7 ounce) jar marshmallow
  creme
3 cups chopped pecans

Mix sugar, syrup and water together in a medium saucepan. Boil until mixture forms a medium hard ball in cold water (about 260° on a candy thermometer). Stir in marshmallow creme until blended. Add pecans and stir thoroughly. Drop onto waxed paper by teaspoonsful and allow to cool. Store in airtight container.

Thelma Dunnam (Spurgeon M., Jr.)

Cherries In The Snow

6 egg whites	2 (3 ounce) packages cream
½ teaspoon cream of tartar	cheese, softened
¼ teaspoon salt	2 cups miniature
2½ cups sugar, divided	marshmallows
2 teaspoons vanilla, divided	1 (21 ounce) can cherry pie
1 pint whipping cream	filling
	½ teaspoon almond extract

Preheat oven to 400°. Beat egg whites, cream of tartar and salt until foamy. Gradually add 1½ cups of the sugar and beat until stiff peaks form. Fold in 1 teaspoon of the vanilla. Spread mixture in a buttered and floured 13x9x2-inch pan. Turn oven off. Put meringue in oven for at least 8 hours or overnight. Later, whip cream in large bowl. In a separate small bowl, cream together the cream cheese, remaining 1 cup sugar and remaining teaspoon of vanilla. Add creamed mixture to whipped cream. Fold in marshmallows. Spoon mixture over baked meringue and refrigerate for 8 hours. When ready to serve, combine cherry pie filling and almond extract. Put 2 teaspoons of cherry filling on top of each serving.

Jean Cragg (Gene)

Caramel Nut Pie

⅔ cup sugar	⅓ cup pecans, chopped
3 eggs, separated	Pinch of salt
2 cups milk	½ teaspoon vanilla
3 tablespoons flour	Baked pie shell

Beat 3 egg yolks. Add ¼ cup milk and ⅓ cup sugar (mixed with flour). Set aside. Brown ⅓ cup sugar. Heat remaining milk just to scalding. Add melted, browned sugar to hot milk very slowly. (If not added slowly, it will boil over.) Add egg yolk mixture and cook, stirring, till thick. Add vanilla and pecans. Pour in baked pie shell, top with meringue and bake till golden brown.

Note: *This recipe was in the original Ministers' Wives' cookbook, "East Texas Cooking." It is heavenly sinful tasting!*

Amy Webb (William C.)

Banana Split Cake

2 cups graham cracker crumbs	4 large or 6 small bananas
1 stick margarine, melted	1 (15¼ ounce) can crushed pineapple, well drained
1 (16 ounce) box confectioners' sugar	1 (12 ounce) carton frozen whipped topping, thawed
2 eggs	½ cup chopped nuts
2 sticks margarine, softened	

Mix graham cracker crumbs and melted margarine and press into a 13x9x2-inch pan. Bake 8-10 minutes at 350°. Cool. Beat confectioners' sugar, eggs and 2 sticks margarine in a large mixing bowl for about 15 minutes. Spread over crumb crust. Slice bananas and lay at random over sugar mixture. Spread pineapples over bananas. Spread whipped topping over fruit. Sprinkle with chopped nuts. Refrigerate before serving. This can be made ahead of time and frozen. Set out 1 hour in refrigerator before serving.

Variation: One pint of strawberries, sliced, can be used in place of or in addition to the pineapples. Chocolate curls and cherries can be used to garnish the top, along with the chopped nuts.

Carolyn Lanagan (David)
Sherlyne Russell (David)

W e had just been sent to the Whitehouse Circuit, our first full-time appointment. Stanley and I visited together in the homes of the members nearly every day, getting acquainted. I was expecting our first baby, so Stanley dropped me by the parsonage to rest for a while. I had unbuttoned my skirt with a hole in front, while lying on the couch. This was in 1949, before people locked their homes. The Whitehouse Church asked us to be home that night for a "pounding." Thinking no one was home that afternoon, the church people came in the back door loaded with refreshments for the Pounding Party. Just as everyone got to the dining room, just off the living room, I jumped up in surprise, as my skirt fell to the floor around my feet! Thank God I was wearing a cotton petticoat that stayed in place!

Virginia Vodicka (Stanley)

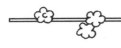

Apricot Breeze

1 (16 ounce) can crushed pineapple	½ cup sugar
1 cup miniature marshmallows	½ cup reserved pineapple juice
1 (6 ounce) package apricot gelatin	2 tablespoons butter
2 bananas, mashed	1 egg, beaten
1 cup chopped pecans	1 (3 ounce) package cream cheese, softened
2 cups boiling water	1 teaspoon vanilla
2 cups cold water	2 cups frozen whipped topping, thawed
2 tablespoons all-purpose flour	

Drain pineapple and reserve liquid. Combine marshmallows and pineapple and let stand at least one hour. Add gelatin, mashed bananas, pecans and boiling water. Mix well, then add cold water. Pour into a 13x9x2-inch pan and refrigerate until firm. Meanwhile, mix flour, sugar, pineapple juice, butter and egg in a medium saucepan. Cook over moderate heat, stirring until thickened. Remove from heat and add softened cream cheese and mix well. Cool completely. Mix vanilla into whipped topping and then fold into the cooled pineapple juice mixture. Spread topping over firm gelatin. Chill. Serves 12.

Janet Kennedy (Tom)

Knowing that I would never receive a "Nobel Award," I was shocked when I received a NO BELLY AWARD from my beloved husband in whom I am well pleased. Many nights after bedtime, when no one was awake, I sneaked to the kitchen looking for cake. Then what to my wandering eyes should appear; my husband had seen me, oh boy did I fear! "I don't want to hurt you," he lovingly said, "but your stomach's protruding, let's go back to bed!" The next day at mealtime, my eyes really flashed, as I gazed in horror at what he had stashed. A NO BELLY AWARD sat in front of my plate, which helped me cut back on the food that I ate. Thanks to my husband who discovered my fate, I jumped from a size 14 to a dress sized 8!

Onita Scott (Leslie)

Strawberry Squares

1 cup all-purpose flour
¼ cup brown sugar, firmly
  packed
½ cup butter or margarine,
  softened
½ cup chopped nuts

2 cups sliced fresh
  strawberries
2 egg whites
1 cup granulated sugar
2 tablespoons lemon juice
1½ cups whipping cream,
  divided

Combine flour, brown sugar, butter and nuts. Spread in a baking pan and bake for 20 minutes at 350°. Stir several times while baking. Combine strawberries, egg whites, granulated sugar and lemon juice in a large mixing bowl. Beat with electric mixer for 10 minutes. Fold in 1 cup of the whipping cream. Pat ⅔ of the crumb mixture in the bottom of a 9-inch square baking pan. Spoon strawberry mixture on top of crumb mixture and top with remaining crumbs. Cover and freeze overnight. Before serving, whip remaining ½ cup of whipping cream. Garnish each serving with a dollop of whipped cream and a fresh berry. Serves 9.

Note: This is also very pretty if you make it in 9 compote glasses and freeze as directed. May easily be doubled or tripled.

Karen Bagley (Bert)

Berried Treasure

2 (3 ounce) packages cream
  cheese, softened
1 (8 ounce) carton sour
  cream

½ cup light brown sugar,
  firmly packed and divided
1 quart fresh strawberries

Combine cream cheese, sour cream and ⅓ cup of the brown sugar in a medium bowl and blend well. Cover and chill for 1-2 hours (may be done the day before and refrigerated overnight). When ready to serve, wash and stem berries; leave whole or cut into large pieces. Spoon berries into 8 compote or dessert dishes. Top with creamed cheese mixture and sprinkle remaining brown sugar on top. Serves 8.

Margaret Hall (A. Sherrill)

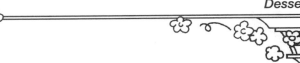

Strawberry Delight

2 cups low-fat cottage
cheese
2 cups unsweetened crushed
pineapple, well drained
1 (0.3 ounce) package sugar-
free strawberry gelatin
(other flavors may be
substituted)

2 cups light frozen whipped
topping, thawed
¼ cup sliced fresh
strawberries (optional)
8 sprigs fresh mint (optional)

Gently fold cottage cheese, crushed pineapple and dry gelatin into the whipped topping. Cover and refrigerate until thoroughly chilled. Spoon into dessert dishes and, if desired, garnish with strawberries and mint sprigs. Serves 8.

Note: This recipe is low in calories, fat and cholesterol. There are approximately 78 calories per serving.

Frances Prickett (Joe)

Mexican Flan

1 (8 ounce) package cream
cheese, softened
1 (14 ounce) can sweetened
condensed milk
1 (12 ounce) can evaporated
milk

2 eggs
1 teaspoon vanilla
1 cup regular milk
Dash of salt
1 cup sugar

In a medium bowl, blend together the cream cheese and condensed milk. Then add the evaporated milk, eggs, vanilla and regular milk; mix well. In a small saucepan, melt the sugar, stirring constantly until it turns to a brown liquid. Pour sugar into a flan pan or a 9-inch square pan and tilt to spread on bottom and sides of pan. Pour custard over sugar and bake at 350° for 1 hour and 15 minutes. Flan may be inverted onto a serving plate for an original look. Garnish with strawberries or a dollop of sour cream or whipped cream.

Note: This is an easy recipe that can be made in quantities for a Mexican fiesta dessert.

Carolyn Lanagan (David)

Chocolate Crunch Supreme

½ cup margarine, softened
1 cup all-purpose flour
1 cup chopped pecans
1 (8 ounce) package cream cheese, softened
1 cup confectioners' sugar
3 cups frozen whipped topping, thawed and divided

1 (3 ounce) package chocolate instant pudding mix
1 (3 ounce) package vanilla instant pudding mix
3 cups milk
Chopped pecans (optional)
Shaved chocolate (optional)

Mix margarine, flour and pecans together; spread in an ungreased 13x9x2-inch pan. Bake at 350° for 15-20 minutes. Cool. While crust is cooling, mix together cream cheese, confectioners' sugar and 1 cup of whipped topping and beat until smooth. Spread on cooled crust and chill. Next, combine pudding mixes with milk and spread on top of cheese mixture. Chill again. Spread remaining 2 cups of whipped topping on top of pudding mixture. Sprinkle with chopped pecans and shaved chocolate, if desired. Cover and refrigerate overnight, if possible, and then cut in squares to serve.

Variation: Replace vanilla pudding mix with another package of chocolate pudding mix or replace both pudding mixes with 2 packages of another flavor such as coconut, pistachio, butterscotch or lemon.

 *Hint: To lighten up this dessert, you can use light cream cheese, light frozen whipped topping, sugar-free pudding mixes and skim milk.*

Sue Bratz (Charles)
Virginia I. Crowe (Thomas W.)
Jane Cunningham (William R.)
Twana Holcomb (Michael)
Julia Miller (William A. "Buddy," Sr.)

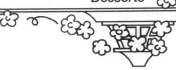

Black Bottom Miniatures

1½ cups all-purpose flour
1½ cups sugar, divided
¼ cup cocoa
½ teaspoon salt
1 cup water
⅓ cup vegetable oil

1 tablespoon vinegar
1 teaspoon vanilla
1 (8 ounce) package cream
  cheese, softened
1 egg

Sift together the flour, 1 cup of the sugar, cocoa and salt. Stir in water, oil, vinegar and vanilla; mix well and set aside. In a separate bowl, combine cream cheese, egg, remaining ½ cup of sugar and dash of salt. Mix well. Line miniature muffin tins with 24 paper liners. Fill cups ⅔ full with cocoa batter. Top each with 1 heaping tablespoon of the cream cheese mixture. Bake at 350° for 30-35 minutes. Makes 24.

Pat Nicholas (Martin)

Ice Cream Delight

⅔ (16 ounce) package
  chocolate sandwich
  cookies

½ gallon ice cream, softened
  (any flavor)
1 (12 ounce) carton frozen
  whipped topping, thawed

Crush cookies in food processor or between sheets of waxed paper. Press into the bottom of a 13x9x2-inch pan. Spoon ice cream on top of crushed cookie layer. Spread until smooth. Spread whipped topping on top of ice cream. Cover and freeze for 2 hours.

Susan Bruster (Tim)

Cinnamon Roll-Ups

15-18 slices white sandwich bread
1 (8 ounce) package regular (not light) cream cheese, softened
1 egg yolk, beaten

1 cup plus 2 tablespoons sugar, divided
1 teaspoon vanilla
1 (8 ounce) can crushed pineapple, drained
Melted butter
2 teaspoons cinnamon

Roll each slice of bread flat with a rolling pin. In a medium bowl, beat cream cheese and egg yolk together until creamy. Add 2 tablespoons of the sugar, the vanilla and the pineapple and mix well. Spread a portion of the mixture on each slice of bread. Roll each slice up like a jelly roll. Cover and refrigerate overnight. Cut in half. Dip in melted butter. Mix remaining 1 cup of sugar with cinnamon and roll each bread roll in the cinnamon-sugar mixture. Place on baking sheet and bake at 350° for 10 minutes.

Joye Eckols (Glen)

Apple Crisp

8 cups sliced tart apples or 2 (16 ounce) cans pie apples, drained
½ cup orange juice
1¾ cups sugar

1½ cups all-purpose flour
1 teaspoon cinnamon
½ teaspoon nutmeg
1 cup butter or margarine, softened

Arrange sliced apples in the bottom of a greased 13x9x2-inch baking dish. Sprinkle with orange juice. For topping, combine sugar, flour, spices and a dash of salt in a large bowl. Cut in the butter with a pastry blender or two knives until mixture is crumbly. Sprinkle over apples. Bake at 375° for 45 minutes.

Tena Spitsberg (Scott)

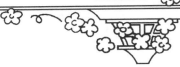

Apple Dumplings

1½ cups sugar, divided
2 cups water
3 tablespoons butter or
  margarine
1¾ teaspoons cinnamon,
  divided

6 small apples
Enough pastry for a 2-crust
  pie (make your own or use
  store-bought)

In a medium saucepan, stir together 1 cup of the sugar, the water, butter and ¼ teaspoon of the cinnamon. Boil for 3 minutes. Keep warm. Peel and core apples. Roll out pastry to ¼-inch thickness. Cut into squares about 6 or 7 inches across. Place apples on pastry squares. Combine remaining ½ cup sugar and 1½ teaspoons cinnamon. Fill cavities of apples with cinnamon-sugar mixture. Dot with butter. Bring opposite points of pastry squares up over the apple. Overlap, moisten and seal pastry. Place pastry-wrapped apples in a baking dish at least 1-inch apart. Pour hot syrup over and around dumplings. Bake at 350° for 45 minutes to 1 hour, until crust is nicely browned and apples are cooked through. Serves 6.

Note: For 4 dumplings, use 4 apples, ⅔ cup sugar, 1¼ cups water, 2 tablespoons butter and ¼ teaspoon cinnamon for the syrup and ⅓ cup sugar and 1 teaspoon cinnamon for the cinnamon-sugar mixture. For 8 dumplings, use 8 apples, 1⅓ cups sugar, 2¼ cups water, 4 tablespoons butter and ½ teaspoon cinnamon for the syrup and ⅔ cup sugar and 2 teaspoons cinnamon for the cinnamon-sugar mixture. You may need extra pastry for 8 dumplings. Follow directions above.

Penny Smith (Donald)

Baked Apples

Apples (Rome is a good
  choice)

Brown sugar
Cinnamon

For each serving, take one apple and core it. Place apple in an apple baker (available at kitchen specialty shops and pottery shops) with one tablespoon of water. Sprinkle brown sugar and cinnamon in the center of the apple. Place apple baker on a cookie sheet and put in a cold oven. Set temperature to 350° and bake for 40 minutes.

Julie Temple (Chappell)

Apples À La Lorraine

2 pounds apples, peeled and thinly sliced	4 tablespoons all-purpose flour
1 stick margarine	2 cups milk
1 cup sugar	2 teaspoons vanilla
	2 eggs

In a large skillet, sauté apples in margarine, cooking slowly for 20 minutes. Add sugar to apples and allow them to brown slightly. Remove from heat and pour apples in an 8-inch square baking dish. Combine flour, milk, vanilla and eggs in a bowl and mix well. Pour over apples. Bake at 300° for 40 minutes. Serve warm with whipped cream or ice cream, if desired. Serves 6.

Judi Stallknecht (Herb)

Popcorn Cake

3 quarts popped popcorn	½ cup margarine
1 (16 ounce) bag M&Ms	1 (16 ounce) bag marshmallows
1 pound dry roasted peanuts	

Mix popcorn, M&Ms and peanuts in a large bowl. Set aside. Melt margarine and marshmallows in a saucepan and stir to mix well. Pour over the popcorn, candy and nut mixture. Mix thoroughly and press firmly into a well-greased Bundt or tube pan. When cool, turn out of pan.

Kathy Reiter (James)
Patsy Weber (Bobbie)

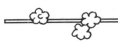

Cracker Pudding

14 Ritz crackers
1 cup chopped nuts
1 cup sugar
1 teaspoon vanilla

½ teaspoon baking powder
3 egg whites
1 (8 ounce) carton frozen
whipped topping, thawed

Crumble crackers until fine. Add next 4 ingredients and mix. Beat egg whites until stiff. Fold into cracker mixture. Pour into a greased 8-inch square pan and bake at 350° for 25-30 minutes. Cool and spread with whipped topping, if desired. May serve with ice cream and omit whipped topping.

Christine M. Garoutte (Victor)
Linda Jordan (Clinton)

Bread Pudding with Sauce

6 slices bread
2 cups milk, warmed
1 egg
½ cup sugar
1 tablespoon butter or
margarine, softened

½ teaspoon cinnamon
½ teaspoon vanilla
½ cup raisins
Sauce (recipe below)

In a large bowl, soak bread in milk. Add egg, sugar, butter, cinnamon, vanilla and raisins. Beat well. Pour into a 13x9x2-inch baking dish and bake at 350° for 45 minutes. Prepare sauce (recipe below) and pour over pudding.

Sauce:
¼ cup butter
5 tablespoons cornstarch
½ cup sugar

2 cups water
1 teaspoon vanilla
½ teaspoon nutmeg

Melt butter in a small saucepan. Blend in cornstarch and sugar. Add water, a little at a time. Cook and stir over medium heat until thick and almost clear. Add vanilla and nutmeg. Cook and stir for 2 minutes. Remove from heat. Cool slightly.

Pat Bingham (John)

Boiled Egg Custard

½ **gallon milk**	1½ **cups sugar**
8 eggs, beaten	**1 tablespoon vanilla**

Scald milk. Mix eggs and sugar, then slowly stir into milk. DO NOT BOIL. Cook slowly and stir constantly until mixture coats the spoon. When it begins to thicken, remove from heat. Strain. Add vanilla and stir until blended. Pour into individual serving cups or a casserole dish.

Note: *If the custard gets too hot, it will curdle. This is easy to do, so be very careful!*

Thelma Dunnam (Spurgeon M., Jr.)

Cherry-Nut Ice Cream

7 eggs	**1 (16 ounce) jar maraschino**
4½ **cups sugar**	**cherries, drained and**
2 (12 ounce) cans evaporated	**chopped (reserve juice)**
milk	**3 quarts homogenized milk**
3 tablespoons vanilla	2½ **cups chopped pecans**

Beat eggs in a large bowl. Add sugar and evaporated milk and beat well to be sure sugar is dissolved. Add vanilla and reserved cherry juice. Pour into freezer can of your 6-quart ice cream freezer and add enough milk to fill almost to the fill line. Freeze according to manufacturer's instructions until about ⅔ frozen, then add cherries and pecans. Complete freezing process. Makes 6 quarts.

Note: *For a 4-quart freezer, use the following amounts of the ingredients: 5 eggs, 3 cups sugar, 1 (12 ounce) can evaporated milk, 2 tablespoons vanilla, 2 quarts homogenized milk, 1 (10 ounce) jar maraschino cherries with juice and 2 cups chopped pecans. Follow directions above. This makes great ice cream for church ice cream suppers!*

Anita Vickers (Jerry)

Bavarian Fruit Ice Cream

3 cups milk
3 cups sugar
1½ cups heavy cream
1 (12 ounce) can evaporated
    milk
Juice of 2 lemons
Juice of 3 oranges

4 bananas, mashed
1½ cups undrained crushed
    pineapple
Chopped strawberries
    (optional)
Chopped peaches (optional)

Heat milk in a large pot, being careful not to scorch. Add sugar and stir until dissolved. Stir in cream and evaporated milk. Cover and chill. When ready to freeze, add fruit juices and fruits. Freeze in your ice cream freezer according to manufacturer's instructions.

Carolyn Curry (Gary)

Hot Cinnamon Sauce

½ cup light corn syrup
1 cup sugar

¼ cup water
1 teaspoon cinnamon
½ cup evaporated milk

Combine syrup, sugar, water and cinnamon in a saucepan. Bring to a full boil over medium heat, stirring constantly. After mixture comes to a boil, cook and stir for 2 minutes. Cool for 5 minutes and stir in evaporated milk. Store in refrigerator. When reheating to serve, be sure not to boil.

Julie Temple (Chappell)

During the early 1930's, we were serving the 4-point Yorktown Circuit in the Southwest Texas Conference. Our 3 children were still young, so they went with us to each church. At one of the churches we usually ate lunch with a woman who ran a boarding house where she served excellent food. Martha Jo, who was 9 at the time, was thin and the most finicky child who ever lived. She would just say, "No, thank you," each time the food was passed to her. Our hostess noticed Martha Jo was not eating, so she asked me what she should fix the next time we came. I told her Martha Jo liked pork and beans, so the next time we came she had cooked a big pot of pinto beans with pork. It was passed to Marthie and she said, "No, thank you." I had failed to tell this dear woman that Marthie only ate Van Camp's canned pork and beans. I was embarrassed. To this day, we often have baked beans for Marthie at family gatherings and label them Van Camp's.

Martha Wells (Joe B.)

One summer in East Texas when it was 100 degrees at daybreak, Alvis invited me to go visiting the new flock. We had been in town for a few weeks and there was a family that had stopped attending when the previous pastor left. Not having money for a baby-sitter, we had to take our 2 sons, John (3 years) and Allen (18 months) with us. We called and made an appointment to go by around 9:30 a.m., before it got any hotter. John was sitting on the floor and I was holding Allen in my lap, bouncing him to keep him still. Suddenly Allen threw-up scrambled eggs on top of John's head. John immediately threw-up on the lady's hand-braided rug. Being pregnant with our third child, it did not take too much for me to join the boys in the "throw-up" act. It took a few seconds to locate the front door. The house was on Main Street, and there I stood on their front porch with my head hanging over the flower bed...very sick! I can't remember whether the family ever came back to church, but I can still remember their name after 40 years, and no doubt, they can still remember the Colemans!

Wanda Coleman (Alvis)

Let the Children Come

P. K. Pages

O, *the Lord is good to me,*
And so I thank the Lord
For giving me the things I need:
The sun, the rain and the appleseed.
The Lord is good to me.

Bunny Salad

1 lettuce leaf
1 (12 ounce) can pear halves, drained
2 tablespoons cottage cheese

1 red grape
2 almond slices
2 raisins

Place lettuce on serving plate. Top with pear (cut side down). Put cottage cheese at wide end of pear for the tail. Put grape at the narrow end for a nose. Use the almonds for ears and the raisins for eyes. Makes 1 serving.

Andrew Neff (Laura and Jerry)

Boiled Pebble Soup

Pebbles
Water

Blades of grass
Pinch of sand

Dolly will love this soup on a cool day. Place a nice amount of small pebbles in your saucepan. Half fill your pan with water. Add 2 blades of grass for each pebble and season with a pinch of sand. Simmer in the sunshine long enough to sing a song with your dolly. Serves 3 hungry dolls or 2 teddy bears.

Kristen Holcomb (Twana and Michael)

Green Bean Casserole

2 (15 ounce) cans green
  beans, drained
1 (10½ ounce) can cream of
  mushroom soup, undiluted

1 (4 ounce) can sliced
  mushrooms, drained
½ cup grated cheese

Grease 1-quart casserole dish. Pour in green beans. Layer with mushroom slices. Cover with mushroom soup. Sprinkle grated cheese on top. Heat in 350° oven for 20-30 minutes until warm and cheese is bubbly. Serves 6-8.

Anna Diller (Helen and David)

Juice Gelatin Squares

1 (12 ounce) can frozen fruit
  juice (any flavor), thawed

3 envelopes unflavored
  gelatin
1½ cups water

Soften gelatin in fruit juice. Boil water and add gelatin mixture to dissolve. Pour into ungreased 13x9x2-inch glass dish. Chill until firm. Cut into squares.

Aaron, Asa, and Adam Calhoun (Bonita and Ken)

When our grandson Mark was of kindergarten age, he came for his first visit to our new appointment. On Sunday morning, I took him to the kindergarten class and told him to wait for me to come back and get him after Sunday School. When I arrived at the classroom door to collect him, lo and behold, he and another little boy were squaring off in a fight. I ran to them, pulled them apart and said, "Mark, what are you doing?" He replied, "This little boy said this wasn't Granddaddy's church, and I said it was!"

Lenora Fay Clark (Lamar)

Lisanne's 10-Minute Pizzas

Non-stick vegetable spray
4 or 5 (10 count) cans
  refrigerated biscuits
1 (32 ounce) jar spaghetti
  sauce (chunky)

1 package pepperoni slices
  (about 50 slices)
2 pounds mozzarella cheese,
  grated

Preheat oven to 350°. Wash your hands! Take a cookie sheet and spray with non-stick vegetable spray. Open canned biscuits and flatten each one well. Lay biscuits on cookie sheet. (You will probably use 2 or 3 cookie sheets.) Make sure there is some room between biscuits. Open spaghetti sauce and place a tablespoonful on each biscuit. Top each biscuit with a slice of pepperoni. Top that with some mozzarella cheese. Place cookie sheets in oven for about 10-15 minutes. When cheese is bubbly and sides of biscuits are brown, enjoy! This is a great treat for after-school youth groups.

Lisanne Reeves (Lisa and R. Dean)

Pizza Crust

1 package active dry yeast
1 cup warm water
2 teaspoons sugar

2 tablespoons vegetable oil
2½ cups all-purpose flour

Topping:
½ cup spaghetti sauce
3 cups shredded mozzarella
  cheese

1 can sliced mushrooms

Dissolve yeast in warm water. Stir in remaining ingredients and then form into ball shape. Place onto floured surface and roll out the dough for the size pizza you want. Lightly grease pizza pan or cookie sheet and lay the dough on it. Allow the dough to rest for 5 minutes while you prepare pizza toppings. (The toppings I prefer are listed above, but you may use any kind you like.) Spread spaghetti sauce over the dough. Sprinkle cheese and mushrooms over top. Bake in a 350° oven for 20-30 minutes or until browned. Let cool about 5 minutes before cutting.

Belinda Carter (Thad)

Dad's Chili

2 pounds ground beef	2 teaspoons salt
1 small onion, chopped	1½ teaspoons cumin
1 (8 ounce) can tomato sauce	1½ teaspoons oregano
2 cups water	1½ teaspoons paprika
½ cup chili powder	1½ teaspoons garlic powder

Mix ground beef and onions together in skillet and cook until meat is done. Add the rest of the ingredients and simmer for about 1 hour.

Note: *This recipe makes really good chili pies. Just add fritos. It's also good over rice or just plain.*

James Danheim (Kathy and Dan)

Chili Cheese Dogs

4 hot dog buns	2 (1 ounce) slices process
½ cup chili	American cheese, cut into 4
4 frankfurters	lengthwise strips

Split buns lengthwise part way through. Spoon 1 tablespoon of chili onto each bun. Place frankfurters in buns. Top each frankfurter with another tablespoonful of chili and 2 strips of cheese. Arrange 4 paper napkins or paper towels in microwave. Place filled buns on napkins, leaving an open center. Microwave at MEDIUM-HIGH (70%) until filling is heated and cheese starts to melt, 2-5 minutes.

Daniel and Aliece Porterfield (Ava and David)

 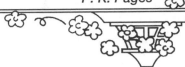

Spaghetti Sauce (Texas Style)

2 pounds lean ground beef
1 large onion, finely chopped
1 medium bell pepper, finely chopped
1½ teaspoons ground cumin
1½ teaspoons oregano
1½ teaspoons marjoram

1½ teaspoons garlic powder
2 tablespoons chili powder
2 (8 ounce) cans tomato sauce
2 cups water
1 bay leaf
Salt and pepper to taste

In a large skillet, sauté onion and bell pepper as you are browning the ground beef. When the meat is lightly browned with onion and bell pepper limp, pour into a colander and drain off fat. Return ingredients to the skillet. With burner still on low heat, add all the spices except the bay leaf, salt and pepper. Mix thoroughly. Add tomato sauce and water; stir. Raise heat until the sauce is boiling. Salt and pepper to taste. Add bay leaf. Simmer (lower heat until sauce is barely bubbling when heat is on) 1 hour or more, adding water as needed. Serve over any type of spaghetti (vermicelli is my favorite).

James Danheim (Kathy and Dan)

Turkey Grilled Cheese Sandwiches

Margarine
2 slices of bread

1 piece of turkey (or your favorite meat)
Cheddar cheese

Spread margarine on 1 side of each slice of bread. Cut Cheddar cheese into slices. Heat your griddle to about medium, depending on your stove. Lay 1 slice of bread (margarine side down) on the griddle. Layer with cheese and then a slice of turkey. Top with other slice of bread (margarine side up). Cook (checking often). When bottom side is toasted turn it over and toast the other side.

Note: *This is fast, easy and good! I usually have two for breakfast.*

Kris Hayes (Kathy and Dan Danheim)

Sausage Balls

**1 pound regular ground
sausage, uncooked
3 cups biscuit baking mix**

**8 ounces grated Cheddar
cheese**

Preheat oven to 350°. Mix all ingredients together. Form into small balls, using about 1 tablespoon of mixture per ball. Bake in 350° oven for about 15 minutes or until golden brown.

Johnathan Diller (Helen and David)

Cheese Crispies

**2 cups grated sharp Cheddar
cheese
½ cup margarine**

**1 cup all-purpose flour
¼ teaspoon salt**

Mix all ingredients together. Roll into 1-inch balls and place on lightly greased cookie sheet about 1 inch apart. Bake at 375° for 12 minutes.

Matthew Neff (Laura and Jerry)

Waffles

**2 cups all-purpose flour
3 teaspoons baking powder
½ teaspoon salt
2 tablespoons sugar**

**2 eggs
1⅔ cups milk
½ cup vegetable oil**

Mix all ingredients together. Blend with beater. Bake in preheated waffle iron using amount of batter indicated in waffle iron instructions. Waffle is done when steam no longer appears. Makes 6 four-sectioned waffles.

Hint: Whole wheat flour may be used. For fluffier waffles, decrease milk to 1⅓ cups. For crispier waffles, increase milk to 2 cups.

Nathan Diller (Helen and David)

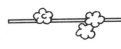

Oatmeal Pancakes

½ cup all-purpose flour
½ cup quick-cooking oats
¾ cup buttermilk
¼ cup milk

1 teaspoon baking powder
½ teaspoon baking soda
½ teaspoon salt
1 egg

Beat all ingredients in a medium bowl with an egg beater or fork until smooth. (For thinner pancakes, stir in 2 to 4 additional tablespoons of milk.) Spray heated griddle with non-stick vegetable spray. (To see if grill is hot enough, sprinkle with a few drops of water. If bubbles skitter around, heat is just right.) For each pancake, pour about ¼ cup of batter onto hot griddle. Cook until pancakes are puffed and dry around edges. Turn and cook other side until golden brown. Makes 10-12 pancakes.

Note: *For a heart-healthy meal, serve with applesauce instead of butter and syrup.*

Matthew Neff (Laura and Jerry)

Egg In A Toast Hole

1 slice of bread
2 teaspoons margarine

1 egg

Butter one side of bread with margarine. Cut a circle out of the bread with a round cookie cutter. Melt 2 teaspoons of margarine on a moderately hot griddle or skillet. Put unbuttered side of bread on the griddle. Immediately break egg into the hole. Cook bread and egg until bottom of bread is golden brown. Then turn and cook until other side is golden brown. You may also cook the "hole" cut out of the slice of bread on the griddle until it is golden brown on both sides. Makes 1 serving.

Patrick Neff (Laura and Jerry)

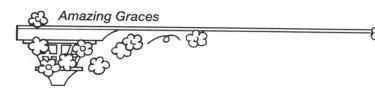

P.K. Muffins

1 (16 ounce) pint vanilla ice
cream

2 cups self-rising flour
Non-stick vegetable spray

Preheat oven to 400°. Soften ice cream and stir in the self-rising flour. Spray muffin tins with non-stick vegetable spray and fill each muffin cup ⅔ full. Bake at 400° for 12 minutes or until lightly browned.

Rebekah James (Merryl and Roy)

Easy Doughnuts

1 (10 count) can refrigerated
biscuits (not flaky style)

Vegetable oil
Confectioners' sugar

Separate the 10 biscuits. Cut a hole out of the middle of each with a biscuit cutter. Heat about ½-inch of oil in a small skillet. (To see when oil is hot enough, sprinkle a few drops of water into the oil. If the water sizzles and pops, then the oil is ready. If the oil begins to smoke, it is too hot!) Place a few doughnuts and holes in the hot oil, but do not crowd. Cook for about 1 minute and then turn and cook for another minute or until golden brown. Remove from oil with slotted spatula to several layers of paper towels and allow to cool slightly. Put confectioners' sugar in small paper bag. Add a few doughnuts or holes to the bag and shake to cover with sugar. Makes 10 doughnuts and 10 holes.

Patrick Neff (Laura and Jerry)

No-Bake Cookies

2 cups sugar
3 tablespoons cocoa
½ cup margarine
½ cup milk
Dash of salt

3 cups quick-cooking oats
½ cup peanut butter
(optional)
1 teaspoon vanilla extract

Bring sugar, cocoa, margarine, milk and salt to rapid boil for 1 minute. Add remaining ingredients. Mix well and working quickly, drop by teaspoonsful onto waxed paper. Makes about 4 dozen cookies.

Aren and Micah Cambre (Jane and Allison)

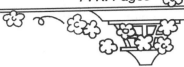

Butterscotch Oatmeal Cookies

¾ cup shortening, softened
1 cup brown sugar
½ cup sugar
1 egg
¼ cup water
1 teaspoon vanilla

1 cup all-purpose flour
1 teaspoon salt
1 teaspoon baking soda
3 cups uncooked oats
1 (12 ounce) package
butterscotch chips

Place shortening, sugar, egg, water and vanilla in a mixing bowl and beat thoroughly. Sift together flour, salt and baking soda and add to shortening mixture. Mix well. Blend in oats and butterscotch chips. Drop by teaspoonsful onto cookie sheet. I line mine with foil. It works well and the cleanup is a lot easier. Bake in moderate oven (350°) 10-15 minutes.

Tony Hayes (Kathy and Dan Danheim)

Neiman-Marcus Bars

1 box yellow cake mix
4 eggs
½ cup margarine, melted

1 (8 ounce) package cream
cheese, softened
1 (16 ounce) box
confectioners' sugar

Mix cake mix, two eggs and margarine. Pat in bottom of 13x9x2-inch pan that is greased and floured. Beat remaining 2 eggs and cream cheese together, then add confectioners' sugar. Spread on top of cake mixture. Bake at 350° for 35 to 45 minutes. Cut into squares. This is so easy to make to be so good!

Kris Hayes (Kathy and Dan Danheim)

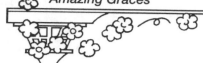

Monster Cookies

½ cup butter or margarine
1 cup sugar
1⅛ cups brown sugar
3 eggs
2 cups peanut butter
¼ teaspoon vanilla
¾ teaspoon light corn syrup

4½ cups regular oats, uncooked
2 teaspoons baking soda
¼ teaspoon salt
1 cup sugar-coated chocolate pieces
1 (6 ounce) package semi-sweet chocolate chips

Cream together butter, sugar and brown sugar. Then add eggs, peanut butter, vanilla and syrup. Beat well. Add oats, baking soda and salt. Stir well. Next add sugar-coated chocolate pieces and chocolate chips. Drop dough by ¼ cupfuls, 4 inches apart onto a lightly greased cookie sheet. Bake at 350° for 12-15 minutes. (Center of cookies will be slightly soft.) Cool. Makes 2½ dozen cookies.

Mary Jane Petty (Ron)

Chocolate Cookie Dirt

1 (8 ounce) package cream cheese, softened
1 cup confectioners' sugar
2 (3½ ounce) packages instant vanilla pudding
3 cups milk
1 (12 ounce) carton frozen whipped topping, thawed

1 teaspoon vanilla
1 (15 ounce) can crushed pineapple, drained
1 (20 ounce) package chocolate sandwich cookies, crushed

Mix all ingredients except cookie crumbs. Put layer of cookie crumbs in bottom of 9x12-inch flower pot. (Naturally a new clay pot or plastic pot would be best.) Add layer of pudding mixture and top with crumbs. Continue to layer. Top it off with silk flowers and serve with a trowel.

Note: Our Aunt Judy makes this every Christmas by request. She tops it off with red poinsettias.

Leslie and Lindsay Lanagan (Carolyn and David)

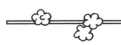
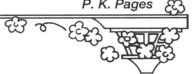

Grandchildren's Yummies

1 pound White Bark
1 cup peanut-flavored cereal
1 cup crisp rice cereal

1 cup dry roasted peanuts
1 cup miniature colored
marshmallows

Melt bark. Mix all ingredients and drop by spoonfuls onto waxed paper. Must work quickly.

Wanda L. Coleman (Alvis)

Peanut Butter Yummies

½ cup peanut butter
2½ tablespoons nonfat dry
milk
2 tablespoons raisins

2 tablespoons honey
¼ cup coconut
Sesame seeds

Combine all ingredients. Form into balls. Roll in sesame seeds. Yummie! Serves 8.

Cookbook Committee

Sugar Paint Icing For Cookies

2¼ cups confectioners'
sugar
4 teaspoons margarine

½ teaspoon vanilla
2 tablespoons milk
Food coloring, if desired

Mix all ingredients and blend thoroughly. Use white or divide into several bowls and tint each bowl a different color. Decorate animal crackers, ginger bread cookies, graham crackers, using water color brushes.

Aaron, Asa and Adam Calhoun (Bonita and Ken)

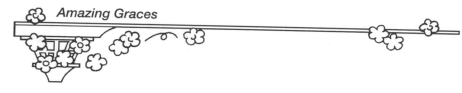

Frozen Bananas

Bananas

Remove the peeling from the banana. Wrap in plastic wrap. Place in freezer. Leave in freezer for an hour or so and remove. Enjoy!!

Note: *Bananas are also good if you dip them in chocolate sauce before freezing.*

Kristen Holcomb (Twana and Michael)

Quick and Easy Banana Pudding

½ **small banana (very ripe)**
3 **tablespoons applesauce**

1 **teaspoon plain yogurt**

Mash the banana and add the applesauce. Stir in plain yogurt. Makes 1 serving.

Cookbook Committee

Microwave Caramel Corn

2 **quarts freshly popped
  warm popcorn**
½ **cup brown sugar**
¼ **cup margarine**
1 **tablespoon water**

2 **tablespoons dark corn
  syrup**
¼ **teaspoon salt**
¼ **teaspoon baking soda**
½ **teaspoon vanilla**

Place popcorn into a 4- to 6-quart microwave-safe utensil. Combine brown sugar, margarine, water, syrup and salt in a 1-quart glass bowl. Microwave on HIGH 1½ minutes; stir. Microwave on HIGH 2 to 2½ minutes. Add baking soda and vanilla. Stir well. Pour mixture immediately over popcorn, stirring to coat evenly. Microwave on HIGH 2 minutes, stirring midway through cooking. Turn out onto a piece of waxed paper or aluminum foil to cool. Break into pieces and store in an airtight container.

Marjorie Willis (Don)

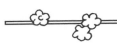 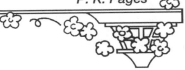

Popcorn Balls

2 cups sugar
1½ cups water
½ cup light corn syrup
1 tablespoon vinegar

½ tablespoon salt
1 tablespoon vanilla
5 quarts popped corn

Butter sides of saucepan. Combine sugar, water, salt, syrup and vinegar. Cook to hard ball stage (250°). Stir in vanilla. Slowly pour over popcorn, stirring just to mix well. Butter hands lightly and shape into balls.

Irma Waddleton (Don)

Graham Cracker Snack

Graham crackers
1 cup chopped pecans

¾ cup sugar
1 cup margarine

Cover a cookie sheet with foil. Lay out graham crackers on cookie sheet and sprinkle pecans over the crackers. In a small saucepan, bring sugar and margarine to a boil (about 2 minutes). Pour the sugar mixture over the crackers. Bake in oven at 350° for 10 minutes.

Pam Besser (Robert)

Popsicles

Fruit juice, powdered drink
mix or soft drink of your
choice

Ice cube tray
Toothpicks

Take your favorite fruit juice, prepared powdered drink mix or even your favorite soft drink and pour into an ice cube tray. Fill holes almost full and put toothpicks in each hole. Place tray in freezer and let it freeze. When they are completely frozen, you have to ask Mom or Dad to remove the popsicles from the tray.

Kristen Holcomb (Twana and Michael)

269

Lime Sherbet / Chocolate Chip Ice Cream

½ gallon lime sherbet, softened

1 (12 ounce) package miniature chocolate chips

Place ice cream in an extra-large bowl. Stir in chips and refreeze.

Jane Cambre (Allison)

Sundae Sauce

1 (6 ounce) package milk chocolate morsels
¼ cup crunchy peanut butter

¼ cup light corn syrup
¼ cup plus 1 tablespoon whipping cream

Melt chocolate. Add peanut butter and mix well. Remove from heat and stir in corn syrup and whipping cream. Store in covered container in refrigerator. Reheat over low heat before serving. Makes 1¼ cups.

Gerry Millikan (Herman)

Yogurt Smoothie

1 ripe banana
1 (8 ounce) carton plain or vanilla yogurt

1 cup orange juice
Sugar or honey to taste

Peel banana and cut into chunks. In a blender container combine banana, yogurt and orange juice. Add sugar or honey to sweeten. Cover and blend for about 2 minutes until smooth.

Brent and Kelsey Ricks (Patricia and Ricky J.)

Strawberry Slush

1 cup frozen strawberries, unsweetened	1 (12 ounce) can diet clear soda

Put strawberries and soda in a blender. Blend until berries are crushed. Serves 2.

Jaunita Lang (Fred)

Roasted Pumpkin Seeds

1 pumpkin 2-3 tablespoons vegetable oil or melted margarine	1-2 teaspoons salt

Cut open pumpkin and scoop out the seeds. Pull the pulp away from the seeds and rinse seeds. Put the seeds in a bowl and add 1 tablespoon oil or margarine and ½ teaspoon salt for every cup of seeds. Stir. Spread seeds in a single layer on a baking sheet and bake for 45 minutes at 250°. Raise temperature slightly if the seeds are slow to brown. Bake until seeds are golden brown and crisp. Eat when cool.

Andrew Neff (Laura and Jerry)

Back when our districts were much smaller, we would go sometimes as a group into a parsonage for a pot luck supper. One such occasion occurred in our parsonage. There were about 30 adults in attendance and 15 youngsters under 12, including our own 3. We rented an 8-millimeter cartoon movie, and our son was the projectionist. The projector was never the same again, but those P.K.'s had one fine time, while we adults talked up a storm. Our den was never quite the same again either. SMILE! While we were at Southwestern University, some of those youngsters, now students at Southwestern, would remind me of that occasion, saying "We remember so many fun things with other P.K.'s. That must have been the golden age." Oh, if they only knew! I didn't dare ask their parents about their monetary, among other, woes.

Lurlyn Fleming (Durwood)

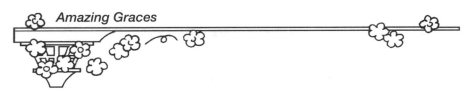

Homemade Butter

1 tablespoon whipping cream   **1 baby food jar**

Pour whipping cream into jar. Shake, shake, shake! Shake until solid butter forms. Spread on bread or crackers.

Merryl James (Roy)

Homemade Chalk

6 egg shells   **1 teaspoon flour**
1 rock   **1 teaspoon very hot tap water**

Wash and dry eggshells. Use rock to grind shells into a powder. Put powder in a dish. Measure and combine flour and hot water in another dish. Add 1 teaspoon of the powder. Mix and mash until the mixture sticks together. Shape and press into a chalk-stick shape. Roll the stick tight in a strip of paper towel. Dry for 3 days until hard as a rock. Write with the chalk. Erase with your shoe.

Merryl James (Roy)

Kid's Make-Up

2 teaspoons white shortening   **1 teaspoon white flour**
5 teaspoons cornstarch   **Glycerin**

Using rubber spatula, blend shortening, cornstarch and flour on a white plate to form a smooth paste. Add 3 or 4 drops glycerin for a creamy consistency. The yield should be enough for a child's face. Using fingers, stroke in one direction, spreading mixture over face. Can be removed easily with shortening, cold cream or baby oil.

Variation: *To make brown make-up, use 1 teaspoon shortening and replace cornstarch with 2½ teaspoons unsugared cocoa.*

Aaron, Asa and Adam Calhoun (Bonita and Ken)

272

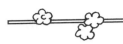 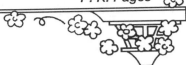

Lint Modeling

3 cups dryer lint
2 cups water

⅔ cup all-purpose flour
3 drops oil of cloves

Combine lint and water in a saucepan. Add flour and stir to prevent lumps. Add oil. Cook over low heat until mixture forms peaks. Pour out and cool on old newspapers. Shape over balloons, boxes or use molds. Use like papier-mâché.

Cookbook Committee

Sculpture Medium

1 part vermiculite (available
at hardware stores)
3 parts plaster

1 paper milk carton
Water

Mix vermiculite and plaster with enough water to pour into milk carton. Allow mixture to set up. Tear away milk carton. Carve with a spoon. It looks like granite!

Cookbook Committee

Play Clay Christmas Ornaments

2 cups baking soda
1 cup cornstarch

1¼ cups cold water

Mix soda and cornstarch together, blending well. Add the cold water and mix well until mixture is smooth. Boil for 1 minute until it has consistency of moist mashed potatoes. Stir constantly. Spoon out on a plate. Cover with a damp cloth and allow to cool. Knead dough and roll out on waxed paper. Cut out designs with a cookie cutter or shape by hand. Let dry until hard, 1-2 days. Paint ornaments with Tempera or water colors. Dry well and coat with clear shellac or clear nail polish. Hangers may be mounted on back with glue or pressed into dough before it dries.

Aaron, Asa and Adam Calhoun (Bonita and Ken)

273

Silly Puddy

4 small bottles glue
Blue food coloring

1 cup liquid starch
Paper towels

First we got 4 bottles of glue. Then we put blue food coloring in the 4 glue bottles. After we added the food coloring, we put the lids back on the bottles and shook them. This made the glue blue. Then we took the lids off and poured the glue into a big bowl. Next we put 1 cup of liquid starch in the big bowl. Then we stirred it with a spoon. It was sticky. Now we had to dry it off with paper towels. It was a little wet. Then we squished it up with our hands. The last thing we did was play with it.

Johnathan, Anna, Sharon and Nathan Diller (Helen and David)

Finger Paint

1 cup flour
1 cup water
½ cup sugar
3 cups boiling water

1 tablespoon boric acid
powder
Oil of cloves
Powdered paint coloring

Combine flour, water and sugar in the top of a double boiler. Pour 3 cups of boiling water into this mixture and stir until thick. Add 1 tablespoon of boric acid powder and several drops of oil of cloves. Add powdered paint coloring. Mix well and cool.

Aaron, Asa and Adam Calhoun (Bonita and Ken)

Cinnamon Ornaments

1 cup applesauce

1 (4.12 ounce) bottle ground
cinnamon

Mix applesauce and cinnamon to form a stiff dough. Roll out to ¼-inch thickness. Cut with cookie cutters. Make hole for ribbon. Carefully put on rack to dry. Let air dry several days, turning occasionally. Makes 12 sweet smelling ornaments.

Aaron, Asa and Adam Calhoun (Bonita and Ken)

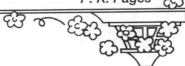

Play Dough

Cooked Version:
2 cups all-purpose flour
1 cup salt
2 teaspoons cream of tartar
2 cups water

2 tablespoons vegetable oil
Food coloring
Perfume

Mix flour, salt and cream of tartar. Mix water, oil, food coloring and perfume. Add liquid to dry ingredients. Cook over low heat. It will start to stick together in a big ball. Takes 3-5 minutes to cook.

Uncooked Version:
7 cups flour
1 cup salt

2 - 3 cups water (food coloring added)

Mix and let children do the stirring. This does not have as smooth a texture as the cooked version and you only have one color.

Aaron, Asa and Adam Calhoun (Bonita and Ken)

Homemade Clay

1½ cups all-purpose flour
1 cup salt
4 teaspoons powdered alum

2 tablespoons vegetable coloring
Water

Combine all ingredients and add enough water to hold ingredients together. When not in use, keep in a covered container. Kneading a little water into clay when surface dries will keep it in good condition.

Kristen Holcomb (Twana and Michael)

 **Amazing Graces**

Index

A

All Occasion Punch 27
All Things Good Dill Dip 13
All-Bran Bread or Rolls 97
Angel Pie 211
APPETIZERS
  Dips
    All Things Good Dill Dip 13
    Artichoke Dip 13
    Cucumber Dip 13
    Hot Sauce 16
    Party Shrimp Dip 14
    Sausage Dip 15
    Shrimp Dip 14
    Spinach Dip 15
    Texas Caviar (Black-Eyed Pea Dip) .. 14
  Hors D'oeuvres
    Asparagus Roll-Ups 19
    Bacon Roll-Ups 20
    Cheese Chili Quiches 16
    Cheese Crispies 262
    Cocktail Pecans 24
    Crab Delight 22
    Crescent Munchies 21
    Crispy Cheese Patties 21
    Olive Cheese Balls 18
    Petite Porkies 20
    Roll-Ups 17
    Sausage Balls 262
    Sausage Rolls 19
    Spinach Balls 18
    Swedish Meatballs 20
    Swiss Crab Bites 22
  Spreads
    Beef and Cheese Spread 24
    Cheese Ball 17
    Cheese Spread For A Crowd 23
    Corned Beef Sandwich Spread 52
    Cucumber Vegetable Spread 24
    Easy Cheese Ball 17
    Salmon Log 23
Apple Butter Cake 189
Apple Cake Quickie 190
Apple Crisp 248
Apple Dumplings 249
Apple Harvest Cake 192
Apple-Ring Pickles 181
Apples À La Lorraine 250
Apples, Baked 249
Apricot Breeze 243
Apricot Cheese Delight 63
Apricot Dream - Cream 67
Apricot Gelatin Salad 63
Arkansas Cherry Salad 56
Artichoke Dip 13
Asparagus / Pea Casserole 155

Asparagus, Escalloped 155
Asparagus Roll-Ups 19
Aunt Selma's Spritz Cookies 227
Avalon Inn Corn Pudding 163

B

Bacon and Egg Sandwiches 51
Bacon Roll-Ups 20
Baked Apples 249
Baked Beans 158
Baked Fruit 175
Baked Grits and Cheese 178
Baked Ham Sandwich 49
Baked Spareribs and Sauerkraut 119
Baked Squash 171
Banana Bread 91
Banana Bread, One Pan 91
Banana Bread, Sugarless 90
Banana Nut Cake 188
Banana Nut Muffins 87
Banana Split Cake 242
Bananas, Frozen 268
Batter Bread 94
Bavarian Fruit Ice Cream 253
BEANS
  Baked Beans 158
  Bean Bundles 156
  Bean Soup 39
  Christmas Beans 157
  Dutch Beans 157
  Eight-Bean Soup 39
  Fancy Ranch-Style Beans 158
  Green Bean Casserole 258
  Green Bean Shrimp 146
  Herbed Green Beans 156
  Rice - Vegetable Casserole 174
  Shoepeg Corn / Green Bean
    Casserole 165
BEEF
  Beef Stew 44
  Braised Beef Tips Over Rice 113
  Classic Beef Stroganoff 114
  Ground
    Best Spaghetti Sauce 103
    Cabbage Casserole 142
    Cabbage Patch Stew 33
    Candlelight Lasagna 104
    Cattleman's Hash 109
    Chili Casserole 108
    Chuck O' Luck 112
    Company Casserole 103
    Cornbread Casserole 107
    Dad's Chili 260
    Dinner In A Dish 110
    Full Meal Deal Soup 35
    Hamburger Soup 34
    Heart-Smart Chili 44

Hearty Meal 111
Meat Loaf For Two 104
Mexican Casserole 107
Microwave Italian Zucchini Meatloaf 105
Okra Gumbo 109
Oodles of Noodles 113
Party Potatoes 167
Plantation Stuffed Peppers 106
Porcupines 105
Potato - Meat Casserole 110
Preacher Soup 35
Quick Parsonage Potluck Stew 45
Ranch-Style Hash 108
Roman Eggplant 166
Sombrero Taco Cups 106
Spaghetti Sauce (Texas Style) 261
Swedish Meatballs 20
Taco Soup 34
Three Cheese Tetrazzini 111
"No Peek" Casserole 112
Peppered Brisket 116
Shanghai Beef 115
Spanish Steak 114
Sunday Brisket 115
Beef and Cheese Spread 24
Beef Stew 44
Beggars' Bundles 129
Berried Treasure 244
Berry Bananawich 46
Berry Turkey Sandwich 45
Best Spaghetti Sauce 103

BEVERAGES
All Occasion Punch 27
Christmas Wassail 28
Coffee Pot Tea 28
Frozen Slush Punch 25
Gelatin Punch 26
Hot Chocolate Mix 29
Hot Cranberry Punch 28
Hot Mulled Cider 29
Hot Vegetable Punch or Moctail
   Appetizer 29
Orange Slush 26
Parsonage Eggnog 27
Picnic Lemonade 27
Red Satin Punch 26
Strawberry Slush 271
Wedding Punch 25
Yogurt Smoothie 270
Biscuits, Cheese Garlic 98
Biscuits, Magic 94
Bishop's Favorite Muffins 85
Black Bottom Miniatures 247
Black-Eyed Pea Cornbread 84
Blackberry Cobbler 223
Blueberry Cheesecake 207
Blueberry Cream Pie 218
Boiled Egg Custard 252
Boiled Pebble Soup 257
Boneless Breasts à la Vineyard 125
Braised Beef Tips Over Rice 113

BREAD
Cornbread
Black-Eyed Pea Cornbread 84
Broccoli Cornbread 84
Delicious Cornbread 81
Heart-Healthy Cornbread 83
Hot Water Cornbread 82
Mary Ann's Mexican Cornbread 83
Mexican Cornbread 82
Sour Cream Cornbread 81
Miscellaneous
Cinnamon Buns 99
Crackers or Matza 100
Easy Doughnuts 264
French Pancake 98
Oatmeal Pancakes 263
Overnight French Toast 99
Waffles 262
Muffins
Banana Nut Muffins 87
Bishop's Favorite Muffins 85
California Muffins 85
Orange Muffins 86
P.K. Muffins 264
Strawberry Muffins 86
Quick
Banana Bread 91
Cheese Garlic Biscuits 98
Cherry Pecan Bread 88
Cranberry Nut Orange Bread 89
Deluxe Gingerbread 205
Light-As-A-Feather Gingerbread 205
One Pan Banana Bread 91
Poppy Seed Bread 89
Pumpkin Bread 90
Quick Onion Bread 98
Strawberry Bread With Spread 87
Sugarless Banana Bread 90
Zucchini Bread 88
Yeast
All-Bran Bread or Rolls 97
Batter Bread 94
Fresh Yeast Bread 95
Kolaches 96
Light Rolls 92
Magic Biscuits 94
Oatmeal Bread 95
Pecan Sticky Buns 96
Pizza Crust 259
Rich Sweet Bread Dough 96
Sour Cream Crescent Rolls 93
Bread Pudding with Sauce 251
Breakfast Casserole 122
Breakfast Pizza 121
Broccoli - Raisin Salad 73
Broccoli and Rice Casserole 159
Broccoli, Chilled Sesame 160
Broccoli Cornbread 84
Broccoli Salad 74
Broccoli Salad Supreme 73
Broccoli Supreme 140

Brownies, Butterscotch 235
Brownies, Caramel Ribbon 235
Buffalo Chip Cookies 233
Bunny Salad 257
Butter, Homemade 272
Butter, Virginia's Better 183
Butterfinger Pie 218
Buttermilk Coconut Pie 221
Buttermilk Pie, Old Time 220
Buttermilk Salad 64
Butterscotch Brownies 235
Butterscotch Oatmeal Cookies 265

C

CABBAGE
Baked Spareribs and Sauerkraut 119
Cabbage Casserole 142
Cabbage Patch Stew 33
Cloggers' Delight Salad 70
Cole Slaw 74
Heart-Healthy Turkey & Cabbage 141
Portuguese Soup 33
Sweet-and-Sour Kraut Salad 75

CAKES
Apple Butter Cake 189
Apple Cake Quickie 190
Apple Harvest Cake 192
Banana Nut Cake 188
Blueberry Cheesecake 207
Carrot Cake 204
Chocolate Chip Cake 195
Chop Suey Cake 202
Cocoa Party Cake 193
Coconut Pound Cake 197
Crème de Menthe Cake 200
Deluxe Gingerbread 205
Earthquake Cake 199
Eggless Raisin Cake — 1910 190
Five-Flavor Cake 195
Fudge Cake 193
Grandmother's Orange Cake Ministry . 198
Individual Cheesecakes 207
Light-As-A-Feather Gingerbread 205
Million Dollar Pound Cake 196
My Cream Cheese Pound Cake 197
Oatmeal Cake 191
Pear Cake 198
Pecan Praline Cheesecake 208
Penny's Special Chocolate Chip Cake 194
Pineapple Pound Cake 196
Pumpkin Cake 203
Punch Bowl Cake 202
Red Velvet Cake 201
Sam's Cake 192
Snowball Cake 200
Strawberry Cinnamon Chiffon Cake 187
Swirl Coffee Cake 206
Three-Day Coconut Cake 189
Turtle Cake 199
Calico Cheese Salad 71
California Muffins 85
Candied Pecan Snacks 237

Candlelight Lasagna 104
CANDY
Candied Pecan Snacks 237
Crispy Rice Bits 238
Divinity 240
Fudge 240
Millionaires 237
Peanut Butter Fudge 239
Peanut Butter Squares 239
Salted Peanut Chews 238
Velveeta Fudge 239
Caramel Nut Pie 241
Caramel Ribbon Brownies 235
Carrot Cake 204
Carrots, Glazed 161
Carrots In Orange Sauce 160
Cattleman's Hash 109
Cauliflower, Cheesy Mushroom 161
Chalk, Homemade 272
CHEESE
Baked Grits and Cheese 178
Beef and Cheese Spread 24
Breakfast Pizza 121
Calico Cheese Salad 71
Cheese Ball 17
Cheese Chili Quiches 16
Cheese Crispies 262
Cheese Fondue Casserole 179
Cheese Garlic Biscuits 98
Cheese Shrimp or Chicken 147
Cheese Spread For A Crowd 23
Chili Cheese Dogs 260
Cream Cheese Raisin Sandwich 51
Crispy Cheese Patties 21
Easy Cheese Ball 17
Lisanne's 10-Minute Pizzas 259
Methodist Grits 178
Olive Cheese Balls 18
Pizza Bagels 48
Quesadillas 49
Three Cheese Chicken Casserole 132
Three Cheese Tetrazzini 111
Tofu Cheddar Enchiladas 152
Turkey Grilled Cheese Sandwiches 261
Cheese Ball 17
Cheese Ball, Easy 17
Cheese Balls, Olive 18
Cheese Chili Quiches 16
Cheese Crispies 262
Cheese Fondue Casserole 179
Cheese Garlic Biscuits 98
Cheese Shrimp or Chicken 147
Cheese Spread For A Crowd 23
Cheesecake, Blueberry 207
Cheesecake, Pecan Praline 208
Cheesecakes, Individual 207
Cheesy Corn Casserole 162
Cheesy Mushroom Cauliflower 161
Cherries In The Snow 241
Cherry Fruit Salad 56
Cherry Ice Box Pie 215

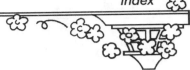

Cherry Pecan Bread 88
Cherry Salad, Arkansas 56
Cherry Salad, Dark Bing 62
Cherry-Nut Ice Cream 252
Chicken à la King 132
Chicken and Artichokes 123
Chicken and Dressing Casserole 130
Chicken Broccoli Casserole 136
Chicken in Soy Sauce 139
Chicken Mexican Dressing 130
Chicken Oriental 137
Chicken Pasta Shells 128
Chicken Pot Pie 134
Chicken Rice Casserole 133
Chicken Spaghetti 135
Chicken Tettrazini 134
Chicken Tortilla Casserole 131
Chicken Wings 139
Chili Casserole 108
Chili Cheese Dogs 260
Chili, Dad's 260
Chili, Heart-Smart 44
Chili, Quick White 43
Chilled Sesame Broccoli 160

CHOCOLATE
Black Bottom Miniatures 247
Buffalo Chip Cookies 233
Caramel Ribbon Brownies 235
Chocolate Chess Pie 219
Chocolate Chip Cake 195
Chocolate Chip Cookies 231
Chocolate Chip Pie 219
Chocolate Cookie Dirt 266
Chocolate Crunch Supreme 246
Chocolate Pie with Magic Meringue 212
Cocoa Party Cake 193
Cream Cheese Dessert Bars 236
Crème de Menthe Cake 200
Eagle Brand Cookie Bars 237
Earthquake Cake 199
Easy Icing 208
Forgotten Cookies 234
Four-Minute Butter Frosting 209
Fudge 240
Fudge Cake 193
Fudge Pie 211
Hot Chocolate Mix 29
Ice Cream Delight 247
Lime Sherbet / Chocolate Chip
  Ice Cream 270
Millionaires 237
Monster Cookies 266
No-Bake Cookies 264
Peanut Butter Squares 239
Penny's Special Chocolate Chip Cake 194
Quick Cookies 225
Sam's Cake 192
Sundae Sauce 270
Turtle Cake 199
Velveeta Fudge 239
Chop Suey Cake 202

Christmas Beans 157
Christmas Corn 164
"Christmas Salad" - Pineapple Cream
  Cheese Mold 66
Christmas Wassail 28
Chuck O' Luck 112
Church Cobbler 224
Chutney, Cranberry 180
Cinnamon Buns 99
Cinnamon Ornaments 274
Cinnamon Roll-Ups 248
Clam Chowder, Quick and Easy 41
Classic Beef Stroganoff 114
Clay, Homemade 275
Cloggers' Delight Salad 70

COBBLERS
Blackberry Cobbler 223
Church Cobbler 224
Peach Cobbler 224
Cocktail Pecans 24
Cocoa Party Cake 193
Coconut Cake, Three-Day 189
Coconut Pie 221
Coconut Pie, Buttermilk 221
Coconut Pound Cake 197
Coffee Cake, Swirl 206
Coffee Pot Tea 28
Cole Slaw 74
Colorful Cookies 232
Company Casserole 103

COOKIES
Aunt Selma's Spritz Cookies 227
Buffalo Chip Cookies 233
Butterscotch Brownies 235
Butterscotch Oatmeal Cookies 265
Caramel Ribbon Brownies 235
Chocolate Chip Cookies 231
Colorful Cookies 232
Corn Flake Cookies 232
Cream Cheese Dessert Bars 236
Cream Cheese Drops 225
Eagle Brand Cookie Bars 237
Easy Time Holiday Squares 236
Forgotten Cookies 234
Grandma's Pumpkin Cookies 230
Monster Cookies 266
Neiman-Marcus Bars 265
No-Bake Cookies 264
Oatmeal Haystacks 233
Old-Fashioned Sugar Cookies 226
Overnight Ginger Cookies 230
Peanut Butter Cookies 229
Pink Snowballs 231
Praline Cookies 234
Quick Cookies 225
Scotch Shortbread 228
Sour Cream Sugar Cookies 227
Sugar Cookies 226
Tansy Cookies 228
Wheat-Free Peanut Butter Cookies 229
Copper Pennies 71

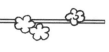

CORN
Avalon Inn Corn Pudding 163
Cheesy Corn Casserole 162
Christmas Corn 164
Corn Casserole 162
Corn Chowder 41
Corn Relish 180
Cream Cheese - Corn Squash
   Casserole 172
Creamed Corn 163
Easy Corn Pudding 163
Fiesta Corn Salad 71
Hominy Casserole 165
Linda's Corn Pudding 164
Monterey Hominy 165
Shoepeg Corn / Green Bean
   Casserole 165
Corn Flake Cookies 232
Cornbread Casserole 107
Corned Beef Sandwich Spread 52
Cornish Hens on Wild Rice 141
Country Style Chicken Kiev 126
Cowboy Rice 175
Crab Delight 22
Cracker Pudding 251
Crackers or Matza 100
Cranberry - Raspberry Congealed Salad .. 66
Cranberry - Raspberry Salad 64
Cranberry Chicken 125
Cranberry Chutney 180
Cranberry Nut Orange Bread 89
Cranberry Salad 61
Cream Cheese - Corn Squash Casserole 172
Cream Cheese Dessert Bars 236
Cream Cheese Drops 225
Cream Cheese Frosting 204
Cream Cheese Icing 201, 203
Cream Cheese Raisin Sandwich 51
Creamed Corn 163
Creamed Tuna 147
Creamy Fish Chowder 42
Creamy Fruit Salad 55
Creamy Ham and Rice for Two 117
Crème de Menthe Cake 200
Crescent Munchies 21
Crispy Cheese Patties 21
Crispy Rice Bits 238
Crock Pot Pork Bar-B-Q 119
Crunchy Squash Casserole 170
Cucumber Dip 13
Cucumber Vegetable Spread 24

D
Dad's Chili 260
Dark Bing Cherry Salad 62
Delicious Cornbread 81
Deluxe Gingerbread 205
DESSERTS
Apple Crisp 248
Apple Dumplings 249
Apples À La Lorraine 250
Apricot Breeze 243

Baked Apples 249
Banana Split Cake 242
Bavarian Fruit Ice Cream 253
Berried Treasure 244
Black Bottom Miniatures 247
Boiled Egg Custard 252
Bread Pudding with Sauce 251
Caramel Nut Pie 241
Cherries In The Snow 241
Cherry-Nut Ice Cream 252
Chocolate Cookie Dirt 266
Chocolate Crunch Supreme 246
Cinnamon Roll-Ups 248
Cracker Pudding 251
Hot Cinnamon Sauce 253
Ice Cream Delight 247
Lime Sherbet / Chocolate Chip
   Ice Cream 270
Mexican Flan 245
Popcorn Cake 250
Quick and Easy Banana Pudding 268
Strawberry Delight 245
Strawberry Squares 244
Diet Strawberry Pie 210
Dinner In A Dish 110
Divinity 240
Dreamy Frozen Fruit Salad 58
Dutch Beans 157

E
Eagle Brand Cookie Bars 237
Earthquake Cake 199
Easy Cheese Ball 17
Easy Chicken Casserole 129
Easy Chicken Cordon Bleu 126
Easy Corn Pudding 163
Easy Curried Chicken 133
Easy Doughnuts 264
Easy Icing 208
Easy Sweet 'N Sour Chicken 123
Easy Time Holiday Squares 236
Egg Cracker Salad 68
Egg In A Toast Hole........................... 263
Eggless Raisin Cake — 1910 190
Eggplant Casserole 166
Eggplant, Roman 166
EGGS
Bacon and Egg Sandwiches 51
Baked Grits and Cheese 178
Boiled Egg Custard 252
Breakfast Casserole 122
Breakfast Pizza 121
Cheese Fondue Casserole 179
Egg Cracker Salad 68
Egg In A Toast Hole 263
French Toast Sandwiches 50
Hot Deviled Eggs 179
Methodist Grits 178
Old-Fashioned Egg Custard Pie 220
Overnight Breakfast Casserole 122
Quiche Lanore 117
Sausage Quiche 121

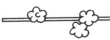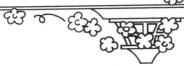
Sausage Strata 122
Eight-Bean Soup 39
Escalloped Asparagus 155

F

Fancy Ranch-Style Beans 158
Festive Cream Cheese Salad 65
Fiesta Corn Salad 71
Finger Paint...................................... 274
Fish Chowder, Creamy 42
Five-Flavor Cake.............................. 195
Forgotten Cookies 234
Four-Minute Butter Frosting 209
French Pancake 98
French Toast, Overnight 99
French Toast Sandwiches 50
Fresh Strawberry Pie 210
Fresh Yeast Bread 95
Fried Green Tomatoes 173
Frosting 209
Frozen Bananas 268
Frozen Chicken Salad Sandwiches 46
Frozen Fruit Salad (Papercup Salad) 59
Frozen Slush Punch 25
Fruit, Baked 175
Fruit Medley 57
Fruit Salad 55
Fruit Salad, Creamy 55
Fruit Salad, Dreamy Frozen 58
Fruit Salad, Frozen (Papercup Salad) 59
Fruit Salad, Mama's 60
Fruity Chicken Salad 69
Fudge 240
Fudge Cake 193
Fudge, Peanut Butter 239
Fudge Pie 211
Fudge, Velveeta 239
Full Meal Deal Soup 35

G

Garlic Chicken Parmesan 127
Gelatin Punch 26
Ginger Cookies, Overnight 230
Gingerbread, Deluxe 205
Gingerbread, Light-As-A-Feather 205
Glazed Carrots 161
Glorified Chicken and Rice 138
Graham Cracker Snack 269
Grandchildren's Yummies 267
Grandma's Pork Chops and Rice 120
Grandma's Pumpkin Cookies 230
Grandmother's Orange Cake Ministry 198
Grape - Blueberry Salad 65
Great Seasoned Rice 176
Green Bean Casserole 258
Green Bean Shrimp 146
Green Chili Chicken Enchiladas 131
Green Chili Open-Faced Sandwiches 51
Green Rice Casserole 176

H

Halibut Lemon Sauté 149
Ham or Chicken Salad Sandwiches 47

Hamburger Soup 34
HEART HEALTHY
Baked Apples 249
Bishop's Favorite Muffins 85
Boiled Pebble Soup 257
Bunny Salad 257
California Muffins 85
Chicken in Soy Sauce 139
Chicken Oriental 137
Chilled Sesame Broccoli 160
Chocolate Crunch Supreme 246
Cole Slaw 74
Corn Relish 180
Cornish Hens on Wild Rice 141
Cranberry Chutney 180
Diet Strawberry Pie 210
Fiesta Corn Salad 71
Grandma's Pork Chops and Rice 120
Halibut Lemon Sauté 149
Heart-Healthy Cornbread 83
Heart-Healthy Turkey & Cabbage 141
Heart-Smart Chili 44
Hearty Meal 111
Holiday Salad 61
Juice Gelatin Squares 258
Lemon - Broiled Orange Roughy 149
Lighthearted Lasagna 143
No-Fat Yogurt Chicken Bake 124
Oatmeal Pancakes 263
Okra Gumbo 109
Oven-Fried Chicken 140
Pink Fluff 57
Preacher Soup 35
Quick and Easy Banana Pudding 268
Quick White Chili 43
Santa Fe Chicken "Steam-Fry" 137
Sour Cream Crescent Rolls 93
Spinach Kitty 170
Spinach Lasagna 151
Split Pea Soup 36
Strawberry Delight 245
Strawberry Muffins 86
Strawberry Slush 271
Sugarless Banana Bread 90
Sugarless Sweetened Deep-Dish Pie .. 214
Tofu Cheddar Enchiladas 152
Turkey-In-The-Orange Salad 69
Vegetable Rice Soup 37
Virginia's Better Butter 183
Zesty Crab Cakes 148
Herbed Green Beans 156
His Majesty's Special 128
Holiday Salad 61
Homemade Butter 272
Homemade Chalk 272
Homemade Clay 275
Hominy Casserole 165
Hoppin' John (New Year's Day Special) .. 159
Hot Chocolate Mix 29
Hot Cinnamon Sauce 253
Hot Cranberry Punch 28
Hot Deviled Eggs 179

Hot Mulled Cider 29
Hot Pineapple Salad 58
Hot Sauce 16
Hot Shrimp Casserole 146
Hot Vegetable Punch or Moctail Appetizer 29
Hot Water Cornbread 82

I

Ice Cream, Bavarian Fruit 253
Ice Cream, Cherry-Nut 252
Ice Cream Delight 247
Ice Cream, Lime Sherbet / Chocolate
   Chip 270

ICINGS
   Cream Cheese Frosting 204
   Cream Cheese Icing 201, 203
   Easy Icing 208
   Four-Minute Butter Frosting 209
   Frosting 209
   Praline Icing 191
   Sugar Paint Icing For Cookies 267
Impossible Pie 217
Individual Cheesecakes 207
Italian Chicken Sandwiches 47

J

Jalapeño Jelly 182
Jelly, Jalapeño 182
Juice Gelatin Squares 258

K

Kid's Make-Up 272
Kolaches 96

L

Layered Salad 72
Lemon - Broiled Orange Roughy 149
Light Rolls 92
Lighthearted Lasagna 143
Lime Angel Pie 217
Lime Sherbet / Chocolate Chip Ice
   Cream 270
Linda's Corn Pudding 164
Lint Modeling 273
Lisanne's 10-Minute Pizzas 259

M

Magic Biscuits 94
Make-Up, Kid's 272
Mama's Fruit Salad 60
Mandarin Salad 76
Marinated Vegetable Salad 77
Mary's Louisiana Cajun Gumbo 40
Meat Loaf For Two 104
Meatloaf, Microwave, Italian Zucchini 105
Methodist Grits 178
Methodist Pie 216

MEXICAN FOOD
   Chicken Mexican Dressing 130
   Chicken Tortilla Casserole 131
   Chili Casserole 108
   Cornbread Casserole 107
   Green Chili Chicken Enchiladas 131
   Green Chili Open-Faced Sandwiches 51
   Hot Sauce 16

   Mary Ann's Mexican Cornbread 83
   Mexican Casserole 107
   Mexican Cornbread 82
   Mexican Flan 245
   Mexican Rice 177
   Monterey Hominy 165
   Quesadillas 49
   Quick Mexican Salad 68
   Roll-Ups 17
   Sombrero Taco Cups 106
   Squash Casserole Ole 171
   Taco Soup 34
   Tofu Cheddar Enchiladas 152
   Tortilla Soup 37
Microwave Caramel Corn 268
Microwave Italian Zucchini Meatloaf 105
Million Dollar Pound Cake 196
Millionaires 237
Monster Cookies 266
Mr. D's Potato Soup 38
Mushroom - Stuffed Fish Rolls 150
My Cream Cheese Pound Cake 197

N

Neiman-Marcus Bars 265
"No Peek" Casserole 112
No-Bake Cookies 264
No-Fat Yogurt Chicken Bake 124
Not-So-Sweet Pecan Pie 212

O

Oatmeal Bread 95
Oatmeal Cake 191
Oatmeal Haystacks 233
Oatmeal Pancakes 263
Okra Gumbo 109
Old Time Buttermilk Pie 220
Old-Fashioned Egg Custard Pie 220
Old-Fashioned Pineapple Pie 222
Old-Fashioned Sugar Cookies 226
Olive Cheese Balls 18
One Pan Banana Bread 91
Onion Pie Casserole 167
Oodles of Noodles 113
Orange - Cranberry Salad 62
Orange Avocado Salad 75
Orange Cake Ministry, Grandmother's 198
Orange Gelatin Salad 60
Orange Muffins 86
Orange Slush 26
Ornaments, Cinnamon 274
Ornaments, Play Clay Christmas 273
Oven-Fried Chicken 140
Overnight Breakfast Casserole 122
Overnight French Toast 99
Overnight Ginger Cookies 230

P

P.K. Muffins 264
Paint, Finger 274
Pancake, French 98
Pancakes, Oatmeal 263
Parsonage Eggnog 27
Party Chicken Critters 124

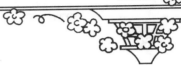

Party Potatoes 167
Party Shrimp Dip 14
PASTA
  Best Spaghetti Sauce 103
  Candlelight Lasagna 104
  Chicken Pasta Shells 128
  Chicken Spaghetti 135
  Chicken Tettrazini 134
  Cloggers' Delight Salad 70
  Lighthearted Lasagna 143
  Oodles of Noodles 113
  Seafood Pasta Salad 67
  Spaghetti Sauce (Texas Style) 261
  Spinach Lasagna 151
  Straw and Hay 116
  Three Cheese Chicken Casserole 132
Peach Cobbler 224
Peach Cream Pie 215
Peach Icebox Pie 214
Peanut Butter Cookies 229
Peanut Butter Cookies, Wheat-Free 229
Peanut Butter Fudge 239
Peanut Butter Squares 239
Peanut Butter Yummies 267
Peanut Chews, Salted 238
Pear Cake 198
PEAS
  Asparagus / Pea Casserole 155
  Black-Eyed Pea Cornbread 84
  Hoppin' John (New Year's Day
    Special) 159
  Split Pea Soup 36
  Texas Caviar (Black-Eyed Pea Dip) 14
Pecan Pie 213
Pecan Pie, Not-So-Sweet 212
Pecan Praline Cheesecake 208
Pecan Snacks, Candied 237
Pecan Sticky Buns 96
Pecan Tarts, Tiny 213
Penny's Special Chocolate Chip Cake 194
Peppered Brisket 116
Perlow 135
Petite Porkies 20
Pickles, Apple-Ring 181
Picnic Lemonade 27
PIES
  Angel Pie 211
  Blueberry Cream Pie 218
  Butterfinger Pie 218
  Buttermilk Coconut Pie 221
  Cherry Ice Box Pie 215
  Chocolate Chess Pie 219
  Chocolate Chip Pie 219
  Chocolate Pie with Magic Meringue 212
  Coconut Pie 221
  Diet Strawberry Pie 210
  Fresh Strawberry Pie 210
  Fudge Pie 211
  Impossible Pie 217
  Lime Angel Pie 217
  Methodist Pie 216
  Not-So-Sweet Pecan Pie 212

Old Time Buttermilk Pie 220
Old-Fashioned Egg Custard Pie 220
Old-Fashioned Pineapple Pie 222
Peach Cream Pie 215
Peach Icebox Pie 214
Pecan Pie 213
Pumpkin Chiffon Pie 222
Sugarless Sweetened Deep-Dish Pie .. 214
Sweet Potato Pie 216
Tiny Pecan Tarts 213
Pineapple Cream Cheese Mold 66
Pineapple Pie, Old-Fashioned 222
Pineapple Pound Cake 196
Pineapple Salad, Hot 58
Pineapple, Scalloped 175
Pink Fluff 57
Pink Snowballs 231
Pizza Bagels 48
Pizza Crust 259
Pizzas, Lisanne's 10-Minute 259
Plantation Stuffed Peppers 106
Play Clay Christmas Ornaments 273
Play Dough 275
Popcorn Balls 269
Popcorn Cake 250
Poppy Seed Bread 89
Popsicles 269
Porcupines 105
PORK
  Bacon and Egg Sandwiches 51
  Bacon Roll-Ups 20
  Baked Ham Sandwich 49
  Baked Spareribs and Sauerkraut 119
  Breakfast Casserole 122
  Breakfast Pizza 121
  Creamy Ham and Rice for Two 117
  Crock Pot Pork Bar-B-Q 119
  Grandma's Pork Chops and Rice 120
  Ham or Chicken Salad Sandwiches 47
  Overnight Breakfast Casserole 122
  Perlow 135
  Petite Porkies 20
  Pork Tenderloin in Red Wine 118
  Portuguese Soup 33
  Quiche Lanore 117
  Sausage Balls 262
  Sausage Dip 15
  Sausage Quiche 121
  Sausage Rolls 19
  Sausage Strata 122
  Straw and Hay 116
  Sweet 'N Sour Sausage 118
  Va.'s Pork Chops and Rice 120
POTATOES
  Mr. D's Potato Soup 38
  Party Potatoes 167
  Potato - Meat Casserole 110
  Potato Salad for 50 70
  Sweet Potato Casserole 168
  Sweet Potato Pie 216
POTPOURRI
  Cinnamon Ornaments 274

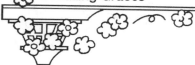

Finger Paint 274
Homemade Chalk 272
Homemade Clay 275
Kid's Make-Up 272
Lint Modeling 273
Play Clay Christmas Ornaments 273
Play Dough 275
Sculpture Medium 273
Silly Puddy 274

POULTRY

Chicken

Beggars' Bundles 129
Boneless Breasts à la Vineyard 125
Broccoli Supreme 140
Cheese Shrimp or Chicken 147
Chicken à la King 132
Chicken and Artichokes 123
Chicken and Dressing Casserole 130
Chicken Broccoli Casserole 136
Chicken in Soy Sauce 139
Chicken Mexican Dressing 130
Chicken Oriental 137
Chicken Pasta Shells 128
Chicken Pot Pie 134
Chicken Rice Casserole 133
Chicken Spaghetti 135
Chicken Tettrazini 134
Chicken Tortilla Casserole 131
Chicken Wings 139
Country Style Chicken Kiev 126
Cranberry Chicken 125
Easy Chicken Casserole 129
Easy Chicken Cordon Bleu 126
Easy Curried Chicken 133
Easy Sweet 'N Sour Chicken 123
Frozen Chicken Salad Sandwiches ... 46
Fruity Chicken Salad 69
Garlic Chicken Parmesan 127
Glorified Chicken and Rice 138
Green Chili Chicken Enchiladas 131
Ham or Chicken Salad Sandwiches ... 47
His Majesty's Special 128
Italian Chicken Sandwiches 47
No-Fat Yogurt Chicken Bake 124
Oven-Fried Chicken 140
Party Chicken Critters 124
Perlow 135
Quick Chick 138
Quick White Chili 43
Santa Fe Chicken "Steam-Fry" 137
Seminary Sandwiches 49
Sour Cream Chicken 127
Spectacular Chicken Supreme 136
Three Cheese Chicken Casserole ... 132

Game

Cornish Hens on Wild Rice 141

Turkey

Berry Turkey Sandwich 45
Cabbage Casserole 142
Heart-Healthy Turkey & Cabbage 141
Lighthearted Lasagna 143

Tasty Turkey Soup 36
Turkey Grilled Cheese Sandwiches . 261
Turkey Tetrazzini 142
Turkey-In-The-Orange Salad 69
Pound Cake, Coconut 197
Pound Cake, Million Dollar 196
Pound Cake, My Cream Cheese 197
Pound Cake, Pineapple 196
Praline Cookies 234
Praline Icing 191
Preacher Soup 35
Preserves, Strawberry 182
Pretzel Salad 59
Pudding, Bread with Sauce 251
Pudding, Cracker 251
Pudding, Quick and Easy Banana ... 268
Pumpkin Bread 90
Pumpkin Cake 203
Pumpkin Chiffon Pie 222
Pumpkin Cookies, Grandma's 230
Pumpkin Seeds, Roasted 271
Punch Bowl Cake 202

Q

Quesadillas 49
Quiche Lanore 117
Quick and Easy Banana Pudding 268
Quick and Easy Clam Chowder 41
Quick Chick 138
Quick Cookies 225
Quick Mexican Salad 68
Quick Onion Bread 98
Quick Parsonage Potluck Stew 45
Quick White Chili 43

R

Ranch-Style Hash 108
Red Satin Punch 26
Red Velvet Cake 201
Reuben Sandwiches 50

RICE

Broccoli and Rice Casserole 159
Cowboy Rice 175
Crispy Rice Bits 238
Great Seasoned Rice 176
Green Rice Casserole 176
Mexican Rice 177
Rice - Vegetable Casserole 174
Texas Gumbo Rice 177
Vegetable Rice Soup 37
Rich Sweet Bread Dough 96
Roasted Pumpkin Seeds 271
Roll-Ups 17
Roman Eggplant 166

S

SALAD

Congealed

Apricot Cheese Delight 63
Apricot Dream - Cream 67
Apricot Gelatin Salad 63
Buttermilk Salad 64
"Christmas Salad" - Pineapple
   Cream Cheese Mold 66

Cranberry - Raspberry Congealed
  Salad 66
Cranberry - Raspberry Salad 64
Cranberry Salad 61
Dark Bing Cherry Salad 62
Festive Cream Cheese Salad 65
Grape - Blueberry Salad 65
Holiday Salad 61
Mama's Fruit Salad 60
Orange - Cranberry Salad.................62
Orange Gelatin Salad 60
Pretzel Salad 59
Dressing
Zesty Salad Dressing 78
Fruit
Arkansas Cherry Salad 56
Bunny Salad....................................257
Cherry Fruit Salad 56
Creamy Fruit Salad 55
Dreamy Frozen Fruit Salad 58
Frozen Fruit Salad (Papercup
  Salad) 59
Fruit Medley 57
Fruit Salad 55
Hot Pineapple Salad 58
Pink Fluff 57
Strawberry Fruit Delight 55
Main Dish
Egg Cracker Salad 68
Fruity Chicken Salad 69
Quick Mexican Salad 68
Seafood Pasta Salad 67
Turkey-In-The-Orange Salad 69
Vegetable
Broccoli - Raisin Salad 73
Broccoli Salad 74
Broccoli Salad Supreme 73
Calico Cheese Salad 71
Cloggers' Delight Salad 70
Cole Slaw 74
Copper Pennies 71
Fiesta Corn Salad 71
Layered Salad 72
Mandarin Salad 76
Marinated Vegetable Salad 77
Orange Avocado Salad 75
Potato Salad for 50 70
Salad Nicholi 78
Spinach and Strawberry Salad 77
Sweet-and-Sour Kraut Salad 75
Valley Salad 72
Salmon Log 23
Salted Peanut Chews 238
Sam's Cake 192
SANDWICH
Bacon and Egg Sandwiches 51
Baked Ham Sandwich 49
Berry Bananawich 46
Berry Turkey Sandwich 45
Chili Cheese Dogs 260
Corned Beef Sandwich Spread 52
Cream Cheese Raisin Sandwich 51

French Toast Sandwiches 50
Frozen Chicken Salad Sandwiches 46
Green Chili Open-Faced Sandwiches 51
Ham or Chicken Salad Sandwiches 47
Italian Chicken Sandwiches 47
Lisanne's 10-Minute Pizzas 259
Pizza Bagels 48
Quesadillas 49
Reuben Sandwiches 50
Seminary Sandwiches 49
Spinach French Loaf 48
Turkey Grilled Cheese Sandwiches 261
Santa Fe Chicken "Steam-Fry" 137
Sauce, Hot Cinnamon 253
Sauce, Sundae 270
Sausage Balls 262
Sausage Dip 15
Sausage Quiche 121
Sausage Rolls 19
Sausage Strata 122
Scalloped Pineapple 175
Scotch Shortbread 228
Sculpture Medium 273
SEAFOOD
Cheese Shrimp or Chicken 147
Crab Delight 22
Creamed Tuna 147
Creamy Fish Chowder 42
Green Bean Shrimp 146
Halibut Lemon Sauté 149
Hot Shrimp Casserole 146
Lemon - Broiled Orange Roughy 149
Mary's Louisiana Cajun Gumbo 40
Mushroom - Stuffed Fish Rolls 150
Party Shrimp Dip 14
Quick and Easy Clam Chowder 41
Salmon Log 23
Seafood Pasta Salad 67
Shrimp and Rice 145
Shrimp Andrea 144
Shrimp Bisque 144
Shrimp Chowder 42
Shrimp Creole 145
Shrimp Dip 14
Swiss Crab Bites 22
Zesty Crab Cakes 148
Seminary Sandwiches 49
Sensational Spinach 168
Shanghai Beef 115
Shoepeg Corn / Green Bean Casserole ..165
Silly Puddy 274
SNACKS
Candied Pecan Snacks 237
Frozen Bananas 268
Graham Cracker Snack 269
Grandchildren's Yummies 267
Juice Gelatin Squares 258
Lisanne's 10-Minute Pizzas 259
Microwave Caramel Corn 268
Peanut Butter Yummies 267
Pizza Bagels 48
Popcorn Balls 269

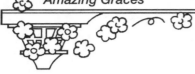

Amazing Graces

Popsicles 269
Roasted Pumpkin Seeds 271
Salted Peanut Chews 238
Snowball Cake 200
Sombrero Taco Cups 106
SOUP
   Bean Soup 39
   Beef Stew 44
   Boiled Pebble Soup 257
   Cabbage Patch Stew 33
   Corn Chowder 41
   Creamy Fish Chowder 42
   Dad's Chili 260
   Eight-Bean Soup 39
   Full Meal Deal Soup 35
   Hamburger Soup 34
   Heart-Smart Chili 44
   Mary's Louisiana Cajun Gumbo 40
   Mr. D's Potato Soup 38
   Portuguese Soup 33
   Preacher Soup 35
   Quick and Easy Clam Chowder 41
   Quick Parsonage Potluck Stew 45
   Quick White Chili 43
   Shrimp Chowder 42
   Split Pea Soup 36
   Taco Soup 34
   Tasty Turkey Soup 36
   Tortilla Soup 37
   Vegetable Rice Soup 37
   Zucchini Soup 38
Sour Cream Chicken 127
Sour Cream Cornbread 81
Sour Cream Crescent Rolls 93
Sour Cream Sugar Cookies 227
Spaghetti Sauce (Texas Style) 261
Spaghetti Sauce, Best 103
Spanish Steak 114
Spectacular Chicken Supreme 136
Spinach and Strawberry Salad 77
Spinach Balls 18
Spinach Dip 15
Spinach Dressing 169
Spinach French Loaf 48
Spinach Kitty 170
Spinach Lasagna 151
Spinach, Sensational 168
Split Pea Soup 36
Spritz Cookies, Aunt Selma's 227
SQUASH
   Baked Squash 171
   Cream Cheese - Corn Squash
     Casserole 172
   Crunchy Squash Casserole 170
   Microwave Italian Zucchini Meatloaf 105
   Rice - Vegetable Casserole 174
   Squash Casserole Ole 171
   Squash Creole 172
   Squash Medley 173
   Zucchini Bread 88
   Zucchini Soup 38

Straw and Hay 116
Strawberry Bread With Spread 87
Strawberry Cinnamon Chiffon Cake 187
Strawberry Delight 245
Strawberry Fruit Delight 55
Strawberry Muffins 86
Strawberry Pie, Diet 210
Strawberry Pie, Fresh 210
Strawberry Preserves 182
Strawberry Slush 271
Strawberry Squares 244
Sugar Cookies 226
Sugar Cookies, Old-Fashioned 226
Sugar Cookies, Sour Cream 227
Sugar Paint Icing For Cookies 267
Sugarless Banana Bread 90
Sugarless Sweetened Deep-Dish Pie 214
Sundae Sauce 270
Sunday Brisket 115
Swedish Meatballs 20
Sweet 'N Sour Sausage 118
Sweet Potato Casserole 168
Sweet Potato Pie 216
Sweet-and-Sour Kraut Salad 75
Swirl Coffee Cake 206
Swiss Crab Bites 22
T
Tansy Cookies 228
Texas Caviar (Black-Eyed Pea Dip) 14
Texas Gumbo Rice 177
Three Cheese Chicken Casserole 132
Three Cheese Tetrazzini 111
Three-Day Coconut Cake 189
Tiny Pecan Tarts 213
Tofu Cheddar Enchiladas 152
Tomatoes, Fried Green 173
Turkey Grilled Cheese Sandwiches 261
Turkey Tetrazzini 142
Turkey-In-The-Orange Salad 69
Turtle Cake 199
V
Va.'s Pork Chops and Rice 120
Valley Salad 72
Vegetable Casserole 174
Velveeta Fudge 239
Virginia's Better Butter 183
W
Waffles 262
Wedding Punch 25
Wheat-Free Peanut Butter Cookies 229
Y
Yogurt Smoothie 270
Z
Zesty Crab Cakes 148
Zesty Salad Dressing 78
Zucchini Bread 88

ORDER FORM

The Texas Conference United Methodist Ministers' Spouses Association

12955 Memorial Drive
Houston, Texas 77079

Please send _____ copy(ies) @ $14.95 each_____
Postage and handling @ $ 2.50 each_____
Texas residents add sales tax @ $ 1.23 each_____
                                            TOTAL =_____

Name_____

Address_____

City _____ State _____ Zip _____

Make checks payable to Texas Conference Ministers' Spouses.

The Texas Conference United Methodist Ministers' Spouses Association

12955 Memorial Drive
Houston, Texas 77079

Please send _____ copy(ies) @ $14.95 each_____
Postage and handling @ $ 2.50 each_____
Texas residents add sales tax @ $ 1.23 each_____
                                            TOTAL =_____

Name_____

Address_____

City _____ State _____ Zip _____

Make checks payable to Texas Conference Ministers' Spouses.

The Texas Conference United Methodist Ministers' Spouses Association

12955 Memorial Drive
Houston, Texas 77079

Please send _____ copy(ies) @ $14.95 each_____
Postage and handling @ $ 2.50 each_____
Texas residents add sales tax @ $ 1.23 each_____
                                            TOTAL =_____

Name_____

Address_____

City _____ State _____ Zip _____

Make checks payable to Texas Conference Ministers' Spouses.